FINANCIAL MANAGEMENT FOR THE DESIGN PROFESSIONAL

FINANCIAL MANAGEMENT FOR THE DESIGN PROFESSIONAL

A Handbook for Architects, Engineers, and Interior Designers

By Lowell Getz, CPA, and
Frank Stasiowski, AIA

WHITNEY LIBRARY OF DESIGN
An imprint of Watson-Guptill Publications/New York

*The authors dedicate this book to their wives:
to Judy Getz who convinced her husband that it's never too late to
undertake the challenge of management consulting and to Anita
Stasiowski who keeps the "home fires burning" while her husband
travels the country and beyond to meet the demands of
design professionals.*

Copyright © 1984 by Whitney Library of Design

First published 1984 in New York by Whitney Library of Design,
an imprint of Watson-Guptill Publications,
a division of Billboard Publications, Inc.,
1515 Broadway, New York, N.Y. 10036

Library of Congress Cataloging in Publication Data

Getz, Lowell, 1932–
    Financial management for the design professional.

    Prepared by Lowell Getz and Frank Stasiowski.
    Bibliography: p.
    Includes index.
    1. Architectural practice—Management—Economic
aspects. 2. Engineering design—Practice—Management—
Economic aspects. 3. Interior decoration—Practice—
Management—Economic aspects. I. Stasiowski, Frank,
1948–   II. Title.
NA1996.G47 1984   720′.68′1   83-19831
ISBN 0-8230-7179-0

Distributed in the United Kingdom by Phaidon Press Ltd., Littlegate
House, St. Ebbe's St., Oxford

Manufactured in U.S.A.

First Printing, 1984

3 4 5 6 7 8 9/89 88 87 86

CREDITS

Pages

88–89: "Professional Risks," The Rough Notes Company, Inc., Indianapolis, IN.

91: "Business Forms Checklist," *Financial Executive*, September 1982.

100–109: Lowell V. Getz, "How to Make Working Capital Work," Texas Society of Architects Newsletter, July 15, 1982.

136–155: Lowell V. Getz, "Effectively Utilizing Your Financial Manager," Professional Service Management Association, March 1978; Lowell V. Getz, "How to Picture Profits [Losses]," *Consulting Engineer*, September 1981.

149: "Financial Analysis of Engineering, Architectural, and Surveying Service," Dun and Bradstreet, 1981.

174: "Tax Shelters: The Basics," Arthur Andersen & Co., Chicago, IL, 1982.

186–187: "Checklist for Internal Control," *Journal of Accounting*, December 1981.

132: "Report Formats," ACCI Business Systems, Inc., Houston, TX.

162: The Murphy Group, Incorporated, Houston, Texas.

Preface

For several years, Professional Services Management Journal Seminars has been giving workshops on finance for principals of architectural, engineering and planning firms. In the course of giving these workshops it was recognized that there is a great need for disseminating even more knowledge on financial techniques to managers with nonfinancial backgrounds. The principals of smaller firms in particular need this information in a manner they can relate to and understand. Often these principals need additional material to direct their thinking after the workshop, and of course, many are unable to attend. This book is designed to help fill that need.

While some of the material was gathered and extracted from workshop notes, this was only the starting point. Much new material was added and the book is directed to meet the needs of both large and small firms. The exhibits are taken from reports and checklists used by workshop leaders in their own firms or consulting practices. Many new exhibits were added and emphasis was placed on reports that can be adapted to either manual or computerized accounting systems.

While the book itself is copyrighted, the forms and checklists are here for you to copy, adapt, and use in your own firm without having to research a problem already solved by others.

Contents

The design professions are changing at a more rapid rate than ever before. Significant changes are occurring that will profoundly determine not only how we do our work, but those practices that will remain financially healthy. The computer is revolutionizing our industry, automating many functions now performed manually, and reaching beyond word and data processing to include computer-aided design and drafting systems. A new generation of professionals who grew up with computers is graduating and moving into design offices to apply their skills and challenge existing methodologies. Growing firms will be required to generate increased working capital to fund the acquisition of new computer systems. Design practices in the eighties will experience narrower profit margins as the economy continues to be influenced by inflationary expectations and resultant high interest rates as well as increased marketing costs incurred in today's more competitive marketplace. Yet, in spite of this, some firms will continue to prosper and grow, much to the amazement of those that do not.

The successful firms have a common attribute: They know where they are going and how they are going to get there. They manage their practice as successfully as they manage their projects. There are many qualified professionals who are capable of providing state-of-the-art services to clients that result in award-winning projects. However, many professionals I've talked with continually comment on how their award-winning projects are their biggest losers financially. David Burstein and Frank Stasiowski's forerunner to this book, *Project Management for the Design Professional*, is an excellent summary of the strong project manager concept that is the heart of successful practice today. Now, taking a step further with the publication of this book, *Financial Management for the Design Professional*, Frank and co-author Lowell Getz have integrated the total financial management of design practice together for the first time. The material is presented in a practical, easy-to-use format that can be directly applied to your practice, complete with many systems, checklists, and charts.

Design and engineering excellence by themselves do not create profits. Project profits are generated by smart project management and must be integrated firmwide into a system which ensures that they will be maintained and enhanced. Financial management of a design practice is thus much more than bookkeeping and billing. Not only must it provide the resources for guiding project managers in monitoring their work, it must establish financial goals and objectives for the firm and continually measure its performance. It must take care of the often overlooked back-of-house functions—from banking relationships to the purchase of supplies that contribute to hidden overhead costs. Regularly applied firmwide, financial management will result in increased profitability with a minimal cost.

The management techniques contained within this book may appear overwhelming to those not familiar with them, yet they are relatively straightforward when worked through once or twice. Each of the forms can be prepared manually or easily constructed on a low-cost microcomputer with a spread sheet software program. Once created, they can be updated with a few keystrokes. By religiously maintaining each step of the financial plan for a few months, those who have operated by the seat of the pants will find new ways of increasing profits by simply being able to see for the first time what is really happening with the firm's finances. The first year we introduced our own computerized accounting system, we were able to increase our net profit before taxes by approximately 3 percent merely by firmwide budget monitoring, better assignment of reimbursables, a reduction in unnecessary overhead items, a faster billing cycle, tighter cash management, and similar items. When you consider the average firm is returning less than 10 percent on gross sales as profit, the impact of such a gain is obvious. We found that once the systems are in place, the management time necessary to maintain them is relatively minimal and that in fact we now spend less time managing them simply because we know where we are at any point in time.

I first met Frank Stasiowski in 1979 when he was a speaker at an American Institute of Architects-sponsored seminar on project management in Denver, Colorado. Since that time, we have retained him periodically as a consultant to our practice. He has conducted in-house seminars on project management to our staff and we have attended many of his *Professional Services Management Journal* seminar programs. Through all of this, it is clear that Frank knows what he is talking about and has a talent for bringing to the profession many practical management techniques.

Lowell Getz is a well-known management consultant to design practices and has spoken at many national architecture and engineering conferences. As a Certified Public Accountant, he has developed financial techniques that are directly applicable to the successful management of the design practice. These are effectively communicated in a language and format that we can all understand and apply.

I trust that you will take to heart the concepts presented by the authors and use them in your everyday practice. They are basic and easily used, and most importantly, they work. The rewards are there for those who make the effort.

David P. Lindsey, AIA
The Callison Partnership, PS

Introduction

"Financial management" is the term used to describe all the functions relating to the monetary aspects of the firm. It goes beyond accounting for current transactions and reporting past results. Modern financial management includes planning for future growth, financing the firm's expansion, monitoring and reporting results to management, and a host of activities that assist other managers to perform their tasks better.

The importance of good financial management was recognized early by industry when it emerged from the Great Depression and World War II. The post-war years witnessed a period of unparalleled expansion in the country's industrial base, and the decisions on how to finance this expansion were often delegated to the accounting personnel inside the company because they were closest to the financial records. Gradually these accounting personnel were recognized as increasingly important to management since their decisions could have a significant impact on the company's performance. As a consequence, their role increased and the concept of *finance* as an expansion of *accounting* was born and carried forward to this day. There is hardly an industrial or commercial entity in the world today where the chief financial officer (regardless of title) is not a senior management official reporting directly to the chief executive.

Design professionals, like other professionals, have been slower to recognize the importance of the financial function of their organizations. Architects, engineers, and interior designers are not trained in business concepts as are the leaders of industrial and commercial enterprises, and the focus of their practice is not primarily on making a profit. Professionals often have little time to spend on business matters and many simply are not interested. Yet they are required to operate their practice in a way that has many of the characteristics of a business, such as complying with governmental regulations, managing people, and developing a market for their services.

In smaller firms one of the principals often takes on the financial and administrative functions in addition to other duties. This can work well, particularly if the principal can supplement his or her education in this area by taking courses or attending seminars on finance and management. At other times the management of a smaller firm is divided between an "outside" principal and "inside" principal according to the temperaments of individuals. The outside principal sells the work, and the inside principal manages the projects. Any combination that works is satisfactory. The point to remember is that the financial and administration functions must be organized and managed in even the smallest firm.

As design firms grow in size and complexity, the importance of the financial function becomes increasingly obvious. Business practices become more complex with increases in size, and many design firm managers recognize that they cannot operate without a full-time person who has been trained in finance. Often this is brought to their attention by their banker or outside auditor.

However, when the principal hires a financial manager for the first time, the results are often not what is expected. The financial problems are still there, and now the principal must cope with someone who is having difficulty adjusting to a professional services environment. The problem is that financial people are trained primarily for work in manufacturing, wholesaling, and retailing, because that is where the majority of jobs are. Professional firms often do not have an atmosphere conducive to the growth of a capable financial function. Principals and professional staff are trained in the disciplines of their profession and talk a common language and have common aspirations. Usually as the firm grows it first operates with a bookkeeper, who is part of the clerical support staff, before hiring a trained financial manager. Often the principals of the firm and other technical staff do not understand the differences in duties between a bookkeeper and financial manager. Like an attorney, personnel manager, or others who are not trained in the disciplines practiced by the firm, the financial manager starts out as an "outsider" and generally remains there until he or she proves worthy as something more than a necessary evil supported by the "productive staff."

As the importance of the financial function is recognized, the financial manager is given an expanded role to play that goes beyond an expertise with numbers to include general management duties. In larger firms the financial manager usually participates in the deliberations of the executive or management committee, even if he or she is not a member. The financial manager also makes reports and presentations at board of directors meetings. The financial manager's advice is often sought at long-range planning sessions and when fundamental decisions on expansion or contraction of operations need to be made. In a few cases, the financial manager has risen to assume the duties of chief executive—not often, but it has happened in larger design firms that are managed more like businesses. It is reasonable to expect that this trend will continue in the future.

1
Characteristics of the Financial Manager

1. What do I look for when hiring a financial manager?

2. Who can assist me in finding the right person?

3. What exactly does a financial manager do?

4. Where can I find out what to pay a financial manager?

5. What problems does a financial manager encounter in a professional services firm that are different from those found in other types of firms?

6. What educational requirements are needed for the job?

7. What other duties does a financial manager perform in a smaller firm?

he financial manager's expertise is vital to the financial health and overall profitability of the firm. This person should not be the "bean counter" who balances the books each month and writes paychecks, but rather the financial planner who continually monitors performance, reports results, and is constantly alert to financial warning signals in order to notify others in management in time to take corrective action. If he or she is not performing those functions there may be two reasons: either the wrong person is in charge of financial activities or else the firm has not given the person the opportunity and encouragement to perform this important task.

Financial Management Alternatives in Smaller Firms

What size does a firm have to be to afford a financial manager? Unfortunately there is no easy answer to this question because it depends on how the firm is organized, whether it is single or multidisciplined, and what its need and requirements are for financial information. Smaller firms should utilize the services of an outside accountant to give them the financial advice that is normally obtained from the full-time financial manager in a larger firm. Outside accountants work with a variety of firms, both large and small, and they can often be of considerable help in showing a principal how to prepare a budget, cash forecast, or other useful financial report. The problem is that while accountants have this information, they often are so busy and preoccupied with auditing and tax work that it never occurs to them that their client may need help in other areas as well. The principals of smaller firms should tap this valuable resource available to them.

By combining administrative functions, such as management of clerical staff, with the financial function it is possible to create the position of business manager in smaller firms. This person handles all business management aspects of the firm, and the job is varied and important enough to attract a capable person. Often there is someone already in the firm who has worked for many years and who is familiar with all aspects of the operations. With additional training it may be possible for that person to grow into the business manager's position.

Another opportunity for the smaller firm to acquire this capability is through an architect or engineer with some business administration training and an aptitude and interest in the business management aspects of the firm. If the person wishes to pursue administrative as well as design activities, an arrangement for splitting these duties might be set up. This is particularly feasible if there is a knowledgeable bookkeeper available to handle the detailed accounting work.

Smaller firms must face the problem of keeping a newly hired financial or business manager productively employed and not bored with the job. This can best be accomplished by giving him or her important extra assignments. For example, every firm needs a plan for ownership succession. Other firms seek to grow by acquiring small firms in the same or other disciplines. They must search out and evaluate these opportunities. The financial manager in smaller firms can be of considerable help if given these added responsibilities.

Role of the Financial Manager

The financial manager is in a unique position. No one else in the firm has such a perspective on everything that goes on within the organization. The financial manager sees everything that relates to money and has first-hand knowledge of the latest information on the financial status of projects. From this vantage point he or she probably knows more about what is going on within the firm than anyone else. As a result, the financial manager is an important source of information.

This person can assist project managers with practically any question dealing with the financial aspects of their projects. Everything from time charges to the smallest detail of reimbursable expenses are in the financial manager's control.

In larger firms he or she is an important resource of information for department or profit center managers because the financial manager can trace every item of expense charged against their budgets. Detailed indirect labor charges are also within the financial manager's purview. Senior management in larger firms cannot possibly know all details so they must rely on the financial manager for summary reports and explanations of financial results as well as analyses of trends and forecasts.

The most difficult problem facing the financial manager in a design firm has nothing to do with the technical aspects of the work. It is simply a matter of communications. Because the financial manager's background and training are different from that of the design professional he or she may have a difficult time communicating with others. It is up to the financial manager to make the necessary changes to improve this communications gap because he or she alone has this background in the organization. It is the financial manager's task to change ways of thinking about accounting problems and technical jargon when mingling with the technical staff. Design professionals need quick information, particularly about projects. The need for absolute accuracy can often be traded away if it means getting approximate information that much sooner. Operating managers often want the financial manager's best guess as to the outcome of the reporting period even before financial statements are complete. Being able to respond to these "unreasonable" requests in an intelligent manner makes the difference between a financial manager who is accepted as part of the management team or one who remains excluded because the technical staff really does not understand what he or she does.

Requirements of a Financial Manager

When looking for a financial manager it is important to have a well-thought-out position description. This is useful for both the firm and prospective employee as it saves the time of both parties. The requirements of the position vary, of course, with the size of the firm and number of people handling financial matters. Exhibit 1–1 is an example of a detailed position description that can serve as a checklist of most duties performed by a financial manager in a larger firm. It can be adapted to the specific requirements of almost any large-to-medium-size firm. Exhibit 1–2 is a position description for a business manager of a smaller firm.

In larger firms this position requires a business administration background with experience in a professional services firm. Financial managers may also have an undergraduate degree in a technical discipline (architecture or engineering) and a graduate degree in business administration. Experience in a service organization rather than in one dealing with products is generally preferable. The financial manager usually reports to the chief executive officer or managing principal of the firm. If the financial manager's duties include such administrative activities as supervision of the support staff and purchasing, this should be made clear at the time of hiring.

Salary surveys are available and should be consulted when establishing a salary range for this position. If the firm uses the services of an employment agency or executive recruiter they can often be of considerable help in determining the appropriate salary for the position. Since the position is generally on a level with other officers of the firm, the usual "perks" should be available to the financial manager in a larger firm. Exhibit 1–3 shows the profiles of a typical financial/business manager.

The importance that management attributes to the position is a significant factor in determining the kind of person hired and his or her attitude after settling into the job. If it is made clear that this position has been created to help the firm achieve financial goals and improve management, then others in the firm will understand its purpose.

Coordination with Other Financial Professionals

The financial manager is the primary contact between the firm and its independent auditor, tax preparer, and management consultant. If the design firm employs an accounting firm to handle these functions, different members of the accounting firm will handle these activities. The audit and tax work will be handled by specialists in these fields, and if other management services are required, as, for example, for the installation of a computerized accounting system, other specialists in the accounting firm will handle this task. The financial manager coordinates these activities and sees that they are accomplished on time and in accordance with management's wishes.

Sometimes a smaller design firm will employ the services of an individual accountant or member of a very small accounting firm. In this case one accountant cannot be expected to have expertise in all these areas. The accounting practitioner

POSITION DESCRIPTION FOR A MEDIUM TO LARGER FIRM

TITLE: Financial Manager (Chief Financial Officer reporting directly to the President)

RESPONSIBILITIES

Planning: Provide projections of short- and long-term financial objectives, develop and maintain financial plans that guide the firm toward attainment of these objectives, and report financial status on a regular basis to allow for adjustments to plans.

Controlling: Develop, direct, and coordinate budgets and projections to ensure that technical functions are consistently executed in accordance with legal requirements and sound business practice. Coordinate audits, provide reports that help all departments perform within the limits of the firm's financial plan, and initiate measures and procedures by which the firm's business is conducted with maximum efficiency and economy.

Financing: Recommend means for providing funds to meet long- and short-term requirements, manage funds in order to meet capital needs of the firm, review current financial position regularly and note any significant deviations from sound management, and develop and recommend appropriate action.

CAPABILITIES

Education: A bachelor's degree in business administration with primary studies in accounting and finance. An MBA and/or CPA desirable.

Experience: At least * years experience in finance and accounting of which at least * years should be in a management position of a service firm requiring financial forecasting, planning, and reporting. Computer experience desirable.

Competence: Established competence with acceptable references from supervisors.

Characteristics: Disciplined time management and attention to detail balanced with the ability to see the organizational whole while having flexibility in approach. Requires a person skilled at communicating with management personnel and directors of the firm. Integrity, technical competence, openness to new approaches, ability to work with others, and willingness to operate with a small staff are paramount.

DUTIES:

  1. Recommend overall financial objectives, strategies, and policies of the firm consistent with approved purposes and objectives.

  2. Recommend the organizational plans and succession plans, both short and long range, for those elements of the organization under his or her direction.

  3. Through continuing contact with departments keep abreast of operating plans that affect financial projections including staffing, capital expenditures, and operating programs.

  4. Ensure that all appropriate firmwide and departmental objectives, policies, and procedures are communicated and explained to all employees under his or her direction.

  5. Advise senior management of impact of legislation and regulations on firm's affairs.

  6. Maintain liaison with such governmental agencies as necessary in order to ensure compliance with local, state, and federal regulations.

  7. Assure that accounting operations are effectively and efficiently performed.

  8. Prepare periodic financial, analytical, and interpretive reports for management, and provide statistical and analytical services to project managers and department heads.

  9. Assure that all legal requirements for proper recordkeeping are met, as well as all recording and reporting requirements for regulatory agencies as required by law.

  10. Work closely with senior management in analyzing the firm's long- and short-term capital requirements.

  11. Maintain adequate funds to meet current requirements and obligations, and consult with senior management in planning future requirements.

  12. Recommend to senior management sources of funds, assist in the negotiation of loans as required, and follow up on the administration and repayment of loans as funds become available and as terms of agreements stipulate.

  13. Develop investment program and manage firm's investments.

  14. Maintain contact with banking executives and financial officers of other firms in order to exchange information of mutual value and interest.

  15. Assure protection of assets through adequate internal controls and develop an insurance program providing protection against insurable risks.

  16. Review and approve proposals before submission to clients.

  17. Help departments formulate pricing policy and provide data for review and analysis.

  18. Prescribe the basic terms and conditions to be used in contracts including but not limited to type of contract, payment terms, and rights granted or obtained.

  19. Prepare or supervise preparation and filing of tax returns and oversee all tax matters.

*Mainly depending on salary offered.

POSITION DESCRIPTION FOR A SMALL FIRM

TITLE: Business Manager (reporting to managing partner)

RESPONSIBILITIES

1. Keeps books of account; prepares financial statements and project management reports.

2. Prepares budgets, analyzes variances, and advises the managing partner so that corrective action can be taken.

3. Prepares workpapers and schedules auditors need to prepare audit and tax returns.

4. Supervises billings, collections, and disbursement of funds.

5. Manages the cash position of the firm and prepares cash reports and forecasts for the managing partner.

6. Reviews liability and employee insurance programs to ensure they are adequate.

CAPABILITIES

A bachelor's degree in business administration. A bachelor's degree in architecture or engineering with MBA highly desirable. Salary based upon experience.

DUTIES

1. Manages the support staff, including secretaries (except partners' secretaries), bookkeeper, librarian, receptionist, and mail room personnel.

2. Takes charge of all purchasing activities and is responsible for adequate supplies.

3. Supervises all other office management functions, such as personnel records, insurance claims, central files, and company automobiles.

may handle the tax work and usually no audit is performed. The financial manager of the design firm may then have to look elsewhere for assistance with management services. Consultants who are specialists in the design profession may have to be retained, or the accounting practitioner may recommend assistance from another firm.

Overall Responsibilities

The financial manager, by virtue of the position, fosters accountability throughout the organization. Someone at a high enough level is now studying the records and bringing to management's attention anything that looks out of the ordinary. Besides being a watchdog, the financial manager is a planner who should look to the future and help the firm achieve its objectives.

In many instances, funds must be raised for growth and maintenance of operations, and it is the financial manager who negotiates loans for additional working capital. When new assets are purchased, such as computer equipment, special purpose loans or leasing arrangements must be made, and the financial manager usually handles these transactions. He or she must also recognize when new equity must be raised and work with the principals to secure additional capital when necessary.

In short, the financial manager's responsibilities extend beyond the day-to-day activities of keeping up with accounting transactions. This person can exert a direct impact on the overall success of the firm.

Discussion Problem

Background. You are the managing principal of a 15-person architectural firm that recently lost its business manager to a higher paying job. The business manager had been with the firm for 10 years and was totally familiar with all its aspects. As a result, the accounting function practically "ran itself," and you had little involvement.

You engaged your auditing firm to conduct a search for a suitable candidate, and after three months they presented you with two candidates, Earl Summers and Stan Taylor. Summers has 10 years of experience with a service firm (dry cleaning chain) and suitable education. He is bright and eager and has excellent references from his former employer. Taylor had his own accounting/bookkeeping firm for 10 years. For the last five years his largest client was a consulting engineering firm. He also has suitable education and references.

THREE TYPICAL PROFILES OF A FINANCIAL/BUSINESS MANAGER

1. JACK BROWN

Background: Bachelor's degree in architecture plus masters in business administration. Began work in large (400-person) architectural firm in project management, but after a year transferred over into finance and administration. After four years, moved to a 150-person architectural/interior design firm as business manager handling all business and financial functions with the help of two bookkeepers and one accounting clerk. After six years was recently hired as vice president–finance of 300-person architectural firm.

Responsibilities: In charge of all accounting for financial functions and manages a seven-person staff working out of two offices. Reports to president of the firm. His first assignment is to install a fully computerized accounting system in both offices that will take the place of the partially computerized system presently in use. The present system is rapidly becoming outdated and unable to handle the present volume of work.

1983 Salary: $55,000 plus approximately 15 percent bonus and profit sharing. Company automobile and the usual perquisites of the other officers in the firm. Currently, owns a 2 percent stock interest in the firm and has been offered the opportunity to buy more stock.

2. SUSAN GRAY

Background: Bachelor's degree in business administration plus Certified Public Accountant. After three years with a public accounting firm she was hired as controller by one of their clients, a freight forwarder. She stayed there one year but did not like the work. Subsequently she was hired by a 70-person consulting engineering firm and land surveyor where she has been employed for the past three years.

Responsibilities: Her primary responsibilities have been to install a project budgeting system and to supervise a cost reduction program as a result of a recent downturn in revenues. For economy reasons, the office manager who was in charge of the support staff was let go, and Gray was put in charge. She now finds it necessary to spend extra hours at the office on weekends to keep up with the increased responsibilities.

1983 Salary: $42,000 plus company automobile. Because of economic circumstances no bonuses were paid last year and none are likely this year. Merit increases have tended to be small and company benefits are limited.

3. SAM GREEN

Background: Graduated from a local two-year business college and immediately went to work for a five-person interior design firm as a bookkeeper and general office assistant. Stayed with the firm for 16 years as it grew into a 40-person organization. Green is highly skilled in the bookkeeping function and thoroughly familiar with the firm.

Responsibilities: His responsibilities have been largely confined to the bookkeeping function while the managing principal handles the broader functions of finance. For example, Green had no background or experience in negotiating a bank line of credit that the firm needed. The managing principal had to handle the task himself. The principals are considering the possibility of hiring a manager in charge of finance and administration.

1983 Salary: $25,000 plus approximately 5 percent bonus. There are no additional benefits other than the usual ones available to all employees.

Summers' experience with a dry cleaning firm will not transfer easily to your firm. Weigh his ability to make changes as distinct from keeping a system operating. For example, did he install a new accounting system for his former employer?

Taylor's experience with an engineering firm will allow him to understand your accounting system more easily. It would be interesting to know why he is giving up his accounting/bookkeeping practice. If you could engage him to handle your work in his accounting/bookkeeping practice for a few months you could try out his services before making a commitment to hire him.

Assignment. List the kinds of questions you would ask each candidate to evaluate which one to hire. Then list advantages and disadvantages of each aspect of both backgrounds as presented.

2
Planning and Monitoring Performance

1. Why is an annual business plan important?

2. What are the pitfalls of "top-down" budgeting?

3. How is budgeting related to the annual business plan?

4. What is "realization budgeting" and how is it used in a professional service firm?

5. Why is a capital budget necessary for all size firms?

6. How are labor costs monitored to assure the most efficient use of personnel?

7. Why is it important to monitor consultant's costs?

8. What is the difference between cash and accrual accounting?

9. How should you value work in progress?

Planning and monitoring performance is important to firms of all sizes as an organized method for controlling operations. However, the method by which a firm accomplishes its planning is also important.

Weakness of "Old-Fashioned" Budgeting

All too often planning is equated with budgeting, and the scenario for the budgeting process goes something like this. The managing principal or chief executive officer calls in the management staff for a discussion about operations for the following year. Generally a certain amount of controlled growth in the organization is expected, and depending upon the economic climate and the anticipated competitive situation, an overall picture develops, say, on the order of 10 to 15 percent growth in revenues and profits in an ordinary year. In a smaller firm the principal in charge of operations develops a budget to meet these goals. In many cases the press of current business does not permit enough time to consult with project managers or anyone else in the organization. The budget is prepared "to please the boss."

In a larger organization the management staff is set to work to develop their individual budgets, and the financial manager is responsible for consolidating these budgets into a firmwide total. Most operating managers will tend to budget their operations conservatively, because they do not want to miss their goals and appear to be less than high achievers. They expect others to pick up the slack and achieve the goals originally decided upon. Since no one does, the firmwide budget may not bear any resemblance to what was discussed in the budgeting meeting. Depending on the managing principal's method of operation, in many cases the financial manager is sent back to the department heads with instructions to revise the budgets to conform to what was originally agreed upon.

In discussing the managing principal's wishes with the department heads, the financial manager may be told the reasons for the conservative estimates, such as completion of certain projects with no likelihood of others taking their place or increased competition from other firms. The financial manager may then find himself in the position of go-between in which he relays instructions and excuses back and forth.

Budgeting accomplished in this manner is "old fashioned" in the sense that it is directed at the top with little participation by the staff. As a result the staff does not feel any responsibility for the results. Budgets are often unrealistic, and they quickly get out of line with actual results so that comparisons between actual and projected budgets are meaningless. This kind of budgeting is not a useful tool of management.

Budgeting as Part of an Annual Business Plan

In order for budgeting to become a meaningful exercise, it must be part of an annual business plan. The annual business plan coordinates all elements of the planning process, of which budgeting is only one part. The annual business plan puts less emphasis on expense control and more on profits. It ties expenses to revenue projections prepared by the most knowledgeable people in the organization so that budgets are realistic. They are then easier to accept and implement.

As shown in the outline in Exhibit 2–1, the annual business plan includes goals and objectives for the firm and individual plans for marketing, operations, finance, personnel, facilities, and administration. The individual plans are prepared by the heads of these functions and coordinated through periodic discussions so that a meaningful document emerges and fits in with the overall goals established at the beginning of the planning process by the managing principal. After input has been obtained from everyone on the management team, the planning document is more realistic, but most importantly, it allows everyone to work toward the same goals. Tracking actual performance against the plan then becomes meaningful. Exhibit 2–2 describes the elements in the planning process by defining the various terms most often used. Exhibit 2–3 is an example of an annual business plan developed by a firm. Exhibit 2–4 is a useful checklist of questions to ask during the planning process.

SAMPLE OUTLINE OF ANNUAL BUSINESS PLAN

1. Goals and Objectives of the Organization
(List answers to such specific questions as where does the firm want to be in five years, how does it expect to get there, what steps in the growth process are to be achieved and by when?)

2. Marketing Plan
(Outline the firm's philosophy on marketing and the organization structure needed to accomplish the marketing plan. Outline tools of the marketing effort and what items need to be produced and expanded. List anticipated project awards by specific marketing areas and dollar amounts. List specific clients wherever possible, amounts expected to be acquired, and estimated dates.)

3. Operations Plan
(List steps to be taken to achieve goals of completing projects on time and within budget. For example, does the firm have a project manager's manual to train new project managers? Outline the procedures to be followed to maximize use of personnel, including sharing of personnel by departments or operating groups. Summarize quality control procedures to be followed. Then develop a monthly forecast of fee income by projecting the balance to be earned on existing contracts and the anticipated earnings on new business acquisitions as outlined in the marketing plan.)

4. Financial Plan
(Based on current backlog, expected new business acquisitions from the marketing plan, and estimated staff capacity, develop a projected income statement and balance sheet for the new year. Develop budgets by operating groups to tie into income statement.)

5. Human Resources and Organization Plan
(Develop estimates of the number of new employees to be hired based on operating and financial plans, taking into account expected employee attrition. List skills needed and expected levels of compensation. Determine where, how, and when these people will be hired. List any techniques or changes in employee benefit plans that may help the firm retain good people.)

6. Administrative Support/Physical Facilities
(Outline support staff requirements needed to accomplish business plan. Determine adequacy of present facilities including new space and equipment needs. Determine how and when new equipment is to be purchased or leased. Review list of all lease expiration dates and determine action for those expiring in the plan year as well as for two to three years thereafter.)

After a firm has had some experience with annual planning, the next step is to develop a three-year plan and eventually a five-year plan. These longer-range plans are obviously very sketchy, but uncertainty of planning in the longer range should not be a hindrance. The importance of long-range planning is not in its accuracy or how closely an individual can guess the future, but in the *discipline* of the planning process. It forces the management of a firm to think about its future direction and to answer questions about growth and diversification, geographical expansion or contraction, new markets, and similar questions. Exhibits 2–5 and 2–6 are checklists to review when preparing plans.

Steps in Planning

Planning is often thought of as an activity that only larger firms have time to do. It is not. All firms can and should develop long-range plans. Since each firm is unique, its planning process and the final plan must take into consideration individual characteristics of a particular firm. However, the cornerstone of all successful plans is that they are simple, extremely realistic, and easily communicated to others.

Although it takes very little time to plan, it can make a substantial difference in the

2-2. *Goals and objectives are difficult to establish because they are the foundaiton on which the firm is built.*

ELEMENTS OF PLANNING

1. Goals: broad statements that describe the nature of the firm and what it hopes to accomplish.

Example for a large firm: "We see ourselves as problem-solvers for clients in all aspects of engineering."

Example for a small firm: "We want a reputation as the premier architects of low-rise office buildings in this state."

2. Objectives: in general terms what the firm hopes to accomplish over the next five years.

Example for a large firm: "We want to become a multidisciplined engineering firm serving clients throughout the United States. We will serve these clients through regional offices located in key cities around the country."

Example for a small firm: "We need to broaden our capabilities by offering an interiors architectural service to clients."

3. Strategies: in more specific terms, what has to be done to obtain the objectives.

Example for a large firm: "We need to open an office in Atlanta to serve as a base for clients in the Southeast."

Example for a small firm: Search for a small (up to 5-person) interiors firm for acquisition or else hire someone to provide this capability and organize a staff.

4. Tactics: very specific actions that need to be taken, including time and budget constraints.

Example for a large firm: "During the next six months we will open an Atlanta office, staffed by four people currently working on the XYZ project and will budget $250,000 over the next 12 months for a marketing effort that will make the office 50 percent self-sufficient by the end of the year."

Example for a small firm: "During the next six months investigate possible acquisition prospects through contacts at the state society and through friends. If nothing definite develops, begin search for candidate for employment (offer about $45,000 for at least 6 years experience in managing a small interiors department)."

success or failure of a firm. The following are points to consider in the planning process:

1. *Start with Yourself.* Make a list of those things you personally want to happen over the next few years. Do you want more income? More challenging projects? A sabbatical? Or a different role? Write down a description of your personal vision of what the firm will look like in three to five years if all goes as you wish.

2. *Establish Time Parameters.* Think in terms of a three- to five-year planning parameter that will help make your plan realistic and keep it simple.

3. *Get Others Involved Early.* Identify those in your firm who have the most impact on its future and ask each to write down his or her personal ambitions and desires and then a description of the firm three to five years from now. It is important not to ask that these written statements be submitted, but that they be used to direct the thinking of the individuals in anticipation of a group planning session.

EXAMPLE OF AN ANNUAL BUSINESS PLAN
FOR A LARGER FIRM

I. INTRODUCTION

A. METHODOLOGY

This annual business plan was developed as follows:

1. Five employee task forces, each consisting of five members, with one from each division, were appointed by the president to study basic issues and topics and to make recommendations to a general Business Planning Committee. The task force efforts were coordinated by the personnel director.

2. A general planning committee meeting was held Saturday, October 28, to hear the reports and recommendations from the five task forces and to participate in general discussions. Extensive notes of the meeting were taken.

3. The personnel director took these notes plus the written reports from the task forces and prepared a draft of the corporate goals and objectives (Sections II and III) for review, modification, and approval of the executive committee.

4. The executive committee sent a copy of the proposed corporate goals to each division/office manager for review and suggested modifications.

5. Each division/office manager provided their own objectives and plans for review and approval of the executive committee.

6. The controller and division/officer managers prepared budgets for the year (not included in this report).

7. These efforts were combined, reviewed, and approved by the executive committee.

B. PURPOSES OF THE ANNUAL BUSINESS PLAN

1. To provide guidance for the officers and managers of the firm to follow in its management of the organization.

2. To be used as a communications tool for the general Business Planning Committee and for all staff. It is intended to be both a road map and a document subject to review and revision throughout the year.

C. CURRENT STATUS OF FIRM

1. Given the apparent success of the firm, it seems essential to review the current strengths and weaknesses to use as building blocks for this year and subsequent years.

Strengths

1. The firm has been in business since 1965 and has established an excellent technical reputation.

2. It is larger than most (perhaps 85 percent) of the consulting environmental firms in the United States.

3. It attempts to provide "one-stop" total environmental services.

4. It has _____ percent repeat business.

5. The firm has been profitable for the past _____ years although margins are thin.

6. It has been successful in penetrating both private and public markets.

7. It has been successful in establishing other offices, although their role, reporting relationships, and ultimate contribution to profits have not been completely determined.

8. It has some capabilities such as _____, which, while they are not unique, do not have as much competiton as other units.

9. It has attracted and retained a significant number of highly qualified and motivated people.

10. It has a young, friendly staff and, for the most part, a pleasant work environment.

11. It has successfully marketed large multidisciplinary projects.

Weaknesses

1. It is in a process of significant change in marketing, line, and project management methods and techniques.

2. Its resources are stretched with the recent active program of geographic expansion, significant percentage of unprofitable projects, and rising overhead costs.

3. It has limited ability to grow and to attract qualified individuals in quantity from outside the immediate area because of uncompetitive salary structures.

4. "Charters" between divisions/offices overlap and/or remain undefined.

5. Line management is viewed as the only route to the top by most of the professional staff, yet management education is not required, perhaps not really encouraged.

6. Affirmative Action/Equal Opportunity programs are ineffective.

7. Space problems hamper growth.

8. Staff turnover is high.

9. Systematic, successful efforts have not been made to answer basic questions such as: (1) Why are we in business? (2) Do we wish to be specialists or generalists? (3) Why have we been successful/unsuccessful in the past? (4) What do we want to be?

10. It has inconsistent attitudes toward profits, billable time, and overhead.

11. It has not learned to successfully manage large multidisciplinary projects and to generate the requisite division/office cooperation.

II. CORPORATE GOALS

A. To continue to build a state-of-the-art professional engineering organization.

B. To foster interdependence with checks and balances on professional performance through:

1. Teamwork
2. Careful planning
3. Quality work
4. Persistent follow through
5. Good business practices

C. To provide the proper working environment and tools to permit the staff to achieve satisfying and stimulating professional careers.

D. To make a major contribution to the national goal of restoring and maintaining the quality of our environment without sacrificing social or economic gains.

E. To build a staff of the most highly qualified and recognized professionals and to encourage all staff members to seek registration and/or certification by their peer professionals.

F. To maintain a commitment to research and development in order to anticipate emerging needs for consulting services.

G. To maintain adequate profit from our activities to ensure sound growth and development.

H. To contribute our efforts and energies to bettering our own communities and to encourage our staff to participate in such activities.

III. CORPORATE OBJECTIVES

A. ORGANIZATION AND MANAGEMENT

1. To further develop the role and effectiveness of the executive committee as a policy review and advisory group.

2. To complete the reassignment of the responsibility for technical achievement, schedules, and budgets of both projects and proposals to operating divisions.

3. To further develop role and effectiveness of corporate marketing committee.

4. To assign all branch offices to division directors.

5. To further define the role, composition, and reporting relationships of branch offices.

2-3. *Continued.*

6. To continue and further develop quarterly evaluations of all organizational units reporting to the president.

7. To hire an outstanding person to head up the environmental division.

8. To eliminate obvious overlaps in "charters" between offices and organizational units.

9. To examine, further define, and strengthen the role, authority, responsibility, accountability, and rewards to both division and project managers.

10. To develop a long range (three- to five-year) corporate business plan.

B. PHYSICAL FACILITIES AND EQUIPMENT

1. To break ground on a new building.

2. To organize and develop a central shipping, receiving, storage, and maintenance activity and facility.

3. To investigate, evaluate, purchase, and install a modern data processing and computer system.

4. To experiment with shifts in overcrowded, particularly capital intensive, areas.

C. MARKETING

1. To evaluate our corporate marketing successes, failures, philosophy, and goals so that long-range plans can be developed. For example, are we to be specialists or generalists or both?

2. To study and determine feasibility of a formal research and development effort as part of an overall marketing program.

3. To identify individuals in each division who are interested and capable of being further developed in client contact and proposal preparation skills and to provide some formal development of these individuals.

4. To develop and install a system for forecasting, budgeting, and controlling marketing costs and benefits.

5. To develop a plan for systematic market research so that future markets can be identified.

6. To refine concept and reporting relationships of marketing managers.

D. HUMAN RESOURCES

1. To intensify efforts and set up formal programs to train and develop current staff in technical, marketing, and management areas.

2. To improve Affirmative Action/Equal Opportunity Employment programs and to conduct at least one formal training program in management staff sensitivity on this issue.

3. To formulate and install a cost effective orientation program for new employees.

4. To further train managers in the processes of motivating and evaluating employees.

5. To reevaluate profit sharing and retirement options and programs and to propose changes if required.

E. PROFITABILITY

1. To establish reasonable long-term project profitability, billable time, and overhead goals and to require accountability by managers at all levels throughout the year.

2. To complete the process of assigning project profitability responsibility to operating division directors.

3. To develop and install an improved project cost control system.

4. To require each division to crosstrain at least 25 percent of its technical staff in one other division.

5. To develop a pragmatic compensation system that rewards interdivisional cooperation.

6. To establish divisional cost and/or profit centers

7. To achieve sales of _____ and profits of _____.

4. *Pick a Planning Leader.* Identify an individual in your firm who is good at conducting brain-storming sessions. The role of this individual is to coordinate and conduct a planning session among top management to synthesize personal goals and desires of the individuals into a concise long-range plan. If such a person is not available in house, choose a consultant as a catalyst to help you with your planning meeting.

5. *Set a Date.* Schedule a full-day planning session for all individuals asked to write down goals in step 3 above. The session must be held outside your facility so that interruptions will be eliminated and so that your commitment to the planning process can be emphasized. The room should be comfortable and provision made for a flip chart, markers, and masking tape. No more than 10 to 12 individuals should ever be invited to the session even in the largest firms.

6. *Don't Do Extensive Research.* The purpose of the planning session is to clarify goals and direction. Subsequent to the session, assignments can be made to research specific aspects for validity of your plan, but your experience and that of your colleagues collectively minimizes the need for extensive preplanning research.

7. *Establish Your Own Yardstick.* Using the flip chart and markers, begin your planning session by asking all individuals to describe verbally what the firm will look like in three, four, or five years. Pick a year (say, three), and list very specific items such as 200 projects, 55 people, $3 million gross fees, two new markets. Be certain to discuss all aspects of the resources, finance, and management in terms of goals and targets. Be realistic, yet stretch your expectations a bit. Also, don't be trapped into cliches such as a goal of continuous growth if the principals of the firm have decided not to grow. The importance of this step is to actively seek and draw out the most realistic picture of what the firm will be like in three to five years from those who will create it.

8. *Set One-Year Expectations.* After agreeing on three- to five-year goals, the leader asks each individual where the firm will be in one year to be on track for achieving the three-year goals. Use the flip chart again, and list in more specific terms exactly where the practice should be in one year.

9. *Give Individual Six-Month Assignments.* Identify specific individuals within the session who agree and commit to the group to carry out specific assignments in order to begin working toward the goals. Set target calendar dates, not elapsed time dates, and establish specifically what is to be done, by whom, and who else will assure that it is done. For example, your three-year goal is to be a recognized expert in a new building type for your firm. In one year, you will have three projects in that building type. By January 1 (30 days) John Smith will develop a written marketing plan to get three projects, and Al Jones will verify that John has carried out the assignment.

10. *Communicate All You've Written.* At the end of your session, summarize in outline form on your flip chart your three-year, one-year, and six-month plans. Using the flip chart forces you to minimize words and to clarify decisions. Take the sheets back to the firm and have them typed. Using this method assures that your written plan will be no more than three to six pages long. It will be simple, clear, and easily understood. Assign each individual in the group session the responsibility to talk personally with four to eight people from the staff about the planning session and personally hand out copies of your typewritten plan to those people. Do not bind your plan in fancy covers or permanent binders. Instead, mark it as a draft: to be updated in June (six months from now). Doing so tells the staff that their input can still have an impact on the firm's direction. When the plan is discussed with the staff, the primary objective is to get their feedback.

CHECKLIST OF KEY STRATEGIC PLANNING QUESTIONS

A. Firm Strategy

1. What is your definition of growth?
2. How does your form of organization affect growth?
3. Form a mental picture of what the practice should be like in three years.
4. How many people can you personally manage?
5. What effect does your ownership transition plan have on growth?
6. What role will *you* play in your visionary practice?
7. What talent will you need that is not now present in the firm?
8. Why is growth important to you?
9. What impact does your management of time have on growth?
10. List three external factors that can help you grow and then three that will hinder growth.
11. Define change.
12. How do you implement change?
13. What conflicts do you perceive between your visionary firm and the present situation?
14. Why do these conflicts exist?
15. What can you do to resolve the conflicts?
16. Define the kind of leader you are.
17. What impact does your leadership style have on growth?
18. How do your clients perceive the firm?
19. Is their perception in line with goals for your visionary firm?
20. Crystallize your thoughts into a one-statement strategic goal for the firm in specific terms.

B. Marketing

1. What are the three primary strengths of the firm?
2. Do your clients perceive these as your strengths?
3. Why do you call them strengths?
4. List three types of work in which the strengths can be maximized.
5. List three more peripheral markets that you are not now serving that could be entered using your strengths.
6. What kind of work should the firm do in order of priority?
7. What geographic area should be covered?
8. Who should be responsible for marketing performance in the firm? Why?
9. Define marketing.
10. Define selling.
11. What is the difference?
12. What image does your firm project? How do you know?
13. What image will your visionary firm project?
14. How do the images differ?
15. Is there a project too large for the firm? Too small? Why?
16. Do you like to sell? List why/why not?
17. Do you have fear of sales failure?
18. List the three things that you personally do best.
19. In one paragraph each convince me that you are best.
20. Write a specific marketing goal statement for the firm.

C. Finance

1. Define profit.
2. How much money should you earn?
3. How much gross income will your visionary firm earn?
4. How does this compare with today?

5. Where will additional fees come from?

6. How much investment will it take to grow?

7. Are your sources of borrowing sufficient to fund the growth?

8. What is your profit goal for next year?

9. How does your profit goal tie in with your personal goal for income?

10. Do you want to communicate the financial status of the firm to the staff?

11. How often do you want to know how well or how poorly the firm is doing? Why?

12. How much should you spend to get the information you want?

13. Should all owners have 100 percent access to all financial data?

14. Should there be a difference between function and ownership? Should all owners manage?

15. How much capital do you want to invest in the operations of the firm?

16. Is return on your investment important to you, and if so, how should it be measured in terms of dollars and cents or in terms of your other goals?

17. List three financial factors affecting growth.

18. What control do you have over each factor?

19. What impact does the economy have on your finances?

20. List three things you can do today to improve the finances of the firm.

21. How can you enlist the help of the entire staff to improve profits?

D. Human Resources

1. What is your primary goal in life?

2. Where do you want to live?

3. How long do you want to work?

4. What is your favorite hobby?

5. What is your favorite work?

6. If you had all the money in the world, what would you do today?

7. What is your family's goal?

8. Do your spouse's goals meet yours?

9. Do you know the answers to the above eight questions for each member of your staff?

10. How can you find out more about your people?

11. Define motivation.

12. Define communication.

13. How do you communicate with your staff?

14. How does the staff perceive you? How do you know?

15. List 10 traits you look for in any person you hire. Rank them from 1 to 10 in importance.

16. How do the traits compare with what you listed as *your* three primary strengths?

17. Identify specific roles needed in your visionary firm that are not now present.

18. What traits should people in those roles have? Why?

19. What is the goal of your recruiting effort?

20. How do you reinforce that goal once an individual is hired?

21. List all benefit programs you now provide your staff.

22. Next to each benefit list how it affects your profit and how it helps you get more work.

23. How do your benefits compare with other architectural, engineering, or planning firms? To other professional firms?

24. Define recognition.

25. List five kinds of recognition you have power to give to each employee.

26. How good a listener are you?

27. In an eight-hour day, how much time do you spend listening? Talking?

28. How does human resources planning affect market and financial planning?

29. Identify one thing you can do better today to improve the human resources effort in the firm.

2-5. *Each of these steps must be addressed in a carefully thought-out plan.*

CHECKLIST OF SIGNIFICANT STEPS IN PREPARING A STRATEGIC FINANCIAL PLAN

1. Identification of financial goals of ownership.
2. List of the management team (personnel) necessary to carry out the financial goals of ownership.
3. Effective communication of ownership goals to the management team.
4. Integrated budget preparation.
5. Execution of the plan.
6. Critical review and update process.

2-6. *Review this checklist for applicability when finalizing profit plans.*

CHECKLIST OF GOALS AFFECTING THE PROFIT BUDGET

1. Capital expenditures (rent versus buy).
2. Investment in other ventures.
3. Estate settlements with deceased partners.
4. Lease/purchase equipment.
5. Market diversity.
6. Economic climate.
7. Merger versus acquisitions.

2-7. *Use this checklist as a guide for considering items that might not be covered under normal operating procedures.*

CHECKLIST FOR MONITORING PERFORMANCE

YES	NO	
☐	☐	Are manpower forecasts prepared on a routine basis?
☐	☐	Do project managers and department heads meet on a periodic basis to plan the utilization of personnel?
☐	☐	Does the firm have adequate accounting procedures that prevent late charges which cannot be billed to clients?
☐	☐	Are project managers evaluated on their performance quarterly or at least twice yearly?
☐	☐	Has the firm prepared a project managers' manual?
☐	☐	Is there a training program for new project managers?
☐	☐	Do project managers carefully monitor consultants' costs as well as performance?
☐	☐	Are reimbursable expenses controlled by including them in the project budget and making the project manager responsible for them?
☐	☐	Are profit margins on projects examined at the close of each project and explanations requested whenever the profit is below budget?
☐	☐	Do project managers understand accrual accounting and how costs are recorded against their projects?
☐	☐	Is work in progress recorded on the basis of selling price? (That is, the value of work in progress should be the same as the amount that will eventually be invoiced to the client.)

11. *Schedule Your Next Planning Session.* Before leaving your one-day meeting, pick a specific calendar date, a specific location, and specific people in order to hold another all-day planning session in six months and repeat the entire process. Following this rule means that you will be devoting two days (sixteen hours) of your staff time per year to planning, which is a price you can afford. It also means that you will respond to the input you receive over the next six months from others in your staff.

By following the planning process, you will see that long-range planning is nothing more than setting goals, establishing one-year objectives, and assigning six-month strategies and action plans on how to achieve your goals. You will determine where your firm is going and when it will get there.

Who Monitors Performance?

Monitoring financial performance is a basic activity of management, and it is performed at various levels in a firm. For example, the project manager monitors the performance of particular projects, and his or her interest is generally confined to these projects. The department head's responsibilities in monitoring performance, like those of the project manager, are generally confined to the overall performance of his department. The financial manager monitors the overall financial condition of the firm, and generally his responsibilities are to bring to the attention of others in management any discrepancies that he discovers. Finally, the principals in a smaller firm and the senior management in a larger firm have the responsibility to keep informed of the overall condition of the firm and to take the necessary action to correct problems as quickly as they are discovered and before it is too late to remedy the situation.

Exhibit 2–7 is a checklist for use in monitoring performance.

What Is Being Monitored?

Labor costs are obviously the most important item to monitor, and there are a number of ways to accomplish this important task. Manpower utilization forecasts are a useful tool to determine in advance what people are scheduled to do in the weeks and months ahead. In larger firms they are prepared by the department heads in consultation with project managers. The manpower forecasts list each individual and the time on each project he or she is expected to spend in the weeks and months ahead, depending on the time frame of the projection. In larger firms with longer-term projects a three-month projection is often prepared, but other firms may have to use a shorter period. Forecasts can and should be revised and updated to achieve maximum use of personnel and a minimum of unutilized or unproductive time. Manpower forecasts may show an overloaded situation with more work to accomplish than people available and vice versa, but their importance is that they give management time to make adjustments. Examples of simple utilization forms are shown in Exhibits 2–8 and 2–9. Remember that once time has been charged on a timesheet it is too late for corrective action.

For control purposes it is important to have all time charges approved by the appropriate project manager or department head (in the case of time not charged to a project by an individual in that department). Labor hours should be reported after the close of each timesheet period including what projects each individual worked on and what hours were charged to overhead accounts. These reports should go to the project managers and department heads concerned and comparisons made against the manpower forecasts and budgeted project hours.

In addition to monitoring hourly charges it is necessary to monitor dollars as well. Revenue and profit forecasts by profit center should be compared with actual figures as shown in the example in Exhibit 2–10, and project costs should be monitored on a profit-and-loss basis as shown in Exhibits 2–11 and 2–12. While there are several ways to monitor performance on a project, the profit-and-loss approach is very clear and direct, and it leaves no room for doubt as to the status of the project. Another type of report for monitoring status on the basis of percentage of completion is shown in Exhibit 2–13.

Department: *Structural*

Period: *Week Ending 7/31*

List Employees by Name	Total Hours	Holidays/ Vacations	Avail. Hours	PROJECTS A Time Needed	PROJECTS A Time Avail.	PROJECTS B, etc. Time Needed	PROJECTS B, etc. Time Avail.	OVERHEAD Business Development Time Needed	OVERHEAD Business Development Time Avail.	OVERHEAD Administration Time Needed	OVERHEAD Administration Time Avail.	Unutilized
J. Smith	80	0	80	40	40	40	40			5*		
M. Jones	80	8	72	60	60	20†	12					
B. Henry	40	0	40	30	30							10‡
A. Aron	80	20	60	40	40	20	20					
T. King	80	0	80	80	80							
R. Keith	80	0	80					80	80			
Total	1,460	240	1,220	540	580	200	180	150	200	100	120	180

*Cannot be accommodated in normal week—consider use of overtime
†Cannot be accommodated in normal week—consider use of contract labor, other employee
‡Consider asking employee to take vacation if productive work cannot be scheduled

2-8. *This report gives the department head a complete picture of the projected utilization status of all members of his or her department. Tradeoffs and adjustments in assignments can then be made for the most effective use of personnel.*

EXAMPLE OF PROJECT MANPOWER BUDGET PREPARED BY PROJECT MANAGER
(Prepared in Hours)

Project Name _____A_____
Project Number _____83-15_____
Project Manager _____L. Brown_____

Budget Period _____4/30_____
Project Starting Date _____1/15_____
Project Ending Date _____5/30_____

List Requirements by Department and Staffing Levels within Departments	Total Project Estimate	Hours Spent to Date	Balance	Projected by Month					Six Months Total Estimate
				Jan.	Feb.	Mar.	Apr.	May	
Structural Dept.									
S. Smith	230	200	30				15	15	30
M. Jones	120	120	0						
B. Henry	80	45	35				30	5	35
Total	980	900	80				50	30	80

Note: Project expenses may be listed below and projected on this same report.

2-9. *This report converts the budgeted hours on a project to a time sequence for planning purposes. In cases where many projects are being scheduled, a chart or graphic presentation is even more effective.*

In addition to labor charges, reimbursable expenses, including consultants' costs, must also be closely monitored. One of the most troublesome aspects of monitoring reimbursable expenses is in closing out a project before all the costs are in. On other than lump sum projects, these late charges come directly out of profits if they cannot be recovered from the client. Therefore, it is important for the financial manager to coordinate closely with the project manager so that a final invoice is not sent until all costs are known. Another important aspect in monitoring consultants' costs is to try to get consultants onto your invoicing cycle so that they do not have to wait an extra 30 days to be paid. To accomplish this, the project manager should discuss the firm's invoicing dates with the consultant so that the consultant can arrange to get his or her invoice in on time. It is simply good business practice to treat consultants as you would wish to be treated. In a few cases the roles may be reversed and the consultant may sometimes be acting as the prime professional. In any event, you want the best service from the consultant so you should give him or her good service in return.

Another area of concern in accounting for consultants' costs is in the proper matching of income and expenses. In the case of lump sum projects, for example, where project managers are calculating revenue on a percentage completion basis, it is very important that they and the financial manager communicate properly. If the percentage completion includes work done by a consultant, then the financial manager must be certain that the expenses include the consultant's costs; otherwise there will be a distortion in the profit on the project.

Profit must also be carefully monitored. It is the ultimate test of financial performance, and if it is lower than the amount budgeted or if the profit turns into a loss, there must be an explanation so that the same mistakes are not repeated. It will be emphasized throughout this text that knowing beforehand when losses are likely to

2-10. *This report is prepared by a profit center manager, that is, the head of an individual office or division or anyone who has profit responsibility for a segment of a larger firm. In smaller firms this report would be prepared for the firm as a whole.*

EXAMPLE OF MONTHLY PERFORMANCE REPORT
(Prepared in Dollars)

List Months Beginning with First One in Fiscal Year	Revenue			Profit/Loss*		
	Original Budget	Revised Budget	Actual	Original Budget	Revised Budget	Actual
January	$100,000	$90,000	$96,000	$15,000	$14,000	$12,000
February	120,000	No Change	115,000	18,000	No change	20,000
December	140,000	No change	140,000	(2,000)	No Change	8,000
TOTALS	$1,600,000	$1,400,000	$1,350,000	$120,000	$110,000	$95,000

*List total dollars of revenue and profit expected to be earned by the profit center each month under various budgets prepared and compare with actual.

occur and informing senior officials so that corrective action can be taken in time is the mark of good management. The project manager must not attempt to cover up an unfavorable situation, because it will usually only get worse if unreported. The urge to cover up will disappear if senior management encourages an open attitude by minimizing criticism of mistakes and emphasizing a helping hand that encourages everyone to assist in solving the problem.

Accrual versus Cash Accounting

It is important to understand the difference between cash and accrual accounting when monitoring performance on projects. This difference has often been described in accountant's technical jargon that is difficult for the design professional to comprehend. A visual explanation is shown in Exhibit 2–14 that makes it easier to understand and also clearly demonstrates the accounting cycle. Beginning with the time-sheets and reimbursable expenses, these items go into a category referred to as "unbilled work in progress." Work in progress can be written off, it can remain in work in progress indefinitely, or as is usually the case, it can be billed to the client and become an account receivable. Accounts receivable can also remain indefinitely in that account, they can be written off as a bad debt, or they can be collected as cash.

The difference in time of when revenue is recognized in the firm determines whether the firm is on a cash or accrual basis. If revenue is not recognized until cash is received, the firm is on a cash basis. Cash expenses are applied against this revenue to determine cash excess or deficiency. If the firm recognizes income at the time the work is performed and it becomes work in progress, then the firm is on the accrual system. Accrual expenses, that is, expenses incurred regardless of when they are paid, are applied against this income to arrive at accrual profit or loss.

2-11. *This report summarizes the status of a project in profit-and-loss format, giving the project manager the essential ingredients he or she needs to know. In this illustration the project manager has overspent the budget on expenses but may be able to recover through a lesser expenditure on labor.*

EXAMPLE OF PROJECT FINANCIAL REPORT

Prepared in Dollars by Accounting Department for Project Managers

Project Name ____A____ Project Number __83-15__ Project Manager __L. Brown__

Report Period ____3/31____

	Current Month		Actual Project To Date	Total Budget	Balance Remaining
	Actual	Budget			
Project Revenue	$15,000	$20,000	$120,000	$150,000	$30,000
Project Expenses					
Direct salaries	5,000	8,000	42,000	60,000	18,000
Overhead	8,000	11,000	70,000	82,000	12,000
Other direct costs					
Consultants	0	0	1,000	1,000	0
Other	500	0	5,000	4,000	<1,000>
Subtotal for Other Direct Costs	500	0	6,000	5,000	<1,000>
Total project costs	13,500	19,000	118,000	147,000	29,000
Profit/Loss	$1,500	$1,000	$2,000	$3,000	$1,000

2-12. *This report shows the status of each project in a one-line summary of profit or loss. In a larger firm with many projects to review this is useful to senior management. Projects that are incurring losses or not meeting budget expectations should be earmarked for further investigation.*

EXAMPLE OF SUMMARY PROFIT AND LOSS BY PROJECT FOR EACH COST CENTER

Prepared in Dollars by Accounting Department for Senior Management in a Larger Firm

	Project Revenue	Project Costs	Profit/ Loss	Profit as % of Project Revenue
Silver City Office				
001 Project A	$402,000	$398,000	$4,000	1%
002 Project B	116,000	120,000	⟨4,000⟩	—
003 Project C	500,000	425,000	75,000	15
008 Project K	950,000	900,000	50,000	5
Total Projects (Silver City office)	$2,000,000	$1,900,000	$100,000	5%
Total Projects (All offices)	$4,000,000	$3,800,000	$200,000	5%

Date __1/1__ Project Number	Project Name	Project Mgr.	Est. Date Completed	Budget Hours	Budget Fee ($)	Totals to Date Hours	Totals to Date Charges ($)	% Hr Spent
1000	Hospital	Baker	10/31	30	$1000	19	$1,933	63%
1010	Office	Jones	10/30	55	846,833	45	830,339	82
1015	Garage	Smith	1/1	150	6,780	33	8,363	22
1020	Warehouse	Thomas	10/16	76	480,000	74	484,329	97
1023	Renovation	Edwards	1/1	5,000	2,000,000	432	9,561	8
1030	Church	Apple	1/1	5,000	846,833	530	91,110	10

2-13. *The project budget status report shows the percentage of hours spent (actual versus budget) in the last column. This percentage is compared with the actual percentage completion determined by the project manager in order to know whether the project is within budget. For example, if Baker estimates that the hospital project is only 50 percent complete based on the work yet to accomplish, this project is overbudget with 63 percent of the hours already used.*

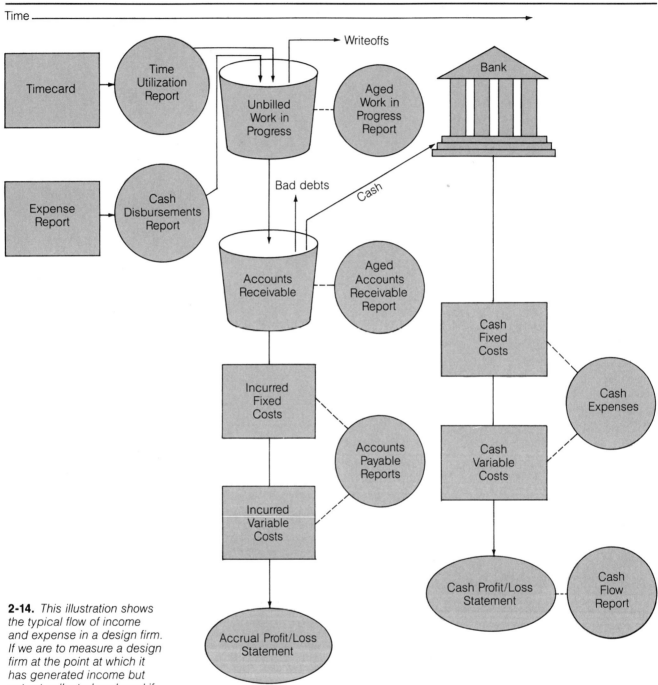

2-14. *This illustration shows the typical flow of income and expense in a design firm. If we are to measure a design firm at the point at which it has generated income but not yet collected cash and if we were to draw a straight line through the boxes and measure the amount incurred for expenses whether paid or not that are fixed and variable, we can measure accrual profit and loss. If we slide the time line to the time at which cash is collected and expenses paid, we can measure cash profit or loss. Each item in a circle represents a report that can be generated to review its status at any point in time.*

When the value of work in progress is determined for revenue purposes, the most generally accepted method is to evaluate it at full value to the client rather than at cost. This means that profit should be added to cost so that the amount of work in progress is the same as the amount that will eventually be invoiced to the client. This is what is recorded as revenue. If work in progress is evaluated at cost only, then revenue will be understated.

Another method of recognizing revenue is at the time the work in progress is invoiced. This is generally not satisfactory because if for some reason invoices were not prepared for several projects during the month, then the revenue picture would be distorted.

Under the accrual system we are recording revenue that has not yet been received as cash. This means that we run the risk of having to write off or eliminate that revenue if, for whatever reason, the client does not pay. In effect, we are "counting our chickens." However, the accrual method is still effective because it forces management to focus its attention on the size of the accounts receivable and work in progress and to do something to enforce collections.

2-15. *Accounts shown in the shaded boxes (accrual basis accounts) are not included on a cash basis balance sheet, since they do not affect cash. The only exception is depreciation, which does not affect cash but which is included in cash basis statements.*

Most larger firms keep their accounting on the accrual basis for internal management reporting purposes. They recognize it as the only way to effectively manage their operations. However, many smaller firms remain on the cash basis because it is easier for their accountants to prepare tax returns. Smaller firms should adopt the accrual method as well. The extra accounting effort is repaid many times by having financial statements that truly reflect the status of operations and tell the principals if the firm is in a profit or loss position. The principals then have information on which to base management decisions. Exhibits 2–15 and 2–16 are examples of cash versus accrual financial statements.

DIFFERENCE IN BALANCE SHEETS BETWEEN CASH AND ACCRUAL BASIS ACCOUNTING

ABC Architects, Inc.
Balance Sheet as of 12/31 with Accrual Basis Accounts Highlighted
(In Thousands)

Assets		Liabilities	
Current assets		Current liabilities	
Cash	$ 31	Accounts payable	$ 12
Short-term investments	10	Accrued expenses	18
Work in progress	683	Deferred income taxes	724
Accounts receivable	824	Note payable	50
Other	12		
TOTAL CURRENT ASSETS	$1,560	TOTAL CURRENT LIABILITIES	$ 804
Fixed assets		Long-term liabilities	
Property & equip. (Net of Depreciation)	$ 57	Long-term debt	100
Other assets	18	Stockholders Equity	
TOTAL FIXED ASSETS	$ 75	Capital stock	100
		Retained earnings	631
		Total stockholders equity	$ 731
TOTAL ASSETS	**$1,635**	TOTAL LIABILITIES AND STOCKHOLDERS EQUITY	**$1,635**

Note: Accrual basis accounts are defined as follows:
  Work in progress: Work performed for which an invoice has not yet been sent.
  Accounts receivable: Invoices sent but not yet paid by clients.
  Accounts payable: Vendor bills received but not yet paid.
  Accrued expenses: Expenses incurred for which the vendor bill has not yet been received.
  Deferred income taxes: Tax liability represented by difference between taxes owed on accrual basis and paid on cash basis.

2-16. *Note that the bottom line of a cash basis income statement is the excess or deficit of cash receipts versus disbursements—a meaningless figure as far as management of the firm is concerned. (A client might pay the day after the statement is prepared and it would not be recorded.)*

DIFFERENCE IN INCOME STATEMENTS BETWEEN CASH AND ACCRUAL BASIS ACCOUNTING

ABC Architects, Inc.
Accrual Basis Income Statement for Year Ending 12/31
Annotated for Adjustments to the Cash Basis
(In Thousands)

To adjust the accrual basis income statement shown to a cash basis, enter the following:

Revenue		
Fee income	$2,000	Record as revenue only amounts received in cash from clients/others.
Other income	12	
TOTAL REVENUE	$2,012	
Expenses		
Direct labor	701	Record as expenses only those amounts actually paid out in cash. The only exception is the expense of depreciation, a noncash item that is usually also recorded in cash statements.
Indirect labor	265	
Payroll burden	203	
Rent	318	
Office supplies & equipment	40	
Insurance	18	
Business development	21	
Telephone	37	
Miscellaneous	33	
After direct costs (including consultants)	344	
TOTAL EXPENSES	$1,980	
Net profit before taxes	32	"Profit" is not proper terminology in cash statements. This figure is actually the excess or deficit of cash receipts over disbursements.

New Concepts in Budgeting

Before we leave the subject of planning and monitoring performance it is important to recognize several budgeting techniques that have been used in other fields of business and that have applicability to professional services. In this case it is important to understand which concepts can be borrowed and used, rather than the actual budgeting techniques themselves.

1. *Zero-based budgeting:* In this system each unit in the organization starts with a zero budget for the new year and then must justify its existence, and therefore the right to a budget, by demonstrating how it can accomplish its tasks and mission in the most economical way. This procedure contrasts with the usual budgeting method of examining last year's budget and making any necessary changes for the new year, which automatically assumes that last year's budget was correct. Zero-based budgeting is actually more complex than what has been described, and it is more suitable to very large organizations and governmental agencies that have certain missions to accomplish. However, the concept of not using last year's budget as a guide for this year and making each overhead cost center prove that it is operating in the most efficient manner is useful and can easily be adapted in almost any firm.

2. *Flexible budgeting:* This is a system used in many manufacturing organizations. Instead of using fixed budgeted amounts, the elements of overhead are converted to unit costs that vary according to the rate of production. That is, when fewer items are produced than anticipated the cost per unit is higher and vice versa. While the techniques of flexible budgeting relate primarily to a manufacturing operation the concept that budgets are not fixed and should be changed to reflect the overall level of a firm's operations can be adapted to any organization. For example, midway through the year the firm may realize that it is not going to come close to reaching its budgeted goals because several large anticipated projects were lost to other firms. A new budget should be prepared for the last half of the year to reflect the lower revenue. Expenses have to be reduced to conform with the lower revenue figure, and in some cases the budget may indicate a breakeven or loss position depending on how quickly expenses can be cut. It is better to recognize the situation early and plan for lower expectations than to compare current performance with a budget that is out of date and meaningless.

3. *Capital budgets:* Most firms, particularly those with heavy capital equipment requirements, use very sophisticated techniques to develop capital budgets that include return on investment calculations, make or buy justifications, and forecasts of obsolescence. Most design professionals do not require such detailed capital budgets, but they all buy capital equipment including office furniture, automobiles, and computers. The capital budgeting process need not be complex, but as a minimum, it should include a listing of all capital expenditures expected during the year and an approximation of the month when the equipment will be purchased. Having a prioritized list will ensure that no purchases are overlooked, and it will enable management to make better decisions when allocating resources to these expenditures.

4. *Contributions budgets:* Charitable contributions are not a significant item of expense, but a firm should decide at the beginning of the year how it wants to budget for donations. Otherwise the question of whether to support a particular charity and how much to give will keep coming up throughout the year as fund drives are carried out. These decisions tend to take an inordinate amount of management time, and a budget will enable a firm to channel its contributions in the most meaningful manner.

Examples of these budgeting concepts are shown in Exhibit 2–17.

| **Firmwide Realization Budgeting** | Firmwide realization budgeting is a technique that is used in other professional services, such as accounting and law, but it is not widely used by design firms. It basically is a budget of the earning power of the firm. Realization budgeting starts with a compilation of potential revenue that can be generated by the firm, as shown in Exhibit 2–18. All individuals in the firm are listed and a percentage utilization is determined for everyone, from zero for such supporting staff as accounting personnel to, say, 85 percent for a draftsman who is expected to be fully occupied on projects. The 85 percent is to allow for vacations, holidays, and sick days. A standard year of 2,080 hours is used and the percentage is multiplied by this standard to arrive at chargeable hours. Multiplying the chargeable hours times a billing rate for each individual gives a gross revenue figure that is multiplied by the percentage the individual is expected to be available, which is generally 100 percent for a full-time individual who is expected to be with the firm for the entire year. The final figure is the potential revenue that can be generated by the individual. Summarizing this for all individuals results in the firmwide revenue potential. Anticipated write-offs of bad debts and work in progress not invoiced must be subtracted based on past history to arrive at the net revenue potential. Net revenue potential is then added to miscellaneous income and the markup earned on reimbursable expenses to arrive at net firmwide revenue. Subtracting anticipated expenses from this figure will give the firm an approximation of the profit potential that can be earned as shown in Exhibit 2–19. |

EXAMPLES OF NEW BUDGETING CONCEPTS

1. Zero-Based Budgeting

Marketing costs in a 15-person architectural firm have averaged 8 to 10 percent of gross revenues. These costs include both the time of marketing personnel as well as expenses. The person in charge of the marketing effort expects to spend $50,000 next year and was the first one to submit a budget. The managing principal read that marketing costs average about 6 percent of revenues in firms of this size according to a recent survey. The managing principal asks for a detailed explanation of the number of calls to be made, new markets reached, schedule of out-of-town trips, types of prospective clients to be called upon, estimated success rate based on the firm's past experience, and a plan for calling on each of the firm's past clients. The marketing director is surprised by this request, but he begins working to comply.

2. Flexible Budgeting

A 25-person architecture and interior design firm budgeted gross revenues of $800,000 in the new year and a net profit of $120,000 (15 percent). One-quarter of the revenue was expected to be earned from two large apartment complexes scheduled for design early in the budget year. Because a major employer in the city expects to shut down operations and move to the West Coast, plans for the apartment complexes were delayed. There is even a possibility they may be cancelled. Although the firm is two months into the budget year the managing principal has asked for a revised budget. Additional hiring has been postponed and expected salary increases deferred. A move to larger quarters has also be cancelled. With some anticipated cost savings a new budget is prepared with revenues estimated at $600,000, and the firm is expected to break even if it can achieve this new revenue figure.

3. Capital Budget

A 10-person architectural firm recognizes that it needs to acquire a computer-aided drafting (CAD) system in order to compete effectively for the design of multi-story office buildings. Previously the firm has done mostly lowrise buildings and apartments. A cost study indicates that total hardware and software costs plus installation will amount to about $250,000. In addition office furniture in the reception area needs to be replaced (cost $3,000) and the managing principal needs a new automobile (cost $20,000). To arrive at a capital budget for planning purposes, the managing principal lists the items of equipment needed and the approximate quarter when they are expected to be purchased:

	BUDGET QUARTER			
	1st	2nd	3rd	4th
CAD system	$250,000			
Furniture	3,000			
Automobile			$20,000	
Other		$1,000		$1,000
TOTAL	$253,000	$1,000	$20,000	$1,000

After examining alternatives, it is decided to use a CAD service bureau for the first half of the budget year and then reexamine the purchase option in the third quarter. All other capital equipment purchases are expected to be made during quarters listed in budget.

4. Contributions Budget

After contributing about $5,000 per year to various charities a 5-person architectural firm decided to establish a budget for this item. The principal started by examining the list of charitable contributions from last year and made the following comments:

United Way	$ 500	Should be the major recipient of contributions; increase to $2,500.
Children's Home	$1,500	Part of United Way; discontinue.
National Hospital	$1,000	This hospital is in another state and was a favorite charity of a former associate; discontinue.
Red Cross	$1,000	Increase to $2,500.
Aid to Refugees	$1,000	This got on the list several years ago; no one knows why; discontinue.

By directing its charitable contributions to a few well-known causes, the firm can decline other inquiries during the year simply because they were not included in the budget.

EXAMPLE OF FIRMWIDE REALIZATION BUDGETING

List Individuals (Group by Dep'ts)	Percent Utilization	Hours per Year	Chargeable Hours	Billing Rate ($)	Gross Revenue ($)	Percent Availability	Potential Revenue ($)
Graphics Dep't							
John Smith	60%	2,080	1,248	$15.00	$18,720	100%	$18,720
Mary Jones	80	2,080	1,664	12.50	20,800	100	20,800
Bill Henry	80	1,040	832	15.00	12,480	50	6,240

Total potential revenue $10,000,000

2-18. *Using existing manpower and expected utilization, calculate expected net revenue as shown above. Then insert the net revenue amount on the top line in Exhibit 2-19 as shown.*

2-19. *Budgeted expenses are developed from the potential revenue figure by using estimates based on past experience and projected costs expected to be incurred during the budgeted period. The difference represents budgeted profit or loss.*

EXAMPLE OF FIRMWIDE REALIZATION BUDGETING
(Continued)

	Annual	Per Month
TOTAL POTENTIAL REVENUE (Net fees)		
Net fees	$10,000,000	$ 833,000
Expense realization income from markup on consultants costs	100,000	8,334
Other income		
Bad debts recovered	0	0
Interest income	2,000	170
Total income	10,102,000	841,504
BUDGETED EXPENSES		
Professional salaries and wages	7,000,000	580,000
Management salaries and wages	800,000	66,000
Management expense		
Rent and utilities	65,000	5,417
Equipment rental	8,700	725
Equipment supplies	0	0
Professional liability insurance	30,000	2,500
Office management travel	1,900	159
Marketing salaries and wages	120,000	10,000
Marketing expenses		
Graphics	8,000	667
Publications	1,000	84
Conventions	2,400	200
Travel expenses	5,000	417
Public relations	2,600	217
Miscellaneous	2,000	167
Total expense	9,737,000	810,000
BUDGETED PROFIT	$ 365,000	$ 30,000

Realization budgeting is a way of looking at the budgeting process from another angle. That is, it's a means of assessing what is capable of being accomplished by the firm rather than what is likely to be accomplished based on the economic outlook. Adjustments to the standard formula may have to be made depending on the firm's operation. For example, if a consistent amount of overtime is worked throughout the year, a factor can be added to the standard number of hours. If, through good management, the firm is able to earn a higher profit on lump sum work than what is generated by using standard billing rates, then the rates should be adjusted to account for that fact. In any event, the calculation of revenue potential gives the firm another method of looking at budgeting.

Discussion Problem

Background. A 10-person architectural firm is interested in expanding by opening an office in a nearby state. The firm has been very successful in its three-year history of operation by concentrating on the design of prison facilities. Profits have averaged 15 percent of revenues after suitable bonuses to the two principals and staff members. However, the market is becoming saturated in the state where the firm is located, since adequate prison facilities have now been built in most areas. The state's budget for new construction has been drastically reduced this year.

The two principals have been considering a geographic expansion for a long time. Another alternative is to expand into different types of work, but they recognize that prison facilities are what they do best and they want to continue to excel in this area. They have recently been approached by a large architectural firm interested in acquiring their specialty.

Assignment. Consider the alternatives available to this firm, and develop a business and financial plan. Begin by preparing a series of goals and objectives for the firm. Carefully think through the various options and examine the advantages/disadvantages of each. As part of the assignment develop a complete realization budget for this 10-person firm.

3

Financial Aspects of Contract Negotiation

1. What types of contracts are most profitable?

2. What is the major drawback to using published standard billing rates?

3. When should retainer-type contracts be used?

4. Who should lead the team when negotiating a government contract?

5. When should an attorney be consulted in the review of contract documents?

6. When should your insurance broker be asked to review contract insurance provisions?

7. When can a simple letter of agreement be used as the contract document?

Financial managers often assume responsibilities in areas closely related to the financial function. This is particularly true in smaller firms where specialists in these areas cannot be hired. For example, the financial manager is often closely involved in contract negotiation procedures when he or she is asked to review contracts prior to signing. Then the financial manager sees that the contract is properly administrated in accordance with the project terms, particularly when invoices are prepared. The financial manager is also responsible for executing any documents required by governmental agencies at the close of a project. Therefore he or she needs to have familiarity with the financial aspects of contracting.

The Impact of Contract Type on Profitability

Design professionals work under various types of contract arrangements, which largely determine the level of profit on a project.

Cost Plus Fixed Fee. This is one of the most common types and in theory it should guarantee a profit of the fixed fee. In reality, overhead costs are not known for certain until after the project is completed, and in many cases, there is a stated or implied limitation on the total amount of the contract established at the beginning. When a total limit is established, cost plus fixed fee contracts become one of the most limiting in terms of profit. This is because the fixed fee is the maximum that can be earned, but any costs incurred beyond the contract limit must be absorbed in the fee. Cost plus fixed fee also exposes the firm's costs to the client and are subject to downward adjustments in case an audit discloses any unallowable costs in overhead.

Lump Sum. These contracts are widely used and are effective when the scope of work is well defined. Unlike cost plus fixed fee contracts, there is no limitation on the profit for these projects, and conversely there is no limitation on the loss. To use a lump sum agreement also requires close scrutiny to be certain that legitimate changes to the original scope are paid for above the lump sum as an extra service.

Percentage of Construction. These contracts used to be more widely accepted, but they are not used as much currently because both parties recognize that they bear no relationship to the cost of the work. While there is no limitation on profits or losses in percentage contracts, the risk is not in the hands nor under the control of the design professional. Instead, the design professional's fee depends on the contractor's bid. In a poor economic climate, this can be disastrous, when contractors are anxious to cut prices in order to obtain work.

Standard Billing Rates. As the basis for contracts standard billing rates have received greater acceptance in recent years. To determine standard billing rates overhead and profit are added to base salary rates to arrive at a flat hourly rate for each individual or classification (such as junior or senior engineer) within the firm. The problem with using billing rates based on classifications is that the rates for the classifications are generally averaged. As people move up the salary scale with periodic increases during the year, the average rates for the classifications must be revised before they are outdated. Generally, standard billing rates should be reviewed and revised, if necessary, on a quarterly basis.

Multiplier Times Salary. This is another common method for pricing services. This method overcomes the objections raised with standard billing rates that have to be constantly revised, but the multiplier contract has the drawback of revealing salary rates to the client and staff who see the invoices. The invoicing procedure also takes longer to complete. An effective way of not revealing salary information on each invoice and yet giving the client the information needed to check the computations is to send the client the individuals' salaries once in a sealed envelope and updated changes as they occur. Then the invoices need only show the hours by individual and a total dollar amount for all labor, which the client can check privately.

Exhibit 3–1 shows a numerical example of the major types of contracts.

In addition, two other types of contract arrangements are sometimes used.

Level of Effort. These contracts are generally found in government work on research projects. These contracts require the design professional to perform a service but without necessarily completing a finished product. They are generally used where a problem must be studied, but there is no indication of what amount of work may be required. Generally, the consultant is given a dollar limitation and told to work at standard rates until there is a resolution or until the money is spent. These kinds of projects are generally profitable since there is little risk of overrun.

Retainers. These contracts are another type of arrangement that generally is satisfactory. In this case the client wants to use the services of one design professional for a number of projects or else keep the professional available or "on call" as problems develop. Payment of a flat monthly fee based on an estimated value of work that is adjusted periodically is one method of retainer. Another is the use of a base figure plus standard hourly rates for work over a certain level. Either arrangement can be worked out to the satisfaction of both parties.

Contract Negotiations

The financial terms of a contract are usually negotiated at the same time as the scope of work. This often means that financial considerations may be sacrificed by the eagerness of the project manager to get the contract signed and the work underway.

Some firms overcome this problem, particularly in negotiating large contracts or contracts with governmental agencies, by having the financial manager designated as leader of the negotiating team. This is not as far-fetched as it may seem when you realize that the contracting officer in charge of negotiating government contracts is a specialist in contracts administration rather than in the disciplines of design. The design professional's negotiating team, of course, includes the technical specialists, but in this case they negotiate through their spokesman, the financial manager. This requires the team to break off the discussions periodically in order to caucus privately to discuss the handling of technical matters. This is a good tactic because it gives the team an opportunity to discuss matters alone and reach a consensus on strategy. With the financial manager in charge, important negotiations on contract price and payment terms will be carried on as equal to equal. This prevents an overly anxious project manager from "giving away the store" during negotiations.

Contract Negotiation in Smaller Firms

While smaller firms cannot afford attorneys and other specialists on their full-time staff, they are not without resources in this area. While contract negotiation is a very specialized function requiring the assistance of experienced personnel, these people are available to the small practitioner. Therefore it is important to know when to call in an attorney to assist with this matter. If the firm does not use the standardized contracts approved by the professional societies, it is well for an attorney prepare a standard form for the firm to use with variations, depending on the types of contracts.

In those cases where the firm must use a contract prepared by the client, a governmental agency, for example, it is well to have an attorney review it, particularly if this is the first time the firm has worked for that client. Another good practice is to have the insurance clauses of any detailed contracts reviewed by your insurance broker and the carrier to make certain that you are fully protected. The insurance company should do this for you at no charge and without any hesitation.

Many firms, particularly smaller ones, work without contracts for some clients, or else they do not have strict procedures that require a contract in hand before the work progresses. A contract need not be a formal document—in many cases a simple one-page letter of agreement will do—but the important point to remember is that some form of agreement is necessary in writing. See Exhibits 3–2 and 3–3 for examples of agreement letters. If the work must proceed without a contract in hand, the next best procedure is for the design professional to write a letter of confirmation to the client outlining the steps taken to proceed with the work and briefly referring to the terms that will be formalized later in the agreement.

While it is possible to collect under a verbal agreement in some cases, it is difficult and expensive, particularly when the client's personnel change and memories fade.

NUMERICAL EXAMPLES OF BASIC CONTRACT TYPES

1. Cost Plus Fixed Fee
Architect agrees to perform work at a rate to cover direct labor costs, overhead, and reimbursable expenses plus consultant's costs. For estimating purposes this amount is expected to be $50,000. In addition, the architect will receive a fee or profit of $5,000 on the project. In a true cost plus fixed fee arrangement the architect receives all costs whether they were above or below the $50,000. Salaries are the actual amounts paid, and overhead is determined on a provisional basis and then adjusted at the conclusion of the project. In any event the architect would only receive $5,000 as profit. There is little risk in the pure cost plus fixed fee contract since all costs are supposedly to be recoverable. Therefore, the profit can be fixed at a relatively low amount.

2. Lump Sum
Architect agrees to do a certain project for a total price of $75,000. Regardless of whether the work takes longer or shorter than estimated the architect receives $75,000 as full compensation. He or she bears the full risk and may recoup an extra reward if efficient or lose money on the project if the estimate is too low to cover the scope of work as defined.

3. Percentage of Construction
The terms of agreement provide for the engineer to receive 7 percent of the cost of construction. For estimating purposes the construction cost is fixed at $2,000,000. The engineer invoices his client monthly based upon his percentage of completion against a project revenue estimate of $140,000. When bids are received and the construction contract is awarded for, say, $1,900,000, the engineer must adjust the latest invoice to reflect a project price reduced to $133,000.

4. Standard Billing Rates
All personnel in the firm are classified into groups according to their levels of skill, and an hourly rate that includes overhead and profit is established as follows: principal engineer $55/hour, senior engineer $45/hour, intermediate engineer $30/hour, and junior engineer $25/hour. Project work is invoiced at these rates plus reimbursable expenses.

5. Multiplier Times Salary
An interior design firm marks up base hourly salary rates by a factor of 1.40 to cover fringe benefits and 2.25 to cover general and administrative expenses. In effect, base salary is multiplied by 3.15 (1.40 times 2.25) to arrive at the billing rate to the client, which includes overhead and profit. Reimbursable expenses are invoiced separately.

Profitable Contract Terms

With the economic climate continually uncertain, the emphasis on solid contract terms is increasingly vital to a firm's financial success. Most clients are demanding more work for less fees, and firms that do not reexamine the terms of their contracts often find themselves without enough income to break even, let alone make a profit.

When negotiating a contract first remember to negotiate scope not price, because the scope of the work should control the price. Next break down price into many small pieces that relate to specific scope items so that portions of the work can be eliminated if a prospective client thinks the price is too high and, more importantly, so that it will become difficult for a client to argue with any small piece of the work when negotiating. Finally, insert as many of the following terms into the contract.

1. Get partial or full payment of fees before starting. It is appropriate and a good negotiating tactic to ask for money up front. The client may not agree, but will understand because many firms are doing the same thing. Also, getting money up front, depositing it, and not crediting it to the client until the last invoice allows you to avoid a bad debt and also earn maximum interest on the deposit.

2. Have the client pay unusual reimbursable costs. In addition to normal reimbursables, ask for reimbursement for items such as liability insurance premiums, computer time, messenger service, and outside project accounting. With government clients this term may reduce overhead, making your contract price more attractive. With private sector clients, it can dramatically increase profits.

3. Include a streamlined form of billing and payment. Having the client agree to a simple monthly payment schedule tied to the scope and schedule of work eliminates time-consuming breakdowns of hours and expenses as well as pages of backup. Then at the end of the project, make any appropriate adjustments.

EXAMPLE OF A LETTER OF AGREEMENT FOR ARCHITECTURAL WORK

Dear Client:

As discussed, we are pleased to outline the scope of architectural services to be provided for you on the subject project. This project will be an office building of a size and scope to be determined by our mutual efforts.

SITE PLANNING AND SCHEMATIC DESIGN

Initially, we will conceptualize a series of alternative site plans that will clearly illustrate the size and scope of the basic project. We can also provide pro formas that will indicate the financial aspects of various alternatves, based upon our recent experience with similar buildings. Once a concept is agreed upon, we will develop the exterior design of the building as well as refine the floor plans in compliance with the program established by you.

After meeting with you, we will provide sketches that will illustrate the proportion and final configuration of the building. At the end of this phase of work, we will also furnish you an ink line presentation loan package.

DESIGN DEVELOPMENT

Upon approval of the schematic design work, and with your authorization, we will enter into the design development phase. In this phase, we will more precisely define the concept of the project and prepare preliminary working drawings for your approval. This phase of the work will include initial engineering recommendations for the structural and air conditioning systems.

CONSTRUCTION DOCUMFNTS

The construction document phase will consist of working drawings and specifications that will detail the requirements for the construction of the entire project, including all necessary bidding information. Toward the end of this phase, we will file the required documents for approval by governmental agencies having jurisdiction over the project.

BIDDING AND NEGOTIATION

During the approval stage of the construction documents, we will assist you in obtaining bids or negotiated proposals. We will also assist you in awarding construction contracts.

CONSTRUCTION PHASE

The construction phase will include our work in relation to the construction contract. In this phase, we will issue change orders as required, make periodic site visits to observe the progress and quality of the work, review shop drawings, and review samples and other submissions to see they conform to the design concepts of the project. We will not make exhaustive or continuous on-site inspections; however, we will endeavor to determine, in general, whether the quality of the work is in accordance with the contract documents.

ENGINEERING AND LANDSCAPE DESIGN

Structural, electrical, and plumbing engineering, as well as landscape and landscape irrigation design, will be included as part of our basic services. Air conditioning will be executed on a design and construct basis, whereby criteria for this work will be established by our consultant, and as such, may be bid on a competitive basis. Upon submittal of the bids, our consultant will assist in the selection of a heating, ventilation, air conditioning (HVAC) contractor, who will then prepare air conditioning drawings to be submitted to our consultant for review.

A fire sprinkler system, if required, will be executed on a design and construct basis in accordance with architect's specifications.

COMPENSATION

Initially, our work on conceptual studies will be billed on the basis of $25 per hour merely to cover our expenses.

When we are all well satisfied with the direction of the project, the professional service fee will be converted to a fixed lump sum amount, based upon a percentage of an agreed-upon budget for the total construction cost of the building shell, structured parking, and on-site improvements. Tenant improvement work is exluded from this amount. This will enable you to know the exact amount of professional service fees, prior to construction, and will serve as your guide in calculating total development costs.

Percentages for the total cost of construction vary in accordance with the size of the office building shell as follows:

40,000 + sq ft	5%
75,000 + sq ft	4.50%
100,000 + sq ft	4.25%
150,000 + sq ft	4%

Fees paid on an hourly basis, which are directly related to the final project, will be deducted from the lump sum amount.

We use the American Institute of Architects (AIA) Standard Form of Agreement between Owner and Architect. This document more precisely defines the architect's professional services and the responsibilities of the owner.

Payments of the fees in the AIA agreement are customarily made on a monthly basis, in proportion to services performed. The total payments at the completion of each phase of our work correspond to the following percentages of the basic fee:

Schematic design phase	15%
Design development phase	35%
Construction document phase	85%
Bidding or negotiation phase	90%
Construction phase	100%

REIMBURSABLE EXPENSES

Reimbursable expenses, for which you will be billed at cost, include blueprints and reproductions, the cost of all fees for government agencies, travel and long distance telephone calls, if required.

ADDITIONAL SERVICES

Additional work that is over and above our normal services, as described above and for which we shall be entitled to extra fees, include the following:

1. Providing space planning, interior design, or decorating services for the lease space.

2. Preparing extensive drawings for alternative bids.

3. Making major revisions to contract documents that are at variance with your previous approvals or instructions.

4. Providing professional services made necessary by the default of a contractor or by major defects in the contractor's work.

5. Contracting the service of a professional artist for an architectural rendering.

None of the above will be undertaken without your full authorization.

Items that are specifically excluded from the scope of our services are as follows:

1. The cost of special testing and inspections required by governing agencies.

2. The cost of a survey of the property and a soils investigation report.

For additional services, authorized by you, the fee will be as follows:

Principal's time	$50 per hour
Partner's time	$40 per hour
Employee's time	$30 per hour

In the event there are additional services by our consulting engineers, their services will be charged as a multiple of one and one-tenth (1.10) times the amount billed to us for such services.

Should either party to this agreement institute legal proceedings on account of alleged failure by the other to perform in accordance with its terms, the party against whom judgment is rendered in a court of law or court of arbitration shall pay for all costs, both legal and otherwise, incurred by the other in the course of said action.

We truly appreciate the opportunity to work with you and believe the results of our joint effort will satisfy your needs in a successful and creative manner.

If the foregoing meets with your approval, please sign and return one copy of this agreement as our authorization to proceed with the work.

Very truly yours,

Principal-in-Charge

Confirmed and accepted

By _____

Date _____

EXAMPLE OF A LETTER OF AGREEMENT FOR INTERIORS WORK

Dear Client:

Thank you for this opportunity to submit this agreement for interior architecture services provided by our firm.

We will consider your signature below as our authorization to proceed with the work.

ARTICLE 1 SCOPE OF WORK

To provide space planning and tenant construction documents for your building complex.

Our firm will provide preliminary services prior to space planning that include preparation of backgrounds, master inventory control book, a check of applicable code requirements, and development of standard wall and millwork details.

Our firm will provide programming services that involve interviewing prospective tenants to determine their space requirements and space planning services that include preparing one-line space plans for review by you or your representative and prospective tenant. A revision to the plan will be submitted if required.

Our firm will provide construction documents for the build-out of the space, including a floor plan, reflected ceiling plan, telephone and electrical outlet plan. Mechanical, electrical, and plumbing design and documentation are to be provided by others. All details and finishes are to be building standard.

ARTICLE 2 COMPENSATION TO OUR FIRM

You will compensate our firm for services provided in Article 1 as follows:

Preliminary services	$35/hr up to $1,400
Programming and space planning	$.15 per rentable sq ft
Tenant construction documents	$.45 per rentable sq ft

Additional services that are authorized by you will be billed at the rate of $50 per hour for principals and $40 per hour for others. Examples of additional services that you may desire are additional revisions or further development to the space plans, design of special millwork, design of renderings or models, graphic design.

Reimbursable expenses are in addition to the compensation listed above and include expenditures made by our firm in the interests of the project. Examples are automobile mileage at $.25 per mile, messenger service at standard commercial rates, reproduction, graphic materials connected with the execution of the work, and long distance phone calls. Reimbursable expenses incurred in performance of additional services shall be invoiced along with additional services. Billing will be on a monthly basis for work accomplished during the preceding month. Invoices submitted by the 20th of the month will be due the first day of the next month. Interest for late payment will be charged and applied to subsequent billings at a rate of 1.75 percent per month on the outstanding total.

Failure to pay within 45 days from date of receipt of statement shall grant our firm the right to refuse to render further services and such acts shall not be deemed a breach of this agreement.

ARTICLE 3 GENERAL PROVISIONS

You will provide information on wall systems, millwork, etc., which is preferred for the project.

You authorize our firm to contract separately with tenants of the project for interior design, move coordination, or other professional services.

This agreement is renegotiable within one year from date of execution.

This agreement may be terminated by either party upon seven days written notice should the other party fail substantially to perform in accordance with its terms through no fault of the other. In the event of termination, our firm will be paid compensation for services performed and reimbursables incurred to termination date.

This agreement shall be governed by the laws of the State of _____.

OUR FIRM   CLIENT

_____   _____
By   By

_____   _____
Date   Date

4. Have the client's in-house staff do some of the work. For example, instead of delivering prints to the client using your messenger, specify that the client's messengers will pick up and deliver all correspondence. If this term were in all contracts, it might be possible to eliminate one messenger from the staff.

5. Shorten the client's schedule and then work overtime. In general, shorter schedules produce more profitable projects by reducing excess perfection. Also by working overtime for private sector clients, you may be able to charge clients at your normal billing rate without incurring additional salary or overhead costs.

6. Shorten the billing/payment cycle. To improve cash flow, ask the client to pay twice a month in accordance with a predetermined payment schedule. Shortening the cycle reduces borrowing, thus saving interest expense, and also indicates sooner whether there is a potential bad debt situation.

7. Agree to split savings on underbid construction amounts. This term requires an independent estimator, but it could save the project's profitability. If you agree to a design fee lower than the original fee estimate without a corresponding scope reduction, you should also not share in losses if the project comes in underbid.

8. Agree to guaranteed interest on late payments. Discuss interest terms with the client and make certain to include a guarantee of interest on late payments. If the client does not agree, negotiate for an advance payment instead.

9. Insert a limit of liability clause. This term can save considerable amounts on professional liability insurance. Limit liability to net fees, rather than gross fees.

10. Insert a provision that measures scope changes precisely. For instance, arrange for the client to sign a record copy of the drawings at specified calendar dates, indicating that decisions made as of that date are known and accepted. Do not tie the signature to completion of a phase, since that is difficult to ascertain.

Few of the above terms taken alone will produce significant improvements in project profitability. However, by adopting as many of these terms as possible you should see an improvement in project profitability.

Another term now used by many design firms is to have the client make payments directly to consultants instead of through the prime professional. This eliminates the problem of one design firm holding funds for another. Also, all design contracts should stipulate a date after which all monetary terms of the contract are subject to renegotiation. This allows for an increase in fees if, for instance, the project is shelved.

Finally, since many projects are based on a letter of agreement, be sure to incorporate these terms plus any additional terms you may have into a one-page typeset sheet that can be attached to all agreements.

| Discussion Problem | **Background.** Your architectural firm is located in the downtown area of a moderate-size midwestern city. Recently there has been a resurgence of interest in many buildings located near your firm, and you have been asked if you would be interested in some large renovation projects. You have done only small renovation projects in the past and are not sure whether this work is a type you want to pursue. |

Background. Your architectural firm is located in the downtown area of a moderate-size midwestern city. Recently there has been a resurgence of interest in many buildings located near your firm, and you have been asked if you would be interested in some large renovation projects. You have done only small renovation projects in the past and are not sure whether this work is a type you want to pursue.

Several younger principals and associates are very interested in pursuing this work. You hesitate because of the many uncertainties associated with renovation projects and what conditions are likely to be encountered during construction. Most of your work has been accomplished on a lump sum basis in the past, but you know that this is risky in projects filled with uncertainty.

You ask your attorney and professional liability insurance advisor to meet with you to discuss the various contracting options available.

Assignment. Prepare a listing of the advantages and disadvantages of the various contract types to present at this meeting. Which type would be most advantageous, and what specific terms would be most important to include? (See pages 47 and 51 for a listing of profitable terms.)

4
Pricing Services to Achieve Profits

1. What does a project manager need to prepare an estimate?

2. How do you use "escalated" rates and why are they important?

3. How much should the project manager allow in an estimate for unforseen contingencies?

4. What is a profit policy and how is it established?

5. What roles does the financial manager play in pricing projects?

6. What procedures should be established to control project expenses?

7. What three other methods beside cost of service can be used to develop price?

For a firm to adequately price its services to achieve profits, two individuals—the project manager and the financial manager—must play a key role.

Project Manager's Role in Pricing

The project manager must develop a realistic estimate for the project that allows for an adequate profit margin. Often in the competitive world this is difficult to accomplish, particularly when a project has been negotiated with a governmental agency or large commercial organization that deals with many design firms. Worse yet, if the project manager has not been part of the negotiating process and is given a job to do for X dollars, he or she is at an even greater disadvantage. Nevertheless, after the contract has been awarded it is up to the project manager to establish a detailed budget and to produce a quality product, delivered on time and within budget.

To assist in preparing an estimate for pricing purposes, it is important that the project manager have a well-defined project scope with a clear understanding from the client that any scope changes will require an adjustment in the project price. It is also necessary to have help in estimating project costs from past experience. Exhibits 4–1, 4–2, and 4–3 are examples of records and forms used by firms to record their experience on past projects that are useful in estimating future work. Another useful technique is to ask project managers to prepare a narrative in the form of a brief memorandum describing the project, the team that worked on it, financial results, and a summary of the team's experience. These data are very useful to project managers when pricing similar projects or additional work for the same client. A sample report is shown in Exhibit 4–4.

When pricing a project, the project manager must be certain to use escalated rates for labor and overhead—that is, the rates should be those in effect during the time the work will be accomplished. Exhibit 4–5 is an example showing how labor rates should be escalated and Exhibit 4–6 shows a format for projecting overhead, particularly in the case of government work where unallowable overhead expenses must be eliminated. The important point to remember is that forward pricing should be based on documented evidence showing how prices have increased in the past and are likely to increase in the future. Of course, known increases in certain overhead items such as payroll taxes and insurance premiums should be factored in using actual amounts rather than estimates.

In larger firms, the question sometimes arises whether to use a single firmwide overhead rate or separate rates for each office or profit center. In most instances, the single firmwide rate is preferable because it is less susceptible to wide fluctuations and a uniform rate is more realistic when work is transferred to different offices.

Reimbursable expenses, which are rapidly rising items, also need to be escalated based on past experience. Exhibit 4–7 shows a calculation of telephone reimbursement that can be used to justify factoring long distance telephone charges by a rate of 1.5 to recover fixed charges. Exhibit 4–8 is a calculation of a reimbursement rate for computer charges. Both of these calculations emphasize the recovery of costs through direct charges to projects. They are useful techniques, but remember that any costs recovered directly through job charges must be excluded when calculating the firm's overhead rate. This is extremely important since firms can unwittingly duplicate the same charges in direct and indirect costs and then be faced with a significant rollback in their overhead rate if it is ever audited. Exhibit 4–9 lists various types of reimbursable expenses.

In developing the estimate it is important to include an amount for contingency planning. It is usually the tightly estimated projects with no contingency allowance that are most likely to overrun. No one can say exactly how much of the estimate should be set aside for contingencies, but a benchmark that some people use is 5 percent. The fact that some amount is provided, depending on what the project can afford, is the important point.

COST VERSUS FEE ANALYSIS OF COMPLETED PROJECTS

Project Number	Project Name	Contract Type	Revenue ($)	Base Labor Cost ($)	Profit/ Loss ($)	Man-hours	Dates of Project	Other Data
1234	Project J	Lump Sum	$6,000	$2,000	$500	150	5/1-6/30	
6789	Project K	CPFF	28,000	8,000	⟨1,200⟩	500	1/1 - 6/30	Excessive Changes
2934	Project Z	CPFF	16,000	6,000	1,000	280	2/15-5/1	
1681	Project R	Time & Mat.	8,000	4,500	1,000	175	3/1 - 4/15	
1905	Project X	% Constr.	42,000	12,000	⟨6,000⟩	740	3/15- 6/15	Bids lower than estimate
1881	Project M	Lump Sum	20,000	7,000	500	380	4/1 - 6/30	
1109	Project Z	Lump Sum	15,000	5,000	⟨800⟩	300	4/1 - 5/15	Delays in obtaining equipment data
Total			650,000	240,000	50,000	1,600		

4-1. *This report gives a concise one-line summary of the financial status of each completed project. It is useful as a historical record to be reviewed when pricing similar projects.*

DESIGN PROJECTS' HOURS PER SHEET

Project Number	Project Name	Design Hours	Number of Sheets (our firm only)	Hours Per Sheet	Project Type	Degree of Difficulty
0016	A	150	7	21	Lump Sum	Average
0017	K	513	28	18	CPFF	Difficult: short deadlines
0123	W	1100	55	20	CPFF	Average
0182	Y	750	21	38	Lump Sum	Complex: equipment difficult to locate in small areas
1176	B	500	20	25	% const.	Difficult: client changes
1212	D	250	15	17	Hourly	Average
1104	O	180	9	20	Hourly	Average

4-3. *Example of a form prepared by the project manager on other-than-per-diem projects to verify profitability. To use this form complete the mandays estimates by department and then convert to a pricing estimate by filling in the lower half of the form with current manday rates, overhead, expenses, and budgeted profit.*

PROJECT EVALUATION FORM

No. _____ 171 _____

Date _____ 3/31 _____

Prepared by _____ TFG _____

Project _____ M _____   Job No. _____ 00212 _____

Type of contract _____ Lump Sum _____

Value of contract _____ $100,000 _____

Construction cost _____ $2,000,000 _____

Value of contract as percentage of construction cost _____ 5 _____ %

Department	Mandays			Drawings	Mandays Per Drawing
	Eng.	**Dr'ft'g**	**Total**		
Mechanical	200	100	300	20	15
Electrical	200	100	300	18	17
Civil					
Structural					
Env. sciences					
Project mgt.					
Administrative					
Total	400	200	600	38	16

PROFIT (LOSS) STATEMENT

Income	$100,000
Expenses	
Labor	
Engineering @ $ 120 /Manday	24,000
Drafting @ $ 64 /Manday	9,000
Total Labor	33,000
Overhead @ 1.6 %	52,800
Misc. costs (Travel, tele, repro, computer, etc.)	2,000
Total expenses	87,800
Net Profit (Loss)	$12,200

4-4. *This report is often the only record of certain information that is not included elsewhere in the project files.*

NARRATIVE REPORT ON COMPLETED PROJECT
(Include in Project Files)

September 17, 1984

TO: Operations Manager

FROM: Project Manager

SUBJECT: Design of Replacement for Silver City Hospital

The following report is provided for the completed project file on the referenced project.

TYPE OF PROJECT

On February 20, Contract No. ABC-123 between our firm and Professional Associates, a group of doctors, was signed to do the preliminary study, concept design, and master space plans to replace the 150-bed Silver City Hospital with a new facility. Our firm was designated as prime professionals for the project, and we used Jones Engineering, Bill Smith and Associates (facilities consultant), and Ray Edwards, a specialist in hospital interiors, as consultants.

The preliminary study was to begin April 1, but because of delays caused by the owners' inability to agree among themselves, the work did not start until May. Through the use of overtime we were able to bring the project back on schedule, and it went out for bids within two weeks of the date originally decided.

TYPE OF CONTRACT

We agreed to provide the above service in two parts. The preliminary study was to be done on an hourly basis and the concept and master space plans on a lump sum.

PROJECT SCHEDULE

The preliminary study was completed on June 1 at a cost of $10,000. After review, the owners decided on August 1 to proceed with the concept design and master space plans and we agreed on a lump sum of $100,000. Final plans were completed and reviewed on January 1.

PROJECT TEAM

Bob Turner served as project manager on the project and was assisted by Sam Bailey. David Eagle worked closely with the subconsultants and was responsible for coordination of their work.

PROJECT COSTS

Our firm did the preliminary study and was budgeted $50,000 for the design phase of the project. Using our standard multiplier, which provides for a 20 percent profit, we earned $2,000 profit on the study. Direct labor for design amounted to $15,000 and reimbursable expenses were $6,000. Total project costs were $48,000 when a 1.8 multiplier for overhead was taken into account. Billings to the client for our portion of the work totaled $50,000. Thus a 4 percent profit on cost was realized.

The final budget versus actual hours were:

CATEGORY	BUDGET	ACTUAL	% USED
Principal architect	20	20	100%
Project manager	200	240	120
Associates	100	150	150
Staff architects	400	430	108
Drafters	200	210	105
Secretaries	80	50	63
	1,000	1,100	110%

SUMMARY

Additional hours were spent in the design phase to accommodate several changes in the clinical and kitchen facilities that were requested by the client. We felt we were entitled to an additional fee for these changes, but the client tended to be difficult throughout the project and insisted it was our misunderstanding of his original intentions. We think that a lot of the problems were caused by the client's lack of experience in working with architects on building projects.

The project gave us an opportunity to work on a highly visible project in a small city. I felt that the client was finally pleased with our efforts and would contact us if we could be of any assistance to them in the future.

4-5. *When using the formulas make certain that the items included under "additional considerations" are answered and included with the work-paper calculations.*

EXAMPLE OF CALCULATION OF LABOR RATE ESCALATION

Situation

1. Current base salary rate for senior engineer is $16/hr and $10/hr for drafter.

2. Estimated project start date is six (6) months from today.

3. Estimated project period is eighteen (18) months.

4. Based on firm's wage increases and the current economy, the estimated increase for both employee classifications is 9%/year.

Problem

1. What is the estimated hourly rate for these classifications for the project period?

Solution

Escalated rate at project start date, six months from today
    9%/year for ½ year = 1.045

Escalated rate at project completion, two years from today
    9%/year for 2 years = 1.188 (compounded)

Use average rate for escalation during the project period
$$\frac{1.045 + 1.188}{2} = 1.1165$$

Escalation on base salary:
    Senior engineer $16 × 1.1165 = $17.86/hour
    Drafter $10 × 1.1165 = $11.17/hour

Additional Considerations

1. Given project team members, is average rate for employee classification a representative figure, or should we use a specific employee rate?

2. Are manhours spread evenly over project period or do more hours need to be expended toward the beginning or end of project?

4-6. *Overhead rate should be calculated with the government unallowable costs included to determine the firm's actual rate and then with the unallowables excluded to determine the rate for government contracting.*

OVERHEAD PLANNING WORKSHEET

FOR THE PERIOD _____

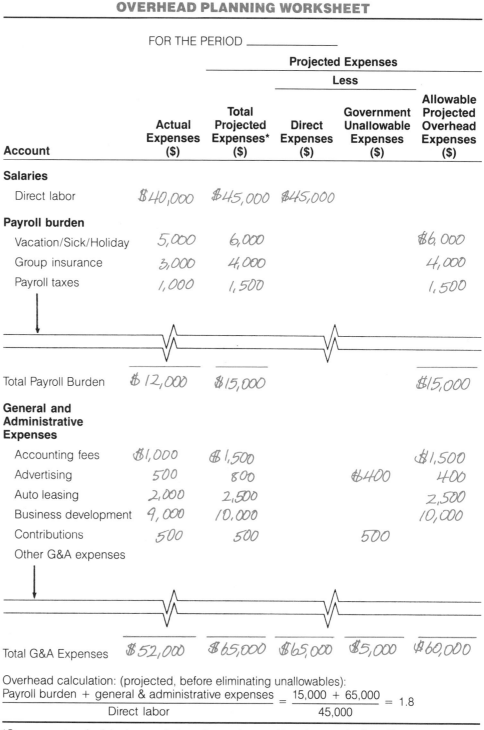

Account	Actual Expenses ($)	Total Projected Expenses* ($)	Projected Expenses Less Direct Expenses ($)	Projected Expenses Less Government Unallowable Expenses ($)	Allowable Projected Overhead Expenses ($)
Salaries					
Direct labor	$40,000	$45,000	$45,000		
Payroll burden					
Vacation/Sick/Holiday	5,000	6,000			$6,000
Group insurance	3,000	4,000			4,000
Payroll taxes	1,000	1,500			1,500
Total Payroll Burden	$12,000	$15,000			$15,000
General and Administrative Expenses					
Accounting fees	$1,000	$1,500			$1,500
Advertising	500	800		$400	400
Auto leasing	2,000	2,500			2,500
Business development	9,000	10,000			10,000
Contributions	500	500		500	
Other G&A expenses					
Total G&A Expenses	$52,000	$65,000	$65,000	$5,000	$60,000

Overhead calculation: (projected, before eliminating unallowables):

$$\frac{\text{Payroll burden} + \text{general \& administrative expenses}}{\text{Direct labor}} = \frac{15{,}000 + 65{,}000}{45{,}000} = 1.8$$

*On a separate schedule show analysis and reasoning used to arrive at projections. That is, certain overhead costs, such as Social Security taxes, have predetermined increases built into them, while others have to be estimated based on recent experience.

4-7. *This is an example of how to price reimbursable telephone expenses in order to recover a portion of the fixed charges in the reimbursement. Overwise fixed charges are included in overhead. When you use this method of reimbursement it is important that the firm use it consistently on all projects.*

TELEPHONE REIMBURSEMENT RATE CALCULATION

ITEM OF COST	MONTHLY AMOUNT
1. New Executone Equipment $29,126 10-Yr depreciation	$242.72/mo
2. Directory advertising	15.24/mo
3. Taxes/Insurance/Maintenance	142.80/mo
4. Receptionist time to place long distance calls 20% × 675/mo =	135.00/mo

1. Executone/mo	$242.72
2. Directory/mo	15.24
3. Taxes/Ins./M't'ce/mo	142.80
4. Receptionist/mo	135.00
Total/mo	$535.76

As a percent of average monthly toll calls = 51.02%

Hence use a multiplier of 1.5 to recover costs

4-8. *This method for arriving at an hourly rate for computer charges includes all related costs in the rate rather than in overhead. When these charges are excluded from overhead, projects that do not require computer services are not burdened with the costs.*

COMPUTER REIMBURSEMENT RATE CALCULATION

	MONTHLY AMOUNT
1. Lease of equipment/mo	$ 596.15/month
2. Service agreement/mo	200.00/month

3. Software cost:
    Structures $1,500   (allotment for future)
    Job cost   350
    Accounting   1,500   Depreciate in 60 mo
    Total $3,350   Cost/mo =
	55.83/month

4. Rental Space 9′ × 8′ = 72 sq ft
    @ $8 + per sq ft + 20% for anticipated yearly cost increase
    Total/month = 9.60 × 72 sq ft =
	691.20/month

5. Utilities (included in rent)	
6. Insurance/mo	2.50/month

7. Cost of running parallel
    a. Double time sheets $ 960.00
    b. Double bookkeeping   2,000.00
    c. Initial setup
       1. New input each job   950.00
       2. Computer training   2,400.00
       3. Misc. other costs   500.00
Total parallel setup cost $6,810.00
    Amortize in 2 yrs
	283.75/month

Total monthly cost	$1,829.43

Working hr/mo =	174 hrs
Actual cost/hr =	10.52/hr
50% efficiency = 2 × actual cost = 21.04/hr	

If it is treated as an employee, the chargeable rate to cover indirect expense and profit would be 2.5 times cost

Hence 2.5 × 21.04 =	52.60/hr
Actual charge rate used =	$60/hr

4-9. *It is advantageous to identify reimbursable expenses and charge for them separately. However, the other costs involved in accounting for reimbursable expenses need to be weighed against the alternative of recovering these costs in overhead.*

Common Reimbursable Expenses

Auto
Computer
Reproduction
Printing
Telephone
Travel and subsistence

Other Reimbursable Expenses

Other fees that directly relate to a project may be charged as reimbursable expenses *as long as the firm follows a consistent policy with all clients:*

Books/maps/charts (purchased for a project)

Courier service

Liability insurance (when increased policy limits are requested the extra costs may be charged to the project)

On-site facilities (cost of trailer, office, administrative personnel)

Postage (large identified mailings)

Professional registration (where needed in order to proceed with the work)

Miscellaneous (any other charges directly related to the project)

The project manager generally plays a part in the contract negotiations, unless he or she is assigned after the project is awarded. In the negotiating sessions it is important that the project manager have the preliminary estimate worked out in advance so as to be in a position to know when and where to negotiate for a reduction in scope if the price must be reduced.

The project manager must also recognize the importance of earning an adequate profit on each project. Profit must be included the same as any other element of "cost," and it must be recognized that any percentage set aside for contingencies must not come out of profit. Members of the firm should understand the meaning of profit, simple as this may sound. Profit is not something that goes in the owner's pocket—it supports the firm during times of low business activity, it pays for unallowable costs, such as interest and promotional expense in government contracts, it buys new equipment, it pays for losses on projects, and it supports the firm's growth and expansion into new areas.

Generally, a profit policy is established on a firmwide basis for various types of projects, and project managers should be well versed in it. The policy may have different rates for different types of work, but usually profit should relate to the degree of risk on a project. For example, a cost plus fixed fee contract generally carries a lower profit margin than, say, a lump sum project. An example of a profit policy is shown in Exhibit 4–10.

The profit percentage should be taken on all items of costs. However, some firms mark up reimbursable costs, including consultants' costs by a factor of, say, 10 percent when incorporating them into the overall price for the project. The 10 percent factor is not a profit in the usual sense, and clients should be made to understand this. Rather, the markup covers the firm's costs for accounting and for managing these items. In some cases the profit policy of the firm needs to be reexamined, particularly on projects requiring a high concentration of effort in a short period of time. When a large portion of the firm's resources must be mobilized quickly to finish a rush project, this project should be estimated at a higher margin of profit than others.

Once the profit policy is established there will still be deviations based on competitive factors and there may even be times when a firm will take a project knowing it will incur a loss. In this case the firm may be trying to enter a new market, or it may

4-10. *Profit policies should be tested periodically against the firm's actual profit experiences to determine whether the policies can be reasonably attained.*

EXAMPLE OF PROFIT POLICY FOR DIFFERENT CONTRACT TYPES

PROFIT RANGE

Cost Plus Fixed Fee   **8–12%**

Where there is no risk of not recovering full costs, use the mid-range. Where an upset limit is imposed, use 12–15%.

Lump Sum   **15–22%**

Depends on competition, degree of difficulty. Needs clear scope of work and agreement on additional charges for extras.

Multiplier/Billing Rates   **20%**

This profit is built into quoted rates. Overhead rate used in this calculation must be examined to make sure it conforms with current actual overhead rate.

Special Projects, Such as Expert Witness Testimony   **35%**

The firm does not actively solicit this work because it is time consuming for the principals. Therefore, a higher-than-normal profit is added to the rates charged and certain minimums established regardless of the time spent in court.

be willing to forego profit in order to keep the staff busy and to cover overhead. The important point is that a decision has been made by the principals of the firm to knowingly deviate from the policy, and therefore the losses will not come as a surprise. Poorly priced projects that, for a host of reasons, result in overruns and losses are to be avoided when determining pricing.

Financial Manager's Role in Pricing

The financial manager plays a significant role in pricing. He or she should review all cost proposals, not only to assure accuracy, but to determine that the correct rates and profit margins are applied. The financial manager should also verify the payment terms and make certain that all salary and overhead escalations have been forecasted and applied properly.

If the firm uses standard billing rates that factor up direct hourly salary rates by overhead and profit, the financial manager, in conjunction with the project manager, must make certain that the client understands what is included in the billing rates. The financial manager must also verify that the standard billing rates realistically reflect the salary averages for the various classifications of personnel.

The financial manager also checks the accuracy of reimbursable expenses when reviewing cost proposals. He or she should make certain that the rates for automobile mileage, printing, and so on keep current with inflation. After the project is underway the financial manager must see to it that people working on the project charge expenses to it, rather than to an overhead account. Procedures should be established so that no expenses are paid without proper approval. The project manager should be responsible for approving all charges to projects and the manager in charge of each overhead function, such as marketing, should be responsible for approving charges affecting these budgets. In smaller firms, the principal in charge of operations should approve all overhead expenses.

Pricing Methods and Techniques

While there are a number of methods for pricing design services, the one most usually used is based on cost. That is, all elements of cost are built up, including direct labor, overhead, and reimbursable expenses, and a profit is added to arrive at an overall contract price. An example of a project estimating worksheet is shown in Exhibit 4–11. Interestingly, most other professionals, including doctors and lawyers, do not price their services this way. Rather, their services are priced using a combination of factors ranging from "what the traffic will bear" to "loss leaders" that attract new clients with a special introductory offer.

PROJECT ESTIMATING SHEET

Prepared by __DB__
Date __11/26/79__

Project __Example__ — Client __DOE__ — Number __1__

4-11. Note that this form is designed to break down projects into whatever detail is necessary for budgeting purposes.

Labor columns are headed (Category of Personnel / Rate per Hour); each labor cell shows hours (top) and direct labor cost (bottom).

Phase/task	Principal A $22/hr	Proj Mgr A $16/hr	Arch/Eng A $13/hr	Technician A $10/hr	Drafting A $8/hr	Secretary A $6/hr	B DIRECT LABOR COSTS	C OVERHEAD (B×1.5)	D OTHER DIRECT COSTS	E EST COST B+C+D	F CONTINGENCIES	G TOTAL BUDGET (E+F)	H PROFIT	I PROJECT VALUE (G+H)
A	20 / 440	20 / 320	200 / 2600	40 / 400	40 / 320	20 / 120	340 hrs / $4200	6,300	2640	13,140	1,314	14,454	1,445	15,899
B1	8 / 176	16 / 256	40 / 520	0 / 0	0 / 0	8 / 48	72 / 1000	1,500	420	2,920	292	3,212	321	3,533
B2	0 / 0	20 / 320	40 / 520	0 / 0	20 / 160	20 / 120	100 / 1120	1,680	160	2,960	296	3,256	326	3,582
B3	12 / 264	40 / 640	120 / 1560	0 / 0	20 / 160	40 / 240	232 / 2864	4,296	490	7,650	765	8,415	842	9,257
B4	20 / 440	60 / 960	400 / 5200	0 / 0	0 / 0	0 / 0	480 / 6600	9,900	3,200	19,700	1,970	21,670	2,167	23,837
B5	0 / 0	0 / 0	40 / 520	400 / 4000	40 / 320	40 / 240	520 / 5080	7,620	4,800	17,500	1,750	19,250	1,925	21,175
C1	8 / 176	20 / 320	120 / 1560	60 / 600	20 / 160	40 / 240	268 / 3056	4,584	420	8,060	806	8,866	887	9,753
C2	20 / 440	40 / 640	160 / 2080	0 / 0	120 / 960	20 / 120	360 / 4240	6,360	260	10,860	1,086	11,946	1,195	13,141
C3	8 / 176	20 / 320	160 / 2080	80 / 800	0 / 0	12 / 72	280 / 3448	5,172	200	8,820	882	9,702	970	10,672
D	8 / 176	12 / 192	80 / 1040	0 / 0	20 / 160	20 / 120	140 / 1688	2,532	200	4,420	442	4,862	486	5,348
E	20 / 440	60 / 960	40 / 520	0 / 0	0 / 0	12 / 72	132 / 1992	2,988	280	5,260	526	5,786	579	6,365
F	20 / 440	40 / 640	80 / 1040	0 / 0	12 / 96	12 / 72	164 / 2288	3,432	520	6,240	624	6,864	686	7,550
G1a	8 / 176	20 / 320	80 / 1040	20 / 200	80 / 640	120 / 720	328 / 3096	4,644	1,200	8,940	894	9,834	983	10,817
G1b	8 / 176	20 / 320	80 / 1040	20 / 200	80 / 640	120 / 720	328 / 3096	4,644	1,200	8,940	894	9,834	983	10,817
G1c	8 / 176	20 / 320	80 / 1040	20 / 200	80 / 640	120 / 720	328 / 3096	4,644	1,200	8,940	894	9,834	983	10,817
G2	20 / 440	80 / 1280	160 / 2080	80 / 800	120 / 960	240 / 1440	700 / 7000	10,500	600	18,100	1,810	19,910	1,991	21,901
G3	8 / 176	40 / 640	40 / 520	20 / 200	20 / 160	60 / 360	188 / 2056	3,084	2,800	7,940	794	8,734	873	9,607
H	60 / 1320	160 / 2560	40 / 520	0 / 0	20 / 160	40 / 240	320 / 4800	7,200	1,400	13,400	1,340	14,740	1,474	16,214
TOTALS	256 hrs / $5632	708 / 11,328	1960 / 25,480	740 / 7400	652 / 5216	944 / 5664	5260 hrs / $60,720	91,080	21,990	173,790	17,379	191,169	19,116	210,285

The first block (Principal through Direct Labor Costs) is headed DIRECT LABOR COSTS; the second block (Overhead through Project Value) is headed FEE COMPUTATION.

The development of price from cost factors plus profit is acceptable, but it is only one method of arriving at price. Other methods include market price, that is, the price at which similar projects are being performed. Obtaining this information is not as difficult as it appears, particularly if you stay attuned to activities in your market and learn the price of projects you were not awarded. Market price may not necessarily be the price you can hope to obtain for a number of reasons, principally competition from others, but it is still important to know what it is in order to help make pricing decisions. Closely related to market price is value pricing, or what the project is worth to the client. An important element in determining value is the amount of construction and operating cost savings that can accrue to the owner from the efforts of the design professional. For example, a design that maximizes energy conservation in a building can save the owner a considerable sum over the life of the building. This amount can be computed by comparing building operating costs against standards developed for similar buildings. Obviously, these factors need to be taken into account and made known to the client even when the design professional is not fully reimbursed for these efforts.

A fourth element in the pricing decision is what the client can afford to spend. In some instances this information may be obtained through various sources of market intelligence, and in some instances, the client might be tempted to come right out and tell you. Regardless of how the information is obtained, it can be a significant factor when deciding to pursue a project and can save a great deal of costly marketing effort on projects that are not worthwhile.

The point to remember is that developing a price from cost is just one element, and it is helpful to know other elements, as well as the client's perception of price, before arriving at a final figure. An example of developing a price based on different methods is shown in Exhibit 4–12.

Discussion Problems

1. Background. Your interior design firm has just incurred a $10,000 loss on a project for a small motel chain. When questioned, your project manager says that the startup costs on this project were higher than expected because of troubles the project manager had in getting the right people assigned to the project. This sounds like an excuse, so you ask to review the data that were used to arrive at the price quoted the client.

The first thing you discover is that there was no allowance for contingency, and the estimate was underpriced by about $10,000 for the amount of work to be done. You were not shown this estimate before (the financial manager is not routinely given an opportunity to review and check the figures), and when questioned, the project manager admitted that he had not reviewed it with a principal of the firm. The firm has been very busy lately and the project manager has been working directly with this client for six months on several projects. He had been quoting estimates for several small motel projects, and since the work was accomplished within budget and on time the client was satisfied and none of the principals questioned the arrangement. This time the project manager received a call to prepare an estimate for a rush project, and in his haste to respond, he overlooked a $7,000 item for computer charges.

Assignment. List what is wrong with the firm's procedures and what you would do to correct them. How would you correct this situation without having the project manager lose initiative in serving the client?

What kinds of reports would you ask the project manager to make for you in order to analyze the reasons for the loss?

2. Background. Your 15-person aviation consulting firm has primary expertise in airport planning facilities and general aviation work. Its projects are split about evenly between private and government work.

4-12. *Developing a price for services using other methods besides costs serves to reinforce the accuracy of the final figure.*

EXAMPLES OF DEVELOPING PRICE FOR SERVICES

Based on Cost
The scope of work is analyzed, and from a detailed estimate of the number of hours required during each phase of the project, the following costs are summarized:

Direct labor	$10,000
Overhead	17,000
Reimbursables	5,000
Consultants	+10,000
Total cost	$42,000
Profit	+ 8,000
Total price	**$50,000**

Based on Market Price
The client is a large developer of small, inexpensively constructed, single-story shopping centers. Over the years, the client has compiled cost data on various architects' costs and profit in order to price these projects. The client expects an architectural firm of the size interested in these projects to have a multiplier of 2.5 times direct labor, which allows for a 7 percent profit factor in the price expected to be quoted. The client makes this information known to any architect who asks.

If your firm is able to meet these criteria and if it wishes to develop this work, it can submit proposals for these projects on the basis of market price.

Based on Value Price
Your engineering firm has special expertise in the design of research and development laboratories for the pulp and paper industry. An overseas manufacturer is interested in establishing a large facility on the east coast of the United States. A laboratory will be built first, and the manufacturer wishes to engage the engineer to conduct a preliminary feasibility and site location study. The manufacturer's U.S. representative wants you because of your reputation among pulp and paper manufacturers.

Depending on competition from other engineering firms with this capability, you may be able to price this project on the basis of value to the client. Consider the level of expertise you can offer, and then set a price based on what this knowledge can save the client in terms of being able to quickly establish a presence in the U.S. market.

Your firm uses a number of fee schedules to price the work according to the wishes of your clients and the type of work as follows:

Schedule A: percentage of construction costs.

Schedule B: actual salaries times a 3.0 multiplier that includes overhead and profit. Other direct costs are marked up by 10 percent.

Schedule C: billing schedule based on standard rates for each classification of personnel, that is, junior engineer, intermediate engineer, and so forth. Other direct costs are marked up by 10 percent.

Schedule D: Special rate schedule for assignments requiring a high degree of senior staff time, such as expert witness testimony. Rates for all technical personnel are the same as the highest hourly rate shown in Schedule C. Support personnel are billed at the highest hourly rate for support personnel. Other direct costs are marked up by 10 percent.

Assignment. When would you use a multiplier (Schedule B) rather than a standard billing rate (Schedule C)? List the advantages and disadvantages of each. Under what circumstances would it be appropriate to quote a lump sum fee arrangement?

List the considerations involved in undertaking an assignment requiring expert witness testimony. How would you justify the higher fee schedule to a client?

PRICING SERVICES TO ACHIEVE PROFITS **65**

5
Project Budgeting

1. What are the advantages of a flexible budgeting policy?

2. What is cost-based budgeting and how is it used?

3. When should other methods of budgeting be used?

4. What types of projects do not require a formal budget?

5. How does a project manager arrive at the mix of people available to work on the project?

6. How should increases in overhead rates be charged against the project budget?

7. When is client price budgeting effective?

To properly control project costs it is essential that budgets be established and control mechanisms be in place to prevent surprises and unexpected cost overruns. The key to successful project control is to have an adequate reporting system that raises warning signals when projects are not proceeding according to plan. The warning signals should alert project managers to take corrective action in enough time to prevent costly overruns. Preparation of good project budgets is the start of this system. Exhibit 5–1 is a checklist for use in preparing project budgets.

What to Look for in Establishing a Budget

When establishing budgets for projects, the project manager must first examine the scope of the project to make certain that it is well thought out and clear to all parties. He or she needs to examine the time frame available to accomplish the task and to plan the work accordingly. Sufficient time must be allowed for project management tasks, concept reviews, and quality control checks. The project manager must also look at the total project budget and make some allowances for contingencies wherever possible. If the project is priced such that the total budget does not have an allowance set aside for contingencies, then the principals in the firm must be aware of it, since these are the projects that often have overrun costs.

When Not to Budget

Budget controls and procedures are important, but there are times when a full-blown project budget is not necessary. Small projects that are completed quickly generally do not have to be budgeted in detail since the total contract amount controls the level of expenditures. Often the client needs the work on an emergency basis, which requires a maximum effort in a short period of time. In this case, the focus is on getting the work done with overtime where necessary and cost is not the primary concern. Another case is where there is an open-ended contract to be performed on a time and materials basis. These "blank-check" contracts are usually small.

The point is that budgeting procedures should be flexible enough to accommodate all kinds of projects. There are certain types of projects where detailed budgets are not necessary. A flexible budget policy will encourage the preparation of accurate and complete budgets for those projects that require them. On other projects they will be prepared to the extent necessary.

Cost-Based Budgeting (Additive)

Cost-based budgeting is the method of preparing budgets by building up the elements of cost and then adding profit to arrive at a total project amount. It is the usual method used in preparing budgets for proposals to governmental agencies. The pricing data prepared at the time of the contract negotiations have now been refined, updated, and broken down into finer detail for the final project budget. Exhibit 5–2 is an example of a relatively simple budgeting form, and Exhibit 5–3 shows one that is more complex; both are illustrative examples. The degree of complexity in budgeting will be determined largely by the types of projects and the amount of control that the firm needs to exercise.

The project manager needs to look over the mix of people available to work on the project and determine the type and classification of people required. He or she needs to determine how flexible people are working in different areas and what levels of experience personnel need to make the best fit. In some cases the project manager needs to allow time for new people to gain experience on projects. If average salary classification rates were used in the pricing proposal, the project manager may have to examine the rates of individuals who are likely to be assigned to the project in order to detect any possibility of higher or lower labor costs than anticipated.

In most instances the overhead rates used in the pricing proposal will be used to prepare the budget, and a single overhead rate should be applied to direct labor that covers fringe benefits plus general and administrative expense (see Exhibit 4–6). It is important for the project manager to understand that the direct labor and overhead rates have been estimated in the price proposal and the financial manager will be accumulating actual costs to compare with the budgets. Refer to Exhibit 2–11 for an example of monitoring actual performance versus budget. Most of these reports can be prepared by computer.

Sometimes costs over which the project manager has little control, such as overhead, get out of line with actual performance. For this reason, many firms compare budget with actual labor costs and reimbursable expenses only and do not hold the project manager accountable for overhead variances. There is no one right way to report project control information. The important thing is for everyone to understand the system and how it affects their performance.

Consultants' contracts should be written so that they abide by the same terms that apply to the prime professional. The project manager should review the consultant's contract with the same care as if it were a client contract. The project manager should make certain there is agreement with the price and work statement. Exhibit 5–4 is a checklist to be used when preparing consultants' contracts.

The amounts set aside for contingency planning and for profit in the pricing proposal are generally carried forward in the budget unless new information is obtained. Any deviations in these two areas should require approval from someone at a level higher than the project manager's.

Client Price Budgeting (Subtractive)

This method of budgeting is the opposite of cost-based budgeting. With subtractive budgeting you start with the total amount for the project and then subtract profit, reimbursable expenses, and overhead to arrive at an amount that is budgeted for direct labor. Dividing this amount by the weighted average salary rates of the people who will be working on the project produces the total budgeted hours available to do the work. The hours are then distributed to the departments and individuals who have been assigned to the project. An example of client price budgeting is shown in Exhibit 5–5.

Generally, it is a good practice to budget a project using more than one method, since each method reinforces the other. The project manager may also have greater confidence in a budget that has been arrived at by more than one method.

5-1. *This checklist can be used as part of the procedural steps to be followed when a project is assigned to a project manager.*

CHECKLIST FOR ESTABLISHING PROJECT BUDGETS

YES	NO	
☐	☐	Is scope of work clearly defined?
☐	☐	Are client responsibilities spelled out as well as the responsibilities of the design professional?
☐	☐	Is the time frame for the project realistic?
☐	☐	Are labor rates based on the latest information available and adjusted to include the time period when the work will be accomplished?
☐	☐	Have reimbursable expense rates been verified with the financial manager to ensure reasonableness?
☐	☐	Is there a letter of agreement from each consultant indicating his or her price?
☐	☐	Has profit on the project been determined in accordance with firm policy?
☐	☐	Is there a contingency allowance?
☐	☐	Has enough time been included for project management?
☐	☐	Has allowance been made for learning time needed by any new people assigned to the project?
☐	☐	Has the budget been compared with the budgets of any similar projects completed recently?
☐	☐	Has the budget been reviewed by a principal in the firm?
☐	☐	Has the financial manager reviewed the budget?

EXAMPLE OF A SIMPLE PROJECT BUDGETING REPORT

Project Name __Project Z__ Project No. __00016__ Date Prepared __6/30__

Project Costs	Total Budget	July	Aug.	Sept.			
Direct salaries							
J. Blue	$6,000	$3,000	$3,000				
J. Green	2,000	1,000		$1,000			
R. White	4,000	1,000	1,000	2,000			
Total	12,000	5,000	4,000	3,000			
Overhead @ 1.5	18,000	7,500	6,000	4,500			
Other direct costs							
Consultants							
Landscape Arch.	4,000		4,000				
Subtotal	4,000		4,000				
Data processing	1,000			1,000			
Travel	500	250		250			
Reproduction	200			200			
Telephone	200	50	50	100			
Miscellaneous	100	50		50			
Subtotal/Other Direct Costs	6,000	350	4,050	1,600			
Fee	2,000	650	700	650			
Contingency	2,000			2,000			
Grand total	$40,000	$13,500	$14,150	$11,750			

5-2. *This report can be used to prepare a budget for a project according to the various categories shown. Start with the grand total in the first column, which is the contract price, and note the allowance for contingency. Then complete the breakdowns for the total budget and spread costs by month thereafter.*

5-3. *This report is used to budget a project by task or phase. In this case daily labor rates include overhead and profit. Note the detail required in budgeting expenses. After the total is budgeted, provision is then made to break the budget down by months in order to compare with actual performance.*

SAMPLE FORM FOR DETAILED BUDGETING BY TASK ELEMENT

Project Name: __Project C__ No. __0216__

Labor Task Element	Time Period		Personnel Classification Assigned[1]	Mandays	Daily Rates[1]	Amount
	Month Start	Month End				
Preliminary Analysis	Sept.	Dec.	Prof. Staff A	10	$600	$6,000
			D	5	200	1,000
Schematics	Jan.	Feb.	Prof. Staff B	20	500	10,000
			E	10	150	1,500
Design Development	Mar.	June	Prof. Staff B	10	500	20,000
			E	20	150	3,000
Construction Documents	June	Aug.	Prof. Staff B	10	500	5,000
			C	20	400	8,000
			D	40	200	8,000
			E	40	150	6,000
Subtotal labor						$68,500

Direct expenses (Show calculations below)

Travel	Location	No. of R/T	Cost per R/T	Extension	
	Large City	4	$500	$2,000	
Subtotal travel					2,000

Subsistence	Location	No. of Days	Daily Rates	Extension	
	Large City	4	$150	$600	
Subtotal subsistence					600

Printing and drafting: In-house materials (Estimate labor separately and include under appropriate task element) — 4,000

Outside services (Include total price for both labor and materials) — 6,000

Data processing service (Complete subcontractors schedule below and enter total here) — 1,000

Communications (Telephone, telegraph, telex, cables, etc.) — 1,000

Subcontractors (Complete subcontractors' schedule below and enter total here) — 10,000

Temporary field/office help[2]

Total direct expenses — 24,600

Total direct expenses at 110% — 27,000

Contingency — *

Total direct labor and expenses (Show monthly breakdown below) — $95,500

Subcontractor Name	Brief Description of Work to Be Performed	Contract Terms[3]	Mandays or Hours	Rate	Amount
A Laboratory	*Soils Investigation*	*Lump Sum*			$10,000

Total labor and expenses (monthly breakdown)

Month	Sept.	Oct.	Nov.	Dec.	Jan.	Feb.	Mar.	Apr.	May	June	July	Aug.
Total labor and expenses	2,000	2,000	2,000	3,000	3,000	4,000	10,000	10,000	10,000	16,000	16,000	17,000

*5% included in each task element.

Notes: [1] Personnel classification and rates

Officers	$800	Supervisors and technicians	$150
Project manager	700	Stenographic and clerical	150
Professional staff A	600		
B	500	All other personnel at actual	
C	400	or estimated rates	
D	200		
E	150		

[2] Survey and coding personnel should be included under the appropriate task element. Use this line for additional personnel who cannot be readily identified, such as temporary help.

[3] Identify basis of payment, that is, fixed price, time and charges, and so on.

Submitted by ___*JPG*___ (Project Manager) Date __8/3__

Reviewed by ___*TVJ*___ (Project Officer) Date __8/12__

Approved by ___*KMR*___ (President) Date __8/18__

CHECKLIST FOR PREPARING CONSULTANT'S CONTRACT

YES   NO

☐   ☐   Are the responsibilities of the consultant clearly defined?

☐   ☐   Is the time frame for the work understood and agreeable?

☐   ☐   Have you worked with the consultant before and are you acquainted with his or her work?

☐   ☐   In your experience, has the consultant quoted a fair price? (If the price is too low the quality of the work will suffer.)

☐   ☐   Are payment terms defined and are they in accord with your payment terms with the client?

☐   ☐   Is the consultant familiar with the terms and conditions of your contract and is the consultant willing to abide by them?

☐   ☐   Does your contract with the client provide for client approval of all consultants hired and has this been done?

☐   ☐   Does your contract contain a provision for obtaining certificates of insurance from consultants and has this been done?

5-5. Using this worksheet enables the project manager to quickly arrive at the breakdown of hours needed to complete the work within the established budget.

CLIENT PRICE BUDGETING

Total project price	$ 20,000	
Less: Profit (15%)	3,000	
Overhead	9,000	
Reimbursables	500	
Contingency (5%)	1,000	
Amount budgeted for direct labor	$6,500	
÷ weighted average salary rates ($10.00)		650 Hours Available

	(Hours)
Architecture	500
Graphics	50
Interiors	100
Total	650

Discussion Problem

Background. Your firm has had difficulty controlling project costs. The managing principal is convinced that the project managers do not budget properly and once the budgets are established they are not changed to accommodate changing circumstances. The excuse given is that there is usually lack of time and that budgets are busy work, which do not contribute to the success of the project.

Although the firm has a computerized accounting and project control system, budgets are prepared by hand and then added to the project information in the computer. When changes occur on a project or adjustments are needed between phases, it is a time-consuming task to rework the budget. As a result many project managers ignore them, thinking that since the total project price has not changed, the changes in different phases will eventually work themselves out. Comparisons between the actual amount spent on phases versus the original budget are often useless.

The managing principal asks the financial manager to develop a computerized program that can be incorporated into the project accounting system. Using the client price budgeting concept shown in Exhibit 5–5 and an electronic spread sheet program, he arrives at a method of budgeting that is simple and easy to change. Client price budgeting emphasizes the labor hours and dollars needed to accomplish the work. The electronic spread sheet program enables changes to be made in any elements of the budget and carried through to the total automatically. Manual calculations are thereby eliminated. Exhibit 5–6 is an example of a budget prepared by computer.

Assignment. List the reasons for preparing a budget and the need for keeping it current as circumstances change on a project. Is time spent on project budgeting a legitimate project cost or should it be included in overhead and spread to all projects? What are the pros and cons of each method?

5-6. *An electronic spread sheet program such as Visicalc allows for changes to be made in any of the budget assumptions, and the computer makes all calculations and extensions automatically, thereby eliminating considerable manual effort.*

SAMPLE BUDGET REPORT

	Hours	Dollars
Direct labor		
Schematic design		
Bill Smith	20	$ 400
Mary Jones	18	350
Etc.		
TOTAL	160	$ 2,000
Design development		
Jay Taylor	10	180
Sam Bailey	18	320
Etc.		
TOTAL	350	$ 5,000
Construction documents		
Al Allen	40	800
Joe Howard	18	350
Etc.		
TOTAL	400	$ 6,000
Bidding negotiations		
Tom Green	18	300
Walter Williams	26	400
Etc.		
TOTAL	80	$ 1,000
Additional service		
Allen Smith	10	180
Gene Bowles	20	350
Etc.		
TOTAL	80	$ 1,000
TOTAL DIRECT LABOR		$15,000
Overhead		24,000
Reimbursable expenses		6,000
Consultants' costs		7,800
TOTAL COSTS		$52,800
PROFIT		7,200
PROJECT PRICE		$60,000

6

Controlling Labor and Other Project Costs

1. What are the elements of a good salary administration plan?

2. How should bonuses be determined?

3. What points should be considered before reducing staff?

4. When reducing personnel, is it best to concentrate on the junior (less experienced) staff?

5. What direct project costs are most likely to overrun?

6. What are the principal causes of project overruns?

7. How do we learn to control overruns?

Since labor makes up such a high percentage of the costs on a project, controlling labor costs will go a long way toward controlling all other project costs.

Controlling Project Labor Costs

Labor costs need to be controlled through careful budgeting and careful supervision, particularly of the less experienced staff members. Each person should be given an individual budget allotment by the supervisor so they are aware of what is expected in a given number of hours. If there is a problem with the budgeted hours it should be discussed and resolved, if possible in advance. In many cases the budgets will have to be adjusted, but it is better to make these adjustments in advance before the work is started. Afterwards there is less flexibility for tradeoffs.

Controlling Firmwide Labor Costs

Labor costs also need to be controlled on an firmwide basis, and this is accomplished through good personnel practices. Most sucessful firms now recognize the need for a human resources function managed by a professional, if the firm is of a size to support it. Hiring and retaining good people is the responsibility of the human resources manager in a larger firm. In smaller firms this responsibility is given to the principal in charge of operations or administration. He or she is responsible for recruiting and recommending proper salary levels for the various categories of personnel in the firm based on surveys and other data. These salary scales must be competitive with those in the marketplace as well as those within the firm. Salary increases should be budgeted and should be based on a number of factors, including (1) prior years' increases, (2) cost of living, (3) competition, and (4) the financial resources of the firm. Exhibit 6–1 is an example of how data on previous years' salary increases are compiled. Most importantly, the decision on salary increases should include the immediate supervisor's evaluation of the individual.

To set up a good salary administration plan you should determine ranges for different categories of personnel, as shown in Exhibits 6–2 and 6–3. Note that the ranges overlap at the top of each classification in order to permit a certain amount of salary increases without necessarily having to promote an individual to the next higher category. A written salary administration policy should accompany the ranges and outline the firm's philosophy and procedures for administering the program. The policy and ranges should then be distributed throughout the firm, and all individuals should know their classification and the requirements needed to advance in classification.

One important method for controlling labor costs is to convert nonbillable to billable time whenever possible. Support staff, such as secretaries and word processing operators, should charge their time to projects whenever they work long enough on a single project to make this worthwhile. Likewise, principals should charge their time directly whenever they are contributing to a project. In this case communication is most important so that project managers know and accept the help they are receiving from the principals.

Bonuses are a widely accepted method of motivating employees, and if used properly they can contribute greatly to the success of the firm and to the proper control of labor costs. Bonuses should be paid on the basis of merit and should generally be large enough to signal an important reward. They should be limited to those people who have made a significant contribution to the firm. To the extent possible they should be directly related to the profitability of the firm and to the individuals responsible for that profit.

When labor costs must be reduced through terminations and layoffs, most firms have found that this is the time when communications between management and staff must be extremely good. The people affected must be told quickly and in a straight-forward manner, and those not affected must be told as well. Otherwise rumors will circulate and the people you are trying to keep will often leave on their own.

Eleven suggestions for determining how to terminate employees, which have been used in several firms, are shown in Exhibit 6–4.

6-1. *This analysis should include employees who worked for the entire period. Employees who were promoted during the year would tend to depress the percentage increase in those categories affected and may require a separate analysis if significant.*

CALCULATION OF PERCENT INCREASE IN SALARIES

Fiscal Year Ending _____

Classification	Number of Employees	Amount (Beginning of Year)	Amount (End of Year)	% Increase
Division manager	1	$40,000	$45,000	
Department manager	2	70,000	74,000	
Senior engineer	4	125,000	130,000	
Engineer/Designer	6	150,000	152,000	
Junior engineer	7	140,000	150,000	
Specialist	—	—	—	
Senior drafter	1	25,000	28,000	
Drafter	3	54,000	60,000	
Senior technician	1	20,000	22,000	
Technician	—	—	—	
Secretary	2	30,000	35,000	
Administrative support	2	35,000	40,000	
Total firm	29	$689,000	$736,000	7%

6-2. *Employees advance along the horizontal levels as they receive periodic salary increases and then are promoted to the next higher grade.*

SALARY ADMINISTRATION RANGES FOR ENGINEERING STAFF

As of _____

Employee Grades	Increasing Levels of Experience and Competency				
Officer	$46,800	$51,500	$56,200	$60,900	$65,600
E-7, E-6	$32,800	$36,000	$39,300	$42,500	$45,700
E-5, E-4	$26,700	$29,100	$31,400	$33,800	$36,100
E-3, D-4, SP-4	$24,600	$26,400	$28,300	$30,100	$31,900
E-2, E-1, D-3	$20,400	$21,900	$23,400	$24,900	$26,400

E = Engineer
D = Designer
SP = Specialists

6-3. *Employees hired or promoted to a grade, such as Drafter-2, advance in that grade until they are promoted to the next higher grade, that is, Drafter-3.*

SALARY ADMINISTRATION RANGES FOR DRAFTERS

As of _____

Employee Grades	Increasing Levels of Experience and Competency				
DR-4	$18,400	$20,200	$22,100	$23,900	$25,700
DR-3	$15,800	$17,200	$18,600	$20,000	$21,400
DR-2	$13,100	$14,100	$15,100	$16,100	$17,100
DR-1	$11,700	$12,300	$12,900	$13,400	$14,000
DR-Apprentice					$12,000

DR = Drafter

6-4. *Use these suggestions as a checklist to determine whether there are other alternatives to outright terminations.*

SUGGESTIONS FOR TERMINATING EMPLOYEES IN AN ECONOMIC DOWNTURN

1. Terminate nonperformers. This should be followed in good times as well as bad, but it is especially important for the morale of an organization to let these people go first in a downturn.

2. Correct existing salary inequities. If anyone's pay is out of line with responsibilities for whatever reason, a good time to correct the situation is when cutbacks and terminations are in the offing.

3. Eliminate overtime. Obviously, in slack periods overtime should be cut back or eliminated consistent with the requirements of ongoing projects. Those people who have counted on a certain amount of overtime to supplement their income will be particularly affected, but this is fairest to all.

4. Loan personnel to other firms, if possible. This is a good solution except during slack periods in the economy few employers need extra help.

5. Reduce working hours. This is also a fair across-the-board solution, but it is often disruptive in a professional services firm where people depend on each other in the course of their work. While the office is open during regular hours, people working shorter hours will not be around for portions of the day.

6. Reduce the number of secretaries per officer/manager. Obviously, each position needs to be evaluated and plans made for doubling up on duties whenever possible. The reduction in number of support staff is one place to start.

7. Encourage voluntary leaves of absence. Through good communication with the staff it may be possible to identify people who because of their personal situations would be willing to take a leave of absence without pay.

8. Promote vacations with/without pay. This is another area where some short-term savings in labor costs are possible.

9. Institute salary cuts/deferrals. When decisions are made to cut salaries it is important for the staff to know that management is included and is taking the largest percentage deductions.

10. Identify labor-consuming tasks/bottlenecks and correct them. If there are any procedural or operating situations where personnel are not being used effectively or people have to wait around for others to complete certain tasks, these problems should be corrected.

11. Cut diagonally across all levels in the organization. Most specialists in human resources suggest that it is better to reduce staff at all levels in the organization when reductions are necessary, rather than cutting off only the junior levels.

Salary Surveys Currently Available

Salary surveys are a useful management tool to evaluate the salary ranges for various classes of employees in order to maintain a competitive and equitable salary structure. Local organizations, chambers of commerce, and personnel search firms conduct surveys and maintain current data for many classifications of employees. In addition state employment offices have information available for employers.

Within the design profession several surveys are used as follows:

1. *Salaries of Scientists, Engineers and Technicians: A Summary of Salary Surveys*, published periodically by Scientific Manpower Commission, 1776 Massachusetts Avenue N.W., Washington, D.C. 20036.

2. *Professional Income of Engineers*, published annually by Engineering Manpower Commission of Engineers Joint Council, 345 East 47th St., New York, NY 10017.

3. *National Survey of Professional, Administrative, Technical and Clerical Pay*, published annually by U.S. Department of Labor, Bureau of Labor Statistics, Washington, D.C. 20210.

4. *Engineering Salaries Survey*, published annually by D. Dietrich Associates, Inc., Box 511, Phoenixville, PA 19460.

5. *Executive Compensation: An RIA Survey*, published annually by The Research Institute of America, Inc., 589 Fifth Avenue, New York, NY 10017.

6. *Professional Engineers' Income and Salary Survey*, published annually by the National Society of Professional Engineers, 2029 K St. N.W., Washington, D.C. 20006.

7. *PSMA/PSMJ Executive Management Salary Survey*, published by *Professional Services Management Journal* (PSMJ), 126 Harvard St., Brookline, MA 02146. Lists salary/fringe data for over 300 design firms.

Controlling Other Project Costs

Costs other than labor on a project, such as computer and report preparation costs, are controlled by the budget. Often these expenditures are not made equally thoughout the project, which is why budgets must be broken down by month or reporting period to compare with actual expenditures. The level of detail needed to control reimbursable expenses, for instance, varies by firm, and each firm has to decide which expenses are likely to overrun and which should therefore be monitored separately. For example, computer costs can become a significant item of expense on a project and can easily get out of hand if not watched. The costs generally associated with the final stages of a project, such as report or document preparation, can also be used up before the project is completed unless budgeted separately and set aside. Experienced project managers recognize the importance of controlling reimbursable expenses and will carefully watch the charges that they approve for payment against their projects.

If the overhead rate must be increased because it was not correctly forecasted when the budgets were prepared, that is not the project manager's fault. He or she cannot be held accountable for it. This will become obvious in the project reporting system when the various elements of costs are isolated. The difference caused by a variance in overhead should be eliminated when judging the project manager's performance on the project.

Project Overruns

Overruns occur when costs get out of line with the budget for any number of reasons and when they cannot be recovered from the client. In that case the project may incur no profit or else suffer a loss. Regardless of the reasons for the overrun the cause is the same—poor estimating or inadequate project management.

In some cases the overrun may not be the fault of the project manager if he or she has been overruled in decisions by higher management. That is then an organizational problem. However, most firms now recognize the importance of the strong project manager type of organization that gives complete operating authority and responsibility to the project manager. In that case the project manager accepts responsibility for project losses. Exhibit 6–5 is a checklist for controlling project overruns.

A good project control system, in which progress on the job is compared against budget and there are reports often enough and in sufficient detail for the project manager and others to recognize potential trouble spots, will go a long way toward preventing project overruns. Simple manual systems can be useful for smaller firms. However as a firm grows and projects are added, it becomes necessary to keep track of such data by computer. Timesharing and service bureaus are available for this task, or the firm may decide to purchase an in-house computer and software to run the system. There are several reference sources available to help in selecting software specifically developed for the design professional. The most comprehensive directory of software for design professionals is *Design Compudata*, published annually by Practice Management Associates, Ltd., 126 Harvard St., Brookline, MA 02146. The 1983 edition contains over 400 vendors. Another source is *A/E Systems Report*, published by MRH Associates, Inc., P.O. Box 11316, Newington, CT 06111. This is a monthly newsletter on automation, and the publisher also sponsors an annual systems show and exposition. Another good source is *Major Software Sources for Consulting Engineers*, published by the American Consulting Engineers Council, 1015 Fifteenth Street, N.W., Suite 802, Washington, D.C. 20005.

Project overruns are a painful and expensive lesson when they occur, and it is important that they be a learning exercise for everyone. Principals in the firm need to know who the capable project managers are who can be trusted to perform well. Experienced project managers need to learn to read early warning signals. Less experienced project managers need to learn from their mistakes. Fault finding is not nearly so important as learning why the loss occurred and what can be done about it in the future so that it will not happen again.

Discussion Problem

Background. Your 10-person interior design firm has been losing projects to a larger architectural and interior design firm located across town. Many of these clients have been of long standing. When asked, several clients have explained that your costs have risen so rapidly over the last few years that your services have become uneconomical. They cannot justify paying a higher price for work that is not that much more superior in quality.

You examine your recent project estimates and budgeting forms and everything looks to be in order. Your overhead rate has increased from 1.5 to 1.8 over the last two years, but it still appears to be comparable with other firms according to some recent survey information you obtained. Salary rates also appear to be about what others are paying for comparable skills. Upon examination of time accounting reports you notice that it takes people longer to accomplish certain tasks than you think necessary. Some of the problem can be traced to the turnover of personnel and the extra training required of new employees. In other cases it appears that overall staff productivity is not keeping pace with that of other firms.

To track the costs for training new employees you establish an overhead account for orientation. Project managers are instructed to have new employees charge this account when they are receiving instruction.

Assignment. What are the advantages of isolating and accounting for training costs? What kinds of training should every new employee receive? What actions should be taken to improve productivity and make the firm more competitive?

List the ways in which a design firm can measure productivity.

CHECKLIST FOR CONTROLLING PROJECT OVERRUNS

YES	NO	
☐	☐	Are procedures in place for review of contracts for technical, legal, and financial aspects?
☐	☐	Are project managers involved at the beginning in contract negotiation and pricing?
☐	☐	Are budgets prepared for each project where appropriate and breakdowns required by month so that comparisons can be made with actual performance?
☐	☐	Do project managers have control over all charges to their projects (including labor and expenses)?
☐	☐	Are meetings held regularly with project managers and principals to discuss the status of projects?
☐	☐	Are project managers encouraged to report problems early so that corrective action can be taken?
☐	☐	Is a financial summary prepared on completion of each project and reviewed with the principals and project manager?
☐	☐	Are project managers graded on their ability to control costs as part of their performance evaluations?
☐	☐	Does the firm encourage project managers to seek further training in project management?
☐	☐	Do project managers read and understand the financial reports prepared for them?

7
Controlling Overhead Costs

1. What are the danger signals to look for that indicate rising overhead costs?

2. How can I compare my overhead rate with that of other similar firms?

3. What are fixed and variable costs, and why is it important to know the difference?

4. How can I control unauthorized purchases?

5. Why is it sometimes dangerous to look for the lowest cost insurance for professional liability?

6. What is a captive insurance company, and when are they practical to consider?

7. How can marketing expenses be controlled and become the most cost effective?

8. How can I avoid overcontrolling the budgets so that people lose initiative?

When overhead costs begin to climb significantly there is generally a reason. However, if a firm can recognize certain danger signals in advance it can save itself the diminished profits or losses that are likely to occur.

How to Recognize Danger Signals

Exhibit 7–1 is a checklist of items to consider in controlling overhead costs. One tipoff that things are not going as planned is when there are wide variances from established budgets. Another is unexpected losses in certain profit centers. There may be unexplainable cost increases in certain overhead accounts. These are danger signals that circumstances are not under control.

Rising indirect labor costs and a corresponding decline in utilization rates (the percentage of direct or chargeable labor to total salaries) are another indication that overhead costs are on the increase. Sometimes there may be significant charges to overhead labor accounts, such as administration or marketing, by people who normally should be charging most of their time to projects. If the firm has an account called "unutilized time" for time that cannot be legitimately charged to anything else and there are significant charges to this account, then that is obviously a danger signal. If there is not enough work to keep the staff busy and people are required to use vacation and sick time, that is another indication that overhead costs are likely to rise. If there are significant project overruns, then that is a sign of lack of proper control that is bound to be reflected in overhead.

Overhead is usually calculated monthly and compared with the budgeted overhead rate established at the beginning of the year. It should be compared on a cumulative year-to-date basis to avoid month-to-month distortions. Generally, an overhead rate is established at the beginning of the year and is not changed unless there are significant changes in the firm's operations. Exhibit 7–2 is an illustration of an overhead rate calculation for two typical firms. The overhead rate should be compared with the firm's historical experience as well as with that of other firms of similar size and characteristics. Two good reference sources for comparing overhead rates and other statistical information with other firms are

1. *Financial Statistics Survey for Professional Services Firms*, sponsored by *Professional Services Management Journal* (PSMJ) and Professional Services Management Association (PSMA) and updated every two years. Write to PSMJ, P.O. Box 11316, Newington, CT 06111 for more information.

2. *Comparative Financial Summary of Publicly Held Companies Engaged in Construction and Related Activities*, V. B. Castellani & Co., 251 Commonwealth Ave., Boston, MA 02116.

Low profitability or losses may be the ultimate signal that overhead costs are climbing out of control. On the other hand, it may not be an overhead cost problem at all, but rather a revenue problem caused by not enough work or lack of project control that is making projects overrun. Therefore, while it is important to monitor overhead closely, the financial manager should be familiar with the other danger signals in order to discover and report the real reasons for any problems that may arise.

Nature of Overhead Costs

Before examining ways to control and reduce overhead costs you need to understand the concept of fixed and variable costs. While all costs are variable given a sufficient period of time, fixed costs are those that do not vary with the volume of operations. Some examples are rent and depreciation expenses that essentially remain unchanged as the firm's revenue increases or decreases. On the other hand, variable costs do change with volume; some examples are supplies and telephone charges that are somewhat related to the amount of work performed. While variable costs may be easier to control in the short run, fixed costs should not be overlooked when examining ways to make permanent reductions.

7-1. *Note the emphasis on preparing budgets and then comparing actual costs against budget.*

CHECKLIST OF ITEMS TO CONSIDER IN CONTROLLING OVERHEAD COSTS

YES	NO	
☐	☐	Do I receive financial information in time enough to take corrective action to prevent losses?
☐	☐	Are project managers aware of their financial performance, and are they constantly monitoring project performance?
☐	☐	Are overhead budgets carefully controlled and not exceeded without advance explanation?
☐	☐	Is management "cost conscious," and is that attitude conveyed to the rest of the staff?
☐	☐	Is there a report on administrative time that identifies the various categories such as marketing and administration?
☐	☐	Do the principals of the firm charge sufficient time to projects?
☐	☐	Are controls in place so that time shown on timesheets reflects what people are actually doing?
☐	☐	Is the support staff of the proper size when compared with other similar firms?
☐	☐	Is there enough work scheduled ahead to keep people busy and not worrying about staff reductions?

It is important to know who has responsibility for controlling costs. In most firms the responsibility for controlling project costs rests with the project manager. Fixed costs should be under the control of the financial manager and variable costs under the control of department or profit center managers. Depending upon how the firm is organized, there may be some variations in this arrangement, but the important point is to assign responsibility so that someone in the organization is looking at individual costs and watching for signs of unusual increases.

Cost Not Affecting Performance

When taking action to control overhead costs, concentrate on meaningful areas. That is, first examine costs of significant size so that any reductions achieved will make an impact on total overhead costs. Otherwise, efforts at cost reduction will be dissipated over an assortment of minor savings that do not amount to much in total. People then become quickly discouraged with the effort. It is also a good practice to begin in areas that do not affect the firm's operating performance. Cuts in these areas are the least painful to make.

Idle Time

YES	NO	
☐	☐	Is idle time of staff members controlled?
☐	☐	Are projects monitored to see that excessive time is not spent by some individuals and departments?
☐	☐	Are charges to overhead accounts, such as marketing and administration, carefully controlled by the people in charge of these activities?

An obvious area to examine first is idle staff time, which is probably the largest waste of money. Either the people should be made productive or else the staff should be reduced. In order to make judgments about this, manpower staffing forecasts as described in Chapter 2 are vital and should be updated at least monthly over a three-month period.

7-2. *Overhead as a factor of direct labor includes all other firmwide costs except such passthrough costs as reimbursable expenses and consultants' fees. It does not include any profit.*

EXAMPLE OF OVERHEAD OF TWO TYPICAL FIRMS
(In Thousands)

	Large Firm	Small Firm
Payroll Burden		
Indirect labor	$1,080	$30
Holiday/vacation/sick leave	400	12
Group insurance	190	6
Payroll taxes	180	3
Tuition reimbursement	20	1
Bonuses, profit sharing	400	7
Other employee benefits	10	1
Total	$2,280	$60
General and Administrative Expenses		
Automobile expenses	30	10
Business development	1,600	70
Contributions	10	2
Data processing	180	15
Office supplies and equipment	1,200	20
Employee recruitment	40	5
Rent and building maintenance	1,800	100
Liability insurance	860	50
Professional dues and subscriptions	100	5
Legal/accounting expenses	200	5
Printing and reproduction	750	15
Telephone	980	20
Depreciation	70	5
State and local taxes	40	1
Miscellaneous expenses	140	7
Total	$8,000	$330
Direct Labor	$6,000	$200

Calculation of overhead Rate:

Payroll burden + general and administrative expense ÷ direct labor

Large firm: $2,280 + $8,000 ÷ $6,000 = 1.7 times direct labor

Small firm: $60 + $330 ÷ $200 = 2.0 times direct labor

When calculating the multiplier for billing purposes, a profit factor is added as follows:

	Large Firm	Small Firm
Direct labor	1.0	1.0
Overhead	1.7	2.0
Profit (@ 20%)	.5	.6
Multiplier	3.2	3.6 times direct labor

Purchasing

YES   NO

☐   ☐   Is purchasing controlled so that only one or two people in the organization can purchase supplies and authorize payment?

☐   ☐   Are purchase orders used for all expenditures except routine purchases?

☐   ☐   Are quantity discounts taken on purchases?

Purchasing is another area that should be brought under control. Purchasing should be centralized within the organization with only one or two people authorized to buy supplies and equipment. This will enable the firm to take advantage of quantity discounts and to shop for the best price, as well as to control unauthorized purchases. Arrangements should be made for emergency purchases by people who run short of supplies when working outside regular office hours, but the large routine purchases should be tightly controlled. The firm should consider the use of a purchase order system if the volume of purchases warrants it.

Another arrangement that some firms have used successfully is of hiring a single vendor for all purchases of high-volume items, such as reproduction or drafting supplies. The firm should calculate what it spends in a year for these supplies and then ask several vendors what discounts they will give if all the firm's business is placed with one supplier. Of course, the firm should only make this offer to vendors that it has used in the past and who have proven their reliability.

General Liability Insurance

YES   NO

☐   ☐   Does the firm have one broker for all insurance?

☐   ☐   Does the broker survey the market to be certain that the firm is purchasing coverage most economically?

☐   ☐   Is the broker routinely notified when new equipment is acquired or office space is to be increased or decreased?

Insurance is another overhead cost area that should be examined for possible savings, or at least periodic increases should be controlled. The firm's insurance broker should be pressed to get the best insurance coverage for the money, since that is the broker's primary purpose. Competitive bids should be obtained for both the employee benefit insurance and the firm's general liability coverage at least once every two years and every year in cases where rates are rising significantly. The firm should try to place all its insurance with a single broker, if possible, so that the total amount is significant enough for the broker to be encouraged to work on the firm's behalf. One good technique for employee benefit insurance is to see if the firm can become a part of a "group within a group"—that is, to place its group insurance within a larger group to take advantage of lower member rates. Members of the American Consulting Engineers Council, American Institute of Architects, and most other professional societies, either locally or nationally, have similar arrangements, or they should be encouraged to obtain them from a group insurance carrier.

Professional Liability Insurance

YES   NO

☐   ☐   Does the firm have a loss prevention program in which all senior staff members participate?

☐   ☐   Are nonstandard contracts reviewed by legal counsel?

☐   ☐   Do principals understand what the professional liability insurance covers and how it is different from general liability?

Professional liability insurance is generally the largest element of insurance cost. While there is little a single firm can do to affect these rates, some things are possible. The firm can participate in loss prevention programs sponsored by the insurance carrier, it can train its own personnel in loss prevention to maintain a good experience record, and it can shop around when various carriers are competing for this business. The problem with switching insurance carriers is in the long time period when the firm has exposure on past projects that must be covered. Another drawback to changing carriers is the volatile insurance market, where carriers enter and leave the market periodically, so that coverage with a new carrier may not be automatically renewed.

One way of achieving some reduction in professional liability premiums is to find out how they are calculated. If they are based on gross revenue encourage clients to accept invoices for service directly from consultants rather than having them pass through the firm's books when the firm is acting as prime professional. The firm can still monitor the consultant's work and act in every way as prime professional on the project, but by elimination of pass-through accounting, the firm's revenues are thereby reduced. This can represent a significant saving.

Another way to reduce professional liability insurance premiums is to investigate the use of project professional liability insurance. In this case the carrier agrees to insure only a particular project and the firm can then claim that premium as a reimbursable expense on the project. If clients will agree to this then they do not have to bear that portion of the overhead rate which includes professional liability insurance on all other projects. This procedure is sometimes useful for larger projects, if your insurance carrier writes this type of coverage.

Another recent development is the use of a single insurance carrier by both the design professionals and the contractor on a project. This prevents disputes between insurance companies if there is a claim, and it can result in lower premiums for all.

Another interesting development is the attempt by several firms to get together to form their own captive insurance company, which is owned by the firm or firms it insures. The captive insurance company invests its own premium income and pays its own claims and can save its owners significant sums of money by handling claims up to a certain limit. The captive insurance company lays off or reinsures the larger losses with other insurance carriers in case of catastrophe. The drawbacks to forming a captive company are that it requires a substantial premium income to support its operations, so it is available only to the largest firms. There are significant administrative expenses as well; in effect, you are going into the insurance business, because you're dependent on the group's experience to determine your premium expense.

It is good to know about the newer developments in the insurance market and then to check with your broker to determine if they are appropriate for your firm.

Exhibit 7–3 is a checklist of insurance coverages that can assist you in structuring a comprehensive program with the assistance of your broker.

Office Space

YES NO
☐   ☐   Has the present office space been examined recently to see whether it is crowded or excessive?

☐   ☐   Does the firm have a plan for its future space requirements?

☐   ☐   Are leases reviewed and decisions made well in advance of expiration dates?

Space requirements are another area that should be examined to keep overhead costs under control. The firm should try to anticipate its space needs as it grows to avoid having to take space at another location. Operating out of two locations can be expensive because of the need to duplicate office services. This is one area in particular where a long-range business plan comes in handy.

Lease arrangements should be made with some provision for growth through subleasing adjoining space or contraction depending on space needs. The firm, for example, must decide whether to stay at its present location or move well in advance

CHECKLIST OF INSURANCE COVERAGE AVAILABLE TO PROFESSIONAL SERVICE FIRMS

Package Policy

1. Multiperil Policy: Provides comprehensive property and general liability insurance tailored to the needs of the insured and subject to a package discount from premiums for similar insurance written under separate policies. Building coverage and personal property coverage are available on a named peril basis or an all-risk basis. An automatic increase in insurance endorsement may be attached to keep coverage in line with inflation. Earthquake coverage where appropriate is available by endorsement. Loss of earnings, rents, and extra expense may also be covered by endorsement, as well as employee dishonesty and money loss.

2. Businessowners' Policy Program: Available for an office building, but subject to certain restrictions. Property coverage is on a replacement cost basis, and there is no coinsurance clause for all risks or named perils protection. Loss of income insurance and comprehensive liability insurance are included.

Building Property Damage

1. Fire Insurance: For design professionals who occupy their own buildings.

2. General Property Form: Applies to described structures and all permanent fixtures constituting a part of the structures.

3. Builders' Risk Form: Available to indemnify professionals who erect their own building for loss or damage from specified perils while under construction. Insurance applies only in course of construction; a permanent policy must be written upon completion, at which time the builders' risk policy is cancelled pro rata.

4. Replacement Cost Endorsement: Provides for full reimbursement for the actual cost of repair or replacement of an insured building without deduction for depreciation. The standard policy indemnifies on an actual cash value basis.

5. Extended Coverage Endorsement: Covers property for same amount as fire policy against all direct loss or damage caused by windstorm and hail, explosion, riot and civil commotion, aircraft, vehicles, and smoke.

6. Vandalism and Malicious Mischief: Written by endorsement with the extended coverage endorsement and extends the policy owner to cover loss or damage caused by vandalism or malicious mischief.

7. Demolition Insurance: For an additional premium, extend the fire policy to cover a loss resulting from the enforcement of any state or municipal law that necessitates, in rebuilding, the demolition of any part of the insured building not damaged by fire. Study your local regulations on this point.

8. Glass Insurance: Insures replacement of plate glass windows and structural glass broken or accidentally or maliciously damaged. Glass is used extensively on the front of modern office buildings, and it should be insured if it appears on your offices.

9. Flood Insurance Policy: Protects owners against financial loss from floods. Flood insurance is written in areas declared eligible by the Federal Insurance Administrator.

10. Sprinkler Leakage: For buildings equipped with sprinkers, insures against all direct loss to buildings or contents as result of leakage or freezing or breaking of sprinkler installations.

11. Earthquake Insurance: Covers loss caused by earthquake, an important coverage in areas where earthquakes occasionally occur.

12. Boiler and Machinery Insurance: Insures against direct damage and loss of income from boiler mishaps.

Contents and Personal Property Damage

1. Fire Insurance: For a tenant who wishes to insure contents, improvements, and betterments under a single policy.

2. Office Personal Property Form: Provides all-risk coverage on contents of offices at named locations; applies to improvements and betterments as well as personal property.

3. Extended Coverage Endorsement: Applicable to contents and personal property just as it is to real property.

4. Vandalism and Malicious Mischief: Determine whether the additional expense of this extension is warranted by the location of the occupied building.

5. Replacement Cost Endorsement: Provides coverage on the basis of replacement cost for owned property.

Professional Activities

1. Scientific Instruments Floater: Intended for scientific instruments of a portable nature; insures each instrument listed on an all-risk basis.

2. Accounts Receivable Policy: Protects the insured against loss resulting from the inability to collect accounts receivable when the books of record have been destroyed, lost, or damaged.

3. Valuable Papers: Covers loss or destruction of valuable papers such as financial data, specifications, client lists, construction plans and blueprints, and manuscripts.

4. Rental Value Insurance: For owners of buildings. Protects building owner against loss of income where rentals have been interrupted or rental values impaired by the occurrence of any of the hazards insured against.

5. Leasehold Interest: For tenants. Protects against loss caused by having to rent property at a higher rate in the event the lease is cancelled as a result of the occurrence of any hazard insured against.

6. Extra Expense Insurance: Insures against payment of additional expense of operating in temporarily rented quarters due to damage to building or contents by fire or other insured hazard.

7. Broad Form Comprehensive General Liability: When added by endorsement, extends basic comprehensive general liability insurance to cover a number of additional hazards. Ask your broker for details about this coverage.

8. Workman's Compensation: Mandated by the state for varying amounts.

9. Business Auto Policy: The business counterpart of the personal auto policy; be sure to include coverage for employee cars and rental cars used on business.

10. Umbrella Liability Insurance: Provides protection against third-party claims not covered by underlying general liability and automobile liability policies and provides excess limits of insurance for claims.

11. Fiduciary Liability Insurance: Pays legal liability arising from claims for alleged failure to prudently act within the meaning of the Pension Reform Act of 1974.

12. Partnerships: Provides cash to carry out a buy-or-sell agreement in the event of the death of a partner. The advice of an attorney is customary in tying the insurance in with a carefully worked-out agreement.

13. Key Man Insurance: Reimburses business for financial loss resulting from death of a key person in the business.

14. Professional Liability Insurance: Covers errors and omissions.

of the lease's expiration. It is important to review the lease and note any milestone dates when notices must be given to the landlord. An analysis of various alternate locations needs to be made and the real estate market tested so that the firm is in a position to make the proper decision when the time comes.

Accounting/Legal Services

YES	NO	
☐	☐	Are you satisfied with the accounting/legal services you are receiving?
☐	☐	Is the cost comparable with what others are paying for similar services?
☐	☐	Does your accountant/attorney keep you informed of the latest tax matters that are important to you?

If the firm is audited by an outside certified public accounting firm, the cost of this service can be significant and it should be examined. As with insurance, the firm should make certain that the money spent on this is giving the most value. Periodically it may be wise to test the market to determine what other firms charge for this service. In some cases, particularly with smaller firms, a regular audit may not be necessary. The accountant may then be asked to "review" the firm's books and records at a significantly lower charge. In that case the accountant will do less work and will not certify as to the fairness of the financial statement presentation, but this narrower examination may be sufficient for the firm's purposes. It will largely depend on whether the firm has a bank loan outstanding and whether the bank will accept a review in place of a complete audit.

After significant items of expense have been reviewed small items should not be overlooked for possible savings, particularly if these items can be looked at in a systematic way by means of a checklist. For example, Exhibit 7–4 is a checklist for reviewing business forms, which can be helpful when investigating all the forms used throughout the firm.

Costs Affecting Performance

After you review the various costs that do not affect performance, it is then necessary to examine others that will have an impact on the firm's operations.

Marketing

YES	NO	
☐	☐	Are marketing costs reviewed and approved by a single individual in the firm?
☐	☐	Is there a budget for marketing (time and expenses)?
☐	☐	Are marketing costs compared as a percentage of total revenue with those of other similar firms?

Marketing costs are a significant item of overhead expense, and this is a very sensitive area to cut. Perhaps the best way is to examine these costs from the standpoint of whether or not the firm is directing its marketing effort in the right channels. Costs should be verified to make certain that they are really going for marketing activities. The marketing director should be responsible for his or her costs and approve all time and expenses charged to that budget. One area to scrutinize in particular for possible savings is that of "entertainment," particularly if the firm cannot realize any real payoff for some of these expenditures.

Support Staff

YES	NO	
☐	☐	Are all personnel on the support staff fully used on meaningful work that benefits the firm?
☐	☐	Are secretaries assigned on the basis of need by the person requiring them?
☐	☐	Is turnover of support staff comparable with that of similar firms?

7-4. *Business forms are a useful tool, but care should be taken to see that only the minimum number and variety are used in a manner consistent with the size of the firm.*

CHECKLIST FOR BUSINESS FORMS

YES   NO

☐ ☐ 1. Do you have a business forms' control program to avoid excess duplication and clerical effort?

☐ ☐ 2. Do you have a forms committee to control forms and improve the paper communication between departments?

☐ ☐ 3. Do you know how many different forms you use?

☐ ☐ 4. Do you know the actual usage for each form?

☐ ☐ 5. Have you identified "key forms," that is, forms without which your operations are severely curtailed?

☐ ☐ 6. Do your external forms present the image you wish to project?

☐ ☐ 7. Do you schedule your requirements to avoid the expense of "rush" orders?

☐ ☐ 8. Do you have specifications written for economy in printing?

☐ ☐ 9. Do your suppliers maintain your forms inventory?

☐ ☐ 10. Do you know the cost per square foot of your forms storage area?

☐ ☐ 11. Do you keep a perpetual inventory of all forms to insure that you never run out of a given form?

☐ ☐ 12. Do you receive sufficient notice prior to depletion of your forms' inventory?

☐ ☐ 13. Do you have a business forms' identification guide, that is, a list of management-approved business forms?

☐ ☐ 14. Have you used a business forms' audit guaranteeing a 10 percent decrease in actual business form costs?

☐ ☐ 15. Do you have an accurate computation of usage to ensure that the proper quantity is printed and thereby avoid obsolescence and excess inventory carrying costs?

☐ ☐ 16. Does each of your forms have a number and revision date?

Support staff expenses are another area to look at in controlling costs. The firm needs to decide on the level of operations it wishes to maintain and then see what, if any, costs can be cut back. It may be possible to combine some functions, but the reductions should not decrease overall efficiency.

Fringe Benefits

YES   NO

☐ ☐ Does the firm conduct an annual review of its fringe benefits policies?

☐ ☐ Are comparisons made with the fringe benefits provided by other similar firms?

☐ ☐ Are employees aware of what the firm is paying them in fringe benefits above salary?

Fringe benefits is an area that cannot be cut without hurting morale, but it should not escape an overall review. The employee benefit plan, for example, should be at least as good as that of other firms in the area in order to retain personnel, but as the costs increase, it is expected that employees will share in that increase. Benefit reductions can be made if they are communicated properly and thoroughly to the staff and as long as the staff recognizes them as fair to all and contributing to the financial health and stability of the firm.

Implementing Cost Reduction Plans

When you review overhead costs and decide on what cuts should be made, it is important to recognize that large sweeping cuts which may relieve a temporary loss will not be effective in the long run. Such cuts will eventually have to be restored if the firm is to operate efficiently. Therefore, it is important to look at the long-term effect of any cost reduction program. The firm should remember not to try to overcontrol operations so that people lose initiative. In addition, long-term staff development needs may have to be reduced, but they should not be eliminated altogether or the firm will ultimately suffer for it. In addition to cutting costs the firm should look for ways to raise revenue, such as entering new markets.

Exhibit 7–5 is a checklist to use when reviewing various overhead accounts for possible cost reductions. Exhibits 7–6 through 7–8 are various reporting forms used to control overhead costs by department or profit center, or however the firm is organized.

7-5. *Do not overlook suggestions from your staff as an important source of ideas for reducing overhead costs.*

CHECKLIST FOR REDUCING OVERHEAD COSTS

Account	Cost-Saving Ideas
1. Accounting fees	
a. Year-end audit	1. Renegotiate the fee each year.
	2. Obtain quotations from other firms.
	3. Ask to have your in-house accounting staff prepare as many workpaper schedules as the auditors will allow.
b. Annual income tax return	1. Do most of the return in-house and ask tax acountant to review.
c. Quarterly payroll tax returns	1. Do in-house.
2. Debt service	1. Investigate other banks for better terms.
3. Insurance	
a. Property/liability	1. Keep coverage at an adequate rate and ask insurance company to provide temporary endorsements for clients who require higher coverage during the time their projects are being worked on.
	2. Obtain quotations from other firms.
	3. Promote good loss experience through in-depth communication with staff.
	4. Arrange for higher deductibles.
	5. Obtain discounts with packaged policies.
b. Group insurance	1. Obtain quotations from several firms.
	2. Investigate professional society insurance programs.
	3. Share cost with employee.
	4. Set up higher deductibles.
c. Officers' life insurance (funds buy/sell)	1. Make sure the coverage is term insurance, not whole life.
	2. Obtain quotations from other firms periodically.
	3. Investigate self-insurance for a portion or all of the risk.

4. Outside services

   a. Retirement program consultation

      1. Use in-house accounting for completing administrative forms and reports.

   b. Branch office services

      1. Negotiate short-term agreements.

      2. Review quotations from many real estate firms.

      3. Investigate whether branch office is the most effective alternative.

5. Rent/lease

   a. Building

      1. Review market rates periodically.

      2. Try to negotiate a limit to the escalation clause at renewal date.

      3. If real estate market is soft, negotiate with a new landlord for free rent, minimum escalation rate, short-term lease, and moving costs.

      4. Eliminate old files to reduce need for storage space.

      5. Make floor plan efficient to reduce need for space.

   b. Equipment

      1. Share equipment with other firms rather than rent equipment that may be idle most of the day.

6. Employment agency fees

      1. Investigate alumni organizations, newspaper advertising, and competition.

7. Dues for professional organizations

      1. Limit to management or else eliminate.

      2. Ask that employee who is an officer in a professional organization be reimbursed by the organization for related travel.

      3. Share cost with employees.

      4. Eliminate or reduce number of meetings attended.

      5. Set up policy of no wives/family attending at company expense.

      6. Institute policy of no entertainment costs charged to firm.

8. Supplies

      1. Investigate quantity discounts for large purchases.

      2. Get quotations from many suppliers.

      3. Control inventory of drafting and field supplies.

      4. Do not store copy paper in copy room to avoid unnecessary waste.

9. Postage/delivery

      1. Does every item have to be mailed first class?

      2. Ensure that postage scale is properly calibrated.

      3. Control overnight deliveries.

PROFIT CENTER OR DEPARTMENTAL SUMMARY REPORT

Month, Year 3/84	Departments/Profit Centers A	B	C	D, etc.	Monthly Costs Actual	Budget	Year to Date Costs	Annual Budget
Gross salary	$30,000	$16,000	$45,000	$20,000	$111,000	$110,000	$148,000	$160,000
Less: Holiday/vacation/sick	5,000	1,000	5,000	2,000	13,000	12,000	17,000	20,000
Available salary	25,000	15,000	40,000	18,000	98,000	98,000	131,000	140,000
Direct salary	18,000	10,000	30,000	12,000	70,000	74,000	95,000	105,000
Utilization rate	72%	67%	75%	67%	71%	75%	71%	75%
Indirect salary	7,000	5,000	10,000	6,000	28,000	24,000	38,000	35,000
Administrative expenses	3,000	2,000	8,000	2,000	15,000	12,000	20,000	30,000
Business development expenses	5,000	1,000	4,000	5,000	15,000	16,000	22,000	25,000
Total expenses	8,000	3,000	12,000	7,000	30,000	28,000	42,000	55,000
Total salaries + expenses	$38,000	$19,000	57,000	27,000	141,000	138,000	190,000	215,000

7-6. *This report compares actual costs against budget so that senior management can review each department or profit center, depending on how the firm is organized. Note how the information on Department A in the first column represents a summary of the more detailed information presented in Exhibits 7-7 and 7-8.*

7-7. *This report shows a more detailed breakdown of costs than that provided in Exhibit 7-6. It is for use by a profit center or departmental manager. Note that the figures shown under "current month" can be traced to the summary data in column 1 of Exhibit 7-6.*

DETAILED PROFIT CENTER OR DEPARTMENTAL REPORT

Month, Year _3/84_   Manager _S. Smith_

	Last Month Actual	Current Month	Budget	Actual Year to Date	Annual Budget
Labor Costs					
Gross salary	$22,000	$30,000	$32,000	$45,000	$60,000
Less: Holiday/ vacation/sick	2,000	5,000	4,000	10,000	15,000
Available salary	20,000	25,000	28,000	36,000	45,000
Direct salary	15,000	18,000	20,000	26,000	34,000
Utilization rate	75%	72%	74%	75%	75%
Indirect salary	5,000	7,000	8,000	9,000	11,000
Other Costs					
Administrative expenses					
Supplies/printing	600	200	300	1,000	2,000
Telephone	300	400	200	600	1,000
Travel	100	400	200	800	2,000
Total costs	$7,000	$8,000	$7,000	$10,000	$15,000

7-8. *This report shows detailed performance by each individual within a profit center or department and supports Exhibit 7-7. The profit center or departmental manager uses this report for a further explanation of the information in Exhibit 7-7. Note that the total figures across the bottom of this report reflect the detail of what appears under the "current month" column for labor costs in Exhibit 7-7.*

INDIVIDUAL UTILIZATION REPORT

Month, Year __3/84__   Manager __S. Smith__

List Individuals by Name	Gross Salary	Hol./Vac./Sick	Avail. Salary	Direct Salary	Utilization Rate	Indirect Salary
J. Terry	$2,400	0	$2,400	$2,400	100%	0
R. Mason	3,000	$400	2,600	1,300	50	1,300
B. Wright	3,600	800	2,800	2,400	85	400
Subtotal	$29,200	$5,000	$24,200	$17,200	72%	$7,000
Loaned personnel						
B. Tarbell	$800	0	$800	$800	100%	0
Total	$30,000	$5,000	$25,000	$18,000	72%	$7,000

Overhead Cost Committees

One technique for controlling overhead, which is used in some larger firms, is an overhead cost committee. These committees are generally established to accomplish the specific task of cutting overhead costs. Usually, the financial manager and several operating personnel are assigned to the committee.

Overhead cost committees can be very beneficial if they are used properly. If they can be formed before a crisis situation develops they do not have to work on a "crash" basis. If senior management personnel are appointed to the committee and its recommendations are carried out, they can be very effective. The committee can serve as an educational forum for the financial manager to explain cost control to others. Very often this is the first exposure that technical people have to the financial operations of the firm. The committee can have a significant impact on performance if it is recognized that cost control is a never-ending task and the committee should work with each segment of the firm on a rotating basis so that all areas are eventually covered.

In smaller firms, the overhead cost committee can be made up of the principals, but the committee must operate separately from the general management of the firm and must meet separately for this purpose. Otherwise management problems and operating crises will crowd out the agenda, leaving no time for this important task.

1. Background. For several years the volume of revenues for Smith Engineers has been steadily increasing, but profit before taxes and discretionary bonus payments has stayed below 5 percent, as shown on the table below.

	Revenues ($000)	Expenses ($000)	Profit before Taxes ($000)	% Profit of Rev.
1981	$402	$394	$ 8	2%
1982	478	460	18	4
1983	492	472	20	4
1984 (est.)	526	514	12	2

Note that the estimate for 1984 is even lower. The managing principal is very concerned that the overhead rate has been steadily increasing and that it is out of line with that of other comparable firms. Although he has no hard numbers to support this conclusion, he bases his assumption on informal talks he has had with other principals at professional society meetings.

The managing principal has decided to look for ways to cut overhead and keep it down. Because this is a small firm and there is no one on staff to assist him he discusses the matter with the firm's independent accountant. The managing principal is aware of the Financial Statistics Survey sponsored by the *Professional Services Management Journal* and the Professional Services Management Association. He obtains the latest copy and gives it to the accountant to assist in the analysis. An extract of key ratios from this report is shown below. The accountant prepares the analysis shown on page 99 that compares the key overhead items for Smith Engineers with other firms in the study. The managing principal then decides to find out why the asterisked items were outside the averages shown in the report.

Assignment. List other reasons beside higher overhead that could account for the low profits. What are the advantages/disadvantages of comparing operating performance with statistical surveys? What other methods could be used to analyze operating performance?

Analyze the data below to determine whether the managing principal was right in his assumption that overhead expense is the reason for the firm's low profitability. What are some other contributing causes?

This extract compares key reporting ratios for firms participating in the survey with Smith Engineers. Definitions of the ratios are provided on the following pages. Asterisked items are outside the ranges and require further analysis.

SUMMARY OF KEY RATIOS[1]

	Participating Firms		Smith Engineers
	Mean	**Median**	
Net profit [before tax and distributions on net revenues] (%)	8.63	8.31	2.3*
Contribution rate (%)	60.1	61.1	59.4*
Overhead rate [before distributions] (%)	144	140	126*
Net multiplier (X)	2.77	2.70	2.09*
Net revenues per total staff ($)	41,415	40,115	24,338*
Net revenues per technical staff ($)	56,672	51,805	35,690*
Chargeable ratio (%)	64	63	59*
Total staff to marketing staff	38.1	53.1	48.1

[1]Extracted from *1982 Financial Statistics Survey for Professional Services Firms*, sponsored by *Professional Services Management Journal* and Professional Services Management Association. Reproduced with permission.

*Indicates figure deviating from averages shown.

This list defines the terms used in the summary of key ratios on page 97.

EXPLANATION OF KEY RATIOS

Net Profit before Tax and Distributions on Net Revenues

This index measures net profit (income) before taxes and distributions based on net revenues. As a result, it bases profit percentage only on your own efforts and not on consultants and reimbursables. It is calculated before distributions for bonuses, profit sharing, and the like.

Contribution Rate

The contribution rate is the portion of each dollar of net revenues remaining after all direct project costs (both labor and expenses) are covered. Thus, it is the contribution of each fee dollar to overhead and profit. The findings indicate that 60.2¢ (mean figure) or 61.1¢ (median) of each $1 of gross income is available for overhead and profit. It is calculated by dividing gross profit by net revenues.

Overhead Rate before Distributions

The overhead rate is the percentage of total office overhead to total office direct labor. For each dollar of project direct labor spent, an equivalent of $1.44 (mean) $1.40 (median) is spent for overhead. Overhead also includes that portion of the principals' time that is not chargeable to projects.

Net Multiplier

This is the effective multiplier firms achieve on direct labor in their most recent fiscal year (it is not the target multiplier). It is calculated by dividing net revenues by direct labor and is more meaningful than a gross multiplier (which includes consultants and reimbursables) in that it represents the actual multiplier you achieve on your own efforts. When determining a project fee, you first calculate the labor required, multiply the result by your net multiplier, then add consultants and reimbursables, and factor in any markups to achieve the total fee quoted to the client. The net multiplier thus covers your direct project labor, any other nonlabor project expenses, overhead, contingencies, and profit. The 2.77 (mean figure) indicates that the participating firms received $2.77 for every $1 in direct labor spent (the median was 2.70).

Net Revenues per Total Staff

This index measures the dollar amount of net revenues each employee or part-time equivalent represents. It is calculated by dividing net revenues by your average total staff incuding principals and part-time equivalents. The average found in the survey was $41,515 per employee (including principals) and the median was $40,115.

Net Revenues per Technical Staff

This index is calculated by dividing net revenues by the average total technical staff (defined as including all planning or design professionals, technicians and job shoppers who work on projects, including principals). The survey results indicate $56,672 in revenues per technical staff member (the median is $51,805). Many feel that this is a more accurate representation than revenues per total staff in that it assigns revenues to those who are directly responsible for generating them.

Chargeable Ratio

The chargeable ratio is determined by dividing total direct labor by direct labor plus vacation, sick leave, and holiday labor expense plus total indirect labor. A calculation could also be made based upon time (hours); however, for survey purposes the dollar figure is more accurate. The average chargeable ratio was found to be 62 percent and the median was 63 percent. A net ratio could be calculated by omitting the vacation, sick leave, and holiday labor expense.

Total Staff to Marketing Staff

This is the number of staff per full marketing person (meaning those who spend at least 75 percent of their time on marketing). The median figure of 53.1 appears quite high when compared with other surveys that found this ratio to be about 22.1.

This extract from the survey report shows individual items of overhead expense as a percentage of direct labor. The use of a percentage comparison is helpful in highlighting those areas where Smith Engineers is outside the survey's ranges.

KEY OVERHEAD ITEMS
(Expressed as Percent of Direct Labor)*

Line Item	Participating Firms		Smith Engineers
	Mean	Median	
Payroll burden			
Mandatory payroll taxes	11.0%	11.1%	10.2%
Vacation, sick leave, holiday	14.1	14.2	10.4
Group insurance	6.1	5.8	6.6[†]
Annual pension expense	4.8	4.0	0
Bonus, incentive payments, profit sharing	14.9	10.8	4.3
All other fringe benefits	2.4	1.4	0
Total Payroll Burden	**48.7%**	**44.9%**	**31.5%**
General & Administrative			
Indirect (nonproject) labor	46.4%	44.9%	51.2[†]
Cost of space	12.5	11.4	16.3[†]
Telephone	3.7	3.5	5.0[†]
Professional liability insurance	4.6	3.8	0.8
Interest on borrowed capital	4.3	2.5	1.0
Bad debt expense	2.9	1.0	3.4
Total other general and administrative	35.7	31.5	31.6
Total general and administrative	**108.8%**	**105.9%**	**109.3%**
Total Indirect Expenses	**159.4%**	**154.7%**	**140.8%**

*Individual items not additive.
†Areas needing attention.

2. Background. Your eight-person architectural firm has experienced a rapid increase in overhead rate at the same time that growth has leveled off because of a downturn in construction activity in your location. Recently you have been losing $5,000 to $10,000 per month on an accrual basis and your bank loan has been higher than ever before. Your forecasts indicate further losses in the months ahead. You have not had to reduce staff yet, but you are concerned about how long you will be able to keep everyone employed. Because of your small size, a layoff of even one person would be disruptive. Everyone understands the situation and has been working extra hours to keep the firm going.

You would like to examine all items of overhead in detail to see if there are expenses that can be trimmed. However, because of the press of current work and the need to make extra business development calls, there is really no time to accomplish this task. Besides, you are not familiar with what is included in many of the overhead accounts since your bookkeeper has been handling this since you founded the firm.

You ask your other principal and the bookkeeper to meet with you on Saturday to review all items of overhead and discuss ways to achieve reductions. Based on what you have learned in Chapter 7, how would you go about preparing for that meeting?

Assignment. List the overhead expenses you would concentrate on to achieve meaningful reductions. How would you involve other members of the staff in an expense-reduction program? What other options are available in addition to cost-cutting?

8
Billing and Collection

1. Why is having sufficient working capital vital to the success of a professional service firm?

2. What is a good rule of thumb for determining how quickly invoices should be mailed following the close of an accounting period?

3. What are some suggestions for expediting billing?

4. What should I look for before signing a client's purchase order?

5. How do I perform a credit check on a new client?

6. How can I expedite payment if I am a consultant and the prime professional has not been paid?

7. What is the seven-step procedure that can be used to improve collections?

8. When do I use the services of a collection agent?

9. What procedure do I follow in paying bills if I have cash flow problems?

The importance of cash flow to a design firm cannot be overemphasized. The rate at which cash enters and leaves the organization can determine the difference between success and failure, regardless of what appears on the financial statements. It is important that technical personnel understand the concept of cash flow and its implications in the overall financial health of the organization.

Working Capital

The cash cycle in a design firm is much simpler than that in other types of organizations since a service firm does not have to be concerned with inventories in various stages of completion. However, labor must be paid immediately after it is performed and vendors of supplies and services must generally be paid within 30 days. This lag between the time the work is performed and when it can be invoiced and still later paid must be financed in one form or another—generally through a bank line of credit or through internally generated funds. In any event it is a cost to the firm. However, as a firm grows and the requirements for working capital increase, it becomes even more difficult to rely exclusively on a bank line of credit.

Banks expect to be partners to share and assist in the firm's growth, but, in a sense, they expect to be favored partners since a bank line of credit must be repaid for some portion of the year, generally 30 days. This demonstrates to the bank that the firm has enough financial strength to meet its obligations and growth objectives and is not completely dependent on outside resources.

Obviously, the faster a firm can invoice and collect for its services the lower the amount needed for working capital. However, no matter how efficiently the firm operates, it will be limited in its growth prospects if it does not have sufficient working capital to support its operations. If we consider the usual operating pattern of doing work one month, invoicing for it the next month, and collecting for it the third month, then working capital would generally be required to support three months' sales. This figure, of course, varies with the nature of the firm's operations.

Expediting Billing Procedures

One area where a firm can take positive action to speed up its cash flow and lower its requirements for working capital is in invoicing clients. Invoices should be sent out as quickly as possible after the close of the accounting period.

A good rule of thumb is that invoices should usually be mailed by the 10th calendar day following the close of the month or end of the reporting period. At least most invoices should be out by that date. It is important to get into the client's monthly paying cycle early enough so as not to have to wait another month to be paid.

Expediting the Approval Process. One method to speed up the billing process is to make certain that approvals of invoices are handled expeditiously. It is important that project managers approve invoices before they are sent, but invoices should not be held up awaiting approval because a project manager is out of town or otherwise not available. Every project manager should designate an alternate who can approve invoices when he or she is absent. In addition, deadlines should be established as a matter of policy when invoices must be mailed, and project managers should know that if invoices have not been approved by that date they will be mailed regardless.

Standardizing Invoicing Procedures. Invoicing procedures should be standardized to the extent possible and invoices should only be typed once. Exhibits 8–1, 8–2, and 8–3 are examples of typical invoice forms. It may be easier, in some cases, to have the project manager approve a marked-up draft of last month's invoice. The financial manager should see that all supporting documentation and progress reports that are required are included and submitted along with the invoice, because the financial manager is the one most concerned with mailing the invoices on time. Using a standard preprinted invoice form will also expedite typing, or if invoices are prepared on a word processor, it is a simple matter to insert the proper figures each

8-1. *Note the inclusion of outstanding invoices on the current invoice as a reminder
that these have not yet been
paid.*

EXAMPLE OF TYPICAL INVOICE FORM
(Multiplier Type Project)

12/31

TO: Able Development Company

PROJECT: Design of Amusement Park (No. 83-025)
INVOICE PERIOD: December
REFERENCE: Letter of Agreement dated 6/30

	Hours	Dollars*	Extension
Labor charges			
Principals			
Jerry Hayes	20	$2,400	
Harry Clay	25	2,625	
Project Manager			
John Gray	18	1,350	
Etc.			
TOTAL LABOR CHARGES			$10,500
Reimbursable expenses			
Travel		260	
Telephone		350	
Etc.			
TOTAL REIMBURSABLE EXPENSES			980
Consultant costs			
Structural Engineer			2,500
AMOUNT DUE THIS PERIOD			13,980
OUTSTANDING INVOICES			4,000
TOTAL AMOUNT DUE			$17,980

*Calculated using multiplier rate.

8-2. *A standardized invoice form permits invoices to be prepared quickly. To save time, if additional information is required by the client, it should be included in a progress report prepared by the project manager at the same time the invoices are being prepared.*

EXAMPLE OF TYPICAL INVOICE FORM
(Published Billing Rate Project)

12/31

TO: Able Development Company

PROJECT: Design of Amusement Park (No. 83-025)

INVOICE PERIOD: December

REFERENCE: Letter of Agreement dated 6/30

	Hours	Dollars*	Extension
Labor charges			
Principals	20	$2,600	
Project Manager	36	2,800	
Etc.			
TOTAL LABOR CHARGES			$12,600
Reimbursable expenses			
Printing			450
Consultants' fees			
Structural Engineer			5,000
AMOUNT DUE THIS PERIOD			18,050
OUTSTANDING INVOICES			3,500
TOTAL AMOUNT DUE			$21,550

*Calculated using standard billing rates.

8-3. *The figure shown under "% completion" should be based on a technical evaluation of the work effort and the amount yet to complete. It should not be based on the hours spent versus the total budgeted hours.*

EXAMPLE OF TYPICAL INVOICE FORM
(Percent of Construction Project)

12/31

TO: Able Development Company

PROJECT: Design of Amusement Park (No. 83-025)

INVOICE PERIOD: December

REFERENCE: Letter of Agreement dated 6/30

Estimated construction cost $2,000,000
fee @ 6%   120,000

Phase	% of Fee	Fee ($)	% Compl.	Fee Earned
Schematic design	20	$24,000	30	$ 7,200
Design development				
Etc.	30	36,000	10	3,600
			TOTAL EARNED	$10,800
			PREVIOUSLY INVOICED	3,000
			CURRENT AMOUNT DUE	$ 7,800

month. It is also important to avoid sending back-up or supporting documentation unless the client specifically requests it. The amount of detail requested on each invoice should be decided upon at the time of contract negotiation, and clients should be encouraged to accept a standard one-page invoice without documentation. Most will, but there will be others, particularly governmental agencies, which require special forms for invoicing, and these, of course, have to be accommodated. Preparing special-purpose invoices to meet the client's need is an extra overhead service and involves extra time and expense that should be brought to the attention of the client even if the firm cannot be compensated for this expense.

Use of Discounts for Prompt Payment. Another consideration in efficient billing procedures is the use of discounts for prompt payment of invoices. Discounts are not widely used by professional service firms because they reduce the already slim profit margins. The cost of offering a discount is expensive even in terms of today's high interest rates, as shown in Exhibit 8–4. While discounts would undoubtedly speed up the turnover of accounts receivable, there are some drawbacks, principally the many cases where clients will take the discount but not pay within the prescribed period. This requires reinvoicing for the discounted amount, at the risk of raising a dispute with the client or else absorbing the loss, neither of which is a completely satisfactory solution.

One thing to keep in mind is that if the firm does work for the government and if discounts are offered, then the government must be given the same discount privileges as any other client. Since government accounting offices are required to take discounts whenever offered, this might be a way to speed up government payments.

Instead of discounts, a preferable technique is to ask for and obtain advance payments whenever possible. Depending on the practice of other similar firms, it is advantageous to obtain a portion of the payment in advance or else a retainer that is then credited against the final payment. It is also important to try to obtain advance payments on government contracts whenever the particular government office will allow it. Some governmental agencies permit advance payments on a quarterly basis, and it does no harm to ask.

Government Letters of Credit. In certain contracts, some government agencies issue what is called a "letter of credit," which is simply a device for arranging for payments from a regional government disbursing office directly into the firm's bank account. This procedure speeds up payments considerably. But the arrangement has to be worked out with the contracting officer in advance, and there is a certain amount of paperwork involved. However, it is advantageous to inquire if these arrangements are available from the agency awarding the contract.

Commercial Letters of Credit. If the firm does work for foreign clients, a commercial letter of credit arrangement should be used that provides for payments directly from a United States bank when payment is authorized by the client. This keeps the firm from having to depend on a foreign client for direct payment when in some cases it is not possible to properly check credit references or banking relationships. In effect, a letter of credit substitutes a bank's credit for that of the client and assures payment once the work has been performed to the client's satisfaction and payment is authorized.

Importance of Payment Terms. One payment method to avoid is the procedure that requires payment upon completion of particular milestones or stages of completion. This procedure often requires the firm to delay invoicing beyond the end of an accounting period, further straining the requirements for working capital.

Payment terms must be clearly defined in the contract and should generally call for monthly invoices and payment within 30 days. Retainers should be withheld from the last payment whenever possible.

It is most important when working under a government or commercial purchase order to recognize that purchase orders were designed primarily to purchase mate-

CASH DISCOUNTS:
HOW TO USE THEM AND WHAT THEY REALLY COST

With interest rates at high levels, the question of cash discounts given or received by design professionals as an incentive for prompt payment becomes important. Cash discounts mean one of two things:

1. A discount given by the design professional to the client who pays during the discount period.

2. A penalty paid by the design professional who doesn't pay the supplier during the discount period.

If the terms of the discount are stated, it is possible to calculate the annual rate of interest lost by the design professional who fails to take the discount given.

$$I = \frac{D}{(G - D)\,(T/365)}$$

I = Annual rate of interest

D = Amount of discount

G = Gross amount of the invoice

T = Time difference between discount and net payment date in days

If, for example, in the case of a design professional's bill for $500 with the terms of 2% discount if paid within 10 days and the net amount due in 30 days, then:

D = 2% of the gross value of the invoice ($10)

G = Gross value of the invoice ($500)

T = Time difference between the discount and net payment date (20 days)

The formula then becomes:

$$I = \frac{\$10}{(\$500 - \$10)\,(20/365)}$$

I = 37.24% per annum

In this example, the client should take the discount as long as the interest rate is higher than what it costs to borrow funds from the bank.

---

rial. They were not designed to purchase services. Therefore if the firm is not careful, it may find that the purchase order was written to provide for payment upon completion of the work. Additional clauses may have to be typed into a purchase order to allow for progress payments.

Obtaining Credit References. To avoid late payments and eventual bad debts, it is wise to ask for credit references from all potential clients for whom the firm has never worked before. In this case the client is coming to the firm requesting work and there should be no hesitation in asking for credit references. This is done all the time in other businesses. The bank references should include the name of the banker who handles the potential client's account. When you need a reference remember that the banker is often more comfortable and will give out more information if he or she is dealing with another banker, so it is often a good practice to ask your banker to obtain the credit check for you. The potential client's banker will generally comment on the length of time the account has been open, average balances maintained, and a brief description of any borrowings and repayment history.

Since banks usually do not give a "bad" credit reference, the negatives to look for in examining the reference are if a loan has had to be renegotiated, if the client has been with the bank only a short time, and if the banker does not know the client very well. In many instances it is necessary to "read between the lines" in judging a potential client's credit status. If a potential client is reluctant to give a bank reference or if the bank has been instructed not to give out information, then the firm will have to make its own judgment before proceeding.

Collecting Receivables

The ability to collect receivables quickly requires considerable effort, but it is vital in these days of record high interest rates. This means that all invoices beyond the current period must be vigorously pursued. Clients must be reminded of any outstanding amounts on current invoices, and separate periodic reminders must be sent out to any clients who do not receive current invoices.

The financial manager should review the accounts receivable list monthly and make certain that something is done to expedite payment on each account past due. In some cases, he or she may know the problem and the reason why a client cannot or will not pay. But the financial manager still needs to investigate the progress that is being made toward reaching a resolution. Project managers must also be involved in the collection process and should work closely with the financial manager to follow up on late payments. The financial manager should not hesitate to get help from anyone in management, including the managing principal if necessary, whenever payment can be expedited in this manner. It is also important for the financial manager to report the status of unpaid invoices periodically to the principals of the firm so that they can help in the collection effort. Project managers will also be more eager to help if they know that a status report on unpaid invoices is sent to the principals each month.

Invoicing for Interest. Collecting interest on late payments is still not widely accepted among professional service firms, but it has been receiving increased attention in recent years. Contracts should be written to provide for interest on late payments, and the interest rate should be whatever it costs the firm to borrow. It is then important to invoice for the interest whenever payments are late.

For the firm to be able to invoice for interest on late payments, this procedure must be discussed during the negotiations, agreed to by the client, and then written into the contract. The interest charges should be clearly identified on the invoice and compounded each month. It is also a good practice to cite the clause in the contract and to show the interest calculation on the invoice, so it will not serve as another excuse for a late-paying client to contact you and request a further explanation. One other tactic to keep in mind is that it is sometimes wise to give up the accumulated interest in exchange for a quick and complete settlement of the outstanding amount. In this case the interest becomes a useful bargaining chip.

Prime Professional/Consultant Relationships in Collection Efforts. In some cases where your firm is a consultant and the prime professional has not yet been paid, it is difficult to press for collection. However, there are still some actions that can be taken. If the prime professional has not been pursuing the collection as actively as you think he should, offer to help, particularly if you have done work for the client previously or have contacts in that office. In certain situations the prime professional will accept your offer, particularly if the amount you have outstanding is more than the prime professional's at that time. In any case anticipate these kinds of delays and try to build them into your costs whenever possible. Finally, you should remember the experience when going after future work and decide if the carrying charges offset the potential profit from the work.

The opposite situation occurs when you are the prime professional and have not been paid and consultants are calling you. In this case make certain to follow up with the client and report back your findings to the consultant. You should then pay him promptly after you are paid in order to maintain his cooperation.

Contacts in Clients' Office. The financial manager should have a contact to call in the client's office to check on the status of invoices, particularly where there are large ongoing relationships. In some cases it may even be necessary for the financial manager to visit the client's office and "walk through" invoices, getting the necessary approvals along the way, particularly in some governmental agencies. This walk-through experience will be helpful in expediting the payment of future invoices.

At times it is difficult to collect the first invoice on government projects because the invoicing routines have not yet been established. In that case, it is wise to invoice for the first payment as soon as possible. This means that if the project started in the middle or toward the end of the month, it is well to send the first invoice at the end of the month even though it may be quite small in order to get the payment routine established.

Collection Techniques. A step-by-step technique that involves calling the client and asking the right questions at various stages of the collection process is described as follows:

First Call

1. Have you received our invoice? This question not only assures you that the invoice has arrived but also gets it to the top of the paying pile because the client has to search for it when the inquiry is made.

2. Is it correct? This question can resolve any discrepancy immediately so you do not have to wait for the invoice to be reviewed in the normal course of the client's paying routine.

3. Do you require any supporting documentation? This question, in conjunction with 2, will tend to assure you that the invoice will receive approval without unnecessary delay.

4. When can we expect payment? This is the first subtle reminder that we are looking for payment.

Second Call

5. We have not received payment. Is anything wrong? This question, asked after payment has not been received within the normal payment terms, is a request to resolve any differences as quickly as possible.

Third Call

6. Shall we stop work? This is a stronger reminder delivered after waiting, say, two to three weeks after the second call.

Fourth Call

7. We have stopped work. Shall we call our attorney? At this point there is a potential bad debt situation that must be resolved quickly before matters reach a point of no return.

In addition to calls, followup letters should be sent to all clients whose invoices are past due. It is very important to have a written record of attempts to collect past-due invoices in case the matter ever gets to court. Exhibit 8–5 has samples of typical collection letters.

Use of Attorneys/Collection Agents. Before a client relationship becomes particularly difficult and payment is seriously past due, it is important to make certain that there is no dissatisfaction with the work. Often a delay in payment can be the first indication that there is a problem. If it is strictly a payment problem and reminders are not working, it may be necessary to stop work or at least threaten to do so until payments are brought up to date. As a last resort, the firm may have to use the services of a collection agency or attorney, but by this time there should be no expectation of future work. Collection agencies and attorneys should be engaged as soon as possible after the firm determines that it has a potential bad debt, because the more time that passes the less likelihood there is of collecting anything on the account. It is well to use a single collection agency for all past-due invoices because design firms rarely have enough poor accounts to make their collections worthwhile to a person in this business. You should obtain liens and judgments against people who do not pay their bills, but throughout the collection process you must balance the amount at stake and the cost of proceeding versus the likelihood of collection.

SAMPLE COLLECTION LETTERS

First Reminder

Dear Client:
In reviewing our accounts receivable I note that our invoice number 118 in the amount of $2,000 is 30 days past due. Enclosed is a copy of the invoice and I would appreciate your taking action to expedite payment.

Second Reminder

(Project manager should speak to client before it is sent.)

Dear Client:
On March 6th I wrote you regarding our invoice number 118 in the amount of $2,000 (copy enclosed). This invoice is now 60 days old and seriously past due. Please call immediately if there is some problem of which we are unaware. Otherwise, we will expect your check by return mail.

Third Reminder

(Project manager should know reason for delay by now. If it is a case of the client simply refusing to pay, this letter should be sent.)

Dear Client:
Our invoice number 118 in the amount of $2,000 (copy enclosed) is 90 days past due and we must now take action to collect it. This is to notify you that if payment is not received by __(date)__ we will turn this account over to our attorney for collection. We must take this action since we can no longer afford to carry past-due accounts at today's high interest rates.

(Be sure to take action on the date specified in the letter.)

Controlling Accounts Payable

Proper control of the bill-paying function is the other side of the cash management picture. It is important that bills be paid on time but no sooner than necessary. This means that all discounts should be taken whenever offered because the effect of a discount of 2 percent for payment within 10 days is the equivalent of an interest savings of 37 percent as shown in Exhibit 8–4. Bills that offer no discount should be paid within 30 days. Not only does this protect the credit reputation of the firm, but in many cases, vendors are now adding charges for late payment of bills.

In the past, many vendors used to offer discounts, but they are rare today because of high interest rates and lower profit margins. Whenever discounts are offered, you should be careful to abide by the payment terms so as not to cause ill will with vendors.

It is important that the firm maintain its credit reputation in order to receive proper service from vendors. It is also important that the firm's credit reputation with banks and credit-reporting agencies, such as Dun & Bradstreet, be maintained so there are no problems with new vendors. Furthermore, it is not unusual for a prospective client who has never worked with the firm to investigate the firm's credit reputation in order to see if it is reputable and the type of corporate citizen that the client wishes to engage.

If the firm is experiencing cash flow problems and is having difficulty paying its bills, credit experts advise that the problem should be discussed with suppliers before they start calling you. It is best to pay off all smaller accounts and then work out payment terms for the larger accounts. When a firm gets itself into this kind of situation it can expect to be placed on a cash-only basis with many of its suppliers. However, when the firm makes an honest effort and works itself out of this position, many of its suppliers will once again grant credit terms because of the competitive nature of the suppliers' business.

Accounts Payable Procedures. The bill-paying function in most firms is generally a clerical or an automated task, which means that management must set procedures for others to follow:

1. It is important to establish times for paying bills so that they do not accumulate interest for late charges.

2. The people handling this function should understand the terms established by the vendor and whether the vendor wants to be paid upon receipt of individual invoices or monthly on receipt of a statement that lists the invoices sent during the month.

3. All bills should first be verified against prior payments to the vendor to avoid duplicate payments.

4. Consider a two-step procedure for better internal control: One person should prepare the bills for payment by checking for duplicate payments, assembling the supporting documentation, noting approvals on documents, and coding for payment, while a second person reviews and approves the documentation and prepares the checks.

Discussion Problem

Background. Average borrowing from the bank has been steadily increasing in your 30-person architectural firm. You are rapidly approaching the limits of your $100,000 line of credit. Several times you had to exceed the limit for short periods when you were waiting for checks from clients. Your bank has been very accommodating, but your interest expense has risen by $10,000 this year. Client invoices are generally mailed during the third week after the close of the accounting period. From conversations with principals in other firms, you recognize that this is an excessive delay and you want to improve it.

You discuss the problem with your business manager and discover that invoices are usually typed three times before they are finally mailed. This is because project managers frequently revise the invoices several times after reviewing the total figures. Often they do not want to charge for the time of individuals who have not contributed sufficiently to the project in spite of the hours having been listed on time sheets. They also take exception to certain reimbursable expenses, particularly computer charges that they feel are excessive. Therefore managers do not hesitate to change invoices several times until they are satisfied.

You arrange a meeting with the project managers and business manager to resolve the problem.

Assignment. List the problems to be discussed at this meeting. What changes in procedures would you institute to resolve the problem? How would you monitor the situation so that you know how much time and expenses are not being charged to clients by the project manager's adjustments to invoices?

9
Cash Management

1. What two outside sources can assist the firm with cash management?

2. What are some suggestions for obtaining a line of credit from a bank?

3. How will the banker determine the size of my credit line?

4. What should I do if I am ever rejected by a bank?

5. What other financing sources are available for equipment loans?

6. What is an ESOP and how can I use it to obtain additional financing?

7. How do I prepare a forecast of cash receipts and disbursements?

8. What service can my bank offer to improve cash management?

Proper management of the firm's cash reserves is extremely important, and keeping a positive cash flow in good times and bad is essential for continued existence.

Use of Outside Sources

There are several outside sources that a firm can use to help with its cash management problems. The principal source is the firm's banker. The banker is usually well experienced in cash management procedures, and sometimes banks will have a specialist on staff to assist customers in improving cash management. To take advantage of this expertise, the banker should be thoroughly familiar with the firm and its operations. Most of a banker's clients are manufacturing and retailing businesses, which means that the banker has relatively little familiarity with firms engaged in providing services. Therefore it will take an effort to make the banker familiar with a professional service firm.

A good practice for the design professional is to keep the banker advised of operations by meeting at least once or twice a year to go over the firm's financial statements and prospects. Quarterly meetings are even better. One thing to keep in mind is that these meetings can be beneficial to both parties. The banker is a good source of marketing information because of membership in the Chamber of Commerce and other organizations as well as associations with many businesses. Often a banker is the first to know about firms moving into and out of the area and what new facilities are being planned.

The firm's outside auditor is another source of assistance in cash management. The CPA sees many types of businesses and is in a good position to make suggestions for improvement of cash management. During the course of an audit the accountant studies the cash flow procedures and can draw on his or her background serving other clients to make good suggestions. One thing to remember is that if you ever want to make any significant changes in your accounting procedures, it is well to talk them over first with your accountant. The accountant is also a good general business adviser because, through audit and tax work, he or she knows more about your firm than possibly anyone else. The accountant can often make good suggestions from the vantage point of an independent outside resource.

Obtaining Credit Lines

Most firms need a line of credit to support their working capital needs and to help expand operations. Generally, the best time to arrange for a line of credit is when the firm does not have an immediate financial need or when banks are eager to loan money. Unfortunately, we cannot always time our requirements to fit the banker's needs and that means we will be competing for funds along with everyone else.

It is important to sell the banker like any other client when preparing a loan request. That means the banker should understand the objectives of the loan and have confidence in your firm. The banker must understand how design firms operate and your firm's position in the marketplace. He or she must learn your firm's strategy and its strengths and must have full and complete financial information, both current and projected. Most importantly, you need to document how the loan will be repaid. The firm should ask for a revolving line of credit, which means that as portions of the loan are repaid, they are available to be reborrowed up to the limits of the credit line.

Bankers will generally want security for the loan, which means a pledge of accounts receivable. Usually, the amount of the loan will be determined by the amount of accounts receivable on the books that the banker considers current, that is, less than 90 days old. In that connection, it is important for the banker to understand the difference between a 90-day-old account and a retainer. A retainer is money withheld from the design professional's invoices to assure compliance with the terms of the contract. Since only a portion of the accounts receivable are paid, the balance remains on the books and should be identified as a retainer rather than a partially paid invoice that grows older each month. If the firm does not distinguish between the two on its accounts receivable aging report and if it is not explained to the banker, he or she cannot be expected to make the distinction. Furthermore, many bankers do not understand the nature of the design profession and the fact that all receivables past 90 days are not potential bad debts. The banker should be made to understand that often a design professional working for a developer, for instance, will not be paid until the developer obtains his financing. The more you can get the banker to understand how your firm operates, the better your chances are for a loan.

Banks will lend a percentage against the accounts receivable, and the interest rate is generally related to the prime lending rate, or the rate that is available to the bank's largest and best customers. In many instances, particularly with smaller or newer firms, banks will request a personal guarantee of the loan by the principals in the firm. The principals should expect to be confronted with this request and must be prepared to deal with it.

In most cases the bank loan officer assembles the information presented, adds whatever analysis he or she makes and/or that of a credit analyst who reviews the application, and submits it to the bank's loan committee, made up of senior officials in the bank. The loan committee makes the final determination, after asking the loan officer for any additional information it may require.

If your application is ever rejected, you should meet with the loan officer to find out why. Possibly, the loan committee may feel it has enough of a particular type of loan and may not want to accept any more of this type in order to diversify its risks. In that case, you might be able to take the application directly to another bank with better results. On the other hand, if there is a weakness in the firm's finances, it will have to be corrected before submitting the application to another bank.

Exhibit 9–1 shows a covering letter for a loan application. Note in particular the kinds of information provided and the explanation of the purpose of the loan.

Other External Sources of Funds

While banks are the obvious source of funds other sources are available. It may help to remember them when the need arises. The Small Business Administration (SBA) is a source of funds for those firms that qualify as small businesses under the regulations. The definition of a small business is based on gross revenues and number of personnel and the criteria often change. All but the larger design firms are in the small business category. SBA loans are generally written through a bank and the SBA guarantees a portion, up to 90 percent usually. The problem with SBA loans is the paperwork involved in filling out the detailed application and the time it takes for the loan to be approved. In some cases the rates for an SBA loan are the same as bank lending rates for comparable loans, but the SBA will often extend the payback terms over a longer period of time, which may be helpful when obtaining loans to purchase equipment.

Equipment loans can often be obtained from a leasing company that operates similarly to a bank, in that they loan a portion of the equipment price and the loan is secured by the equipment. Venture capital companies are another source of funds. They are groups of investors who specialize in investing in startup situations and in small and emerging companies. They are generally not interested in service firms, however. Venture capital companies want to secure their investments with fixed assets, and they also want an equity participation for their risk, which closely held firms, like professional design offices, are reluctant to give.

Internal Sources of Funds

Sources of funds within the firm can come from additional equity sold to new or existing stockholders or additional partners in the case of a partnership. Employee Stock Ownership Plans (ESOPs) are an excellent source of internally generated funds that appear to fit the requirements of many firms, although they are still not widely used. An ESOP consists of a trust made up of all the employees and formed for the primary purpose of buying shares in the firm. Instead of a regular profit-sharing plan that places its funds in outside investments, the profits declared by the firm are placed with the ESOP, which, in turn, buys shares of the firm's stock and thereby returns the funds to the firm. In effect, there is no cash outflow when profit-

9-1. *This letter should go to a specific individual at the bank whom you either know or else have explained your requirements to in advance.*

EXAMPLE OF TRANSMITTAL LETTER FOR LOAN APPLICATION

The Cato Group
Interior Architecture/Facilities Planning/Project Coordination

First City Bank of Anytown

Dear Banker:

Enclosed are financial statements and data on our firm. Specifically included in this package are

1. End of year and current financial statements

2. Accounts receivable aging schedule

3. Cash flow projection showing the effects of borrowing and repayment

4. A listing of major clients and prospective new projects

5. Personal financial statements for the principals

6. Corporate brochure including resumes of the principals

Our desire for bank financing is threefold: (1) We require working capital in order to continue our growth and to anticipate the requirements of upcoming projects. The nature of an interior architecture firm such as ours necessitates heavy expenditures prior to the startup as well as during the performance of a project. This is because a portion of our interior design work is performed for building developers at a reduced rate until tenants are located and signed. Our role as consultant to larger architectural firms also delays our receipt of payments because the prime professional is paid before the consultant is paid. (2) We would like to convert our existing short-term loans to a more stable line of credit so that we do not have to keep renewing the loans on an individual basis. (3) Although our current banking relationship is in New Orleans, our office is in Houston. We recognize the importance of developing a strong banking relationship in Houston.

Initially, we are requesting $100,000. This would be in the form of a revolving line of credit. We would expect to pay not more than two points over the current prime lending rate. We anticipate the length of the loan to be one year (renewable terms) with interest payments on a quarterly basis.

After establishing a good relationship with your bank, we would seek to enlarge our revolving line of credit based on our firm's continuing needs and its ability to secure new and larger projects.

If you require any additional information, please do not hesitate to call me.

Yours very truly,

John L. Smith, Managing Principal

JLS:jc

sharing funds are turned over to an ESOP as there is when it is placed with a regular profit-sharing plan.

A major stockholder can also divest holdings over time by selling shares to the ESOP that can borrow from a bank to finance the purchase. ESOP borrowings are backed by the financial strength of the firm and the firm's pledge to pay off the note through periodic contributions to the plan. An alternative is for the ESOP to hold a life insurance policy on the major stockholder with premiums paid through contributions. The policy enables the ESOP to buy the major stockholder's holdings from his or her estate.

A prime advantage of the ESOP is that it expands the ownership of the firm to all employees, which improves morale and productivity. At the same time an ESOP can maintain the closely held nature of the firm by a provision that requires departing employees to offer to sell their shares back to the plan upon termination. While there is dilution of equity as more shares are created, it should be offset by the growth in the firm sparked by the owner-employees. Control of the ESOP rests with the trustees appointed by the board of directors. Since the trustees are usually the major stockholders, control of the firm does not pass from their hands.

Another advantage of the ESOP is that it is able to finance equipment purchases with pre-tax dollars. For example, if the firm needs $100,000 for capital equipment, the ESOP borrows the funds (backed by the firm as a guarantor of the note) and buys stock in the firm. The firm uses the money to buy the equipment and makes periodic tax deductible contributions of profit-sharing funds to the ESOP to repay the note. Assuming for simplicity the firm was in a 50 percent tax bracket, it would require $200,000 in earnings to pay off a note plus interest at a bank, whereas it only requires $100,000 in earnings through the ESOP. When depreciation on the equipment is considered, a significant portion of the equipment cost can be paid for through tax deductions, depending on the firm's tax bracket.

A further benefit of having an ESOP is that it allows the firm to take an extra 1½ percent investment tax credit under the current laws if that extra 1½ percent is invested in the plan. The investment tax credit is allowed on the purchase of new and, in some cases, used equipment. The mechanics of electing the additional investment credit need to be handled by your accountant.

If interested, a firm should explore the formation of an ESOP with its accountant and attorney. Generally, the firm must be of sufficient size for the ESOP to support the costs involved. In addition to accountant and attorney fees involved in the setup and operation of the plan, a yearly valuation of the stock must be made by an independent appraiser. This is necessary in order to have a realistic price for the transactions.

Raising Capital in Smaller Firms

Smaller firms are limited in the ways they can raise equity funds to support the firm and expand operations. A partnership must provide an opportunity for new partners to be admitted. In the case of a corporation, outside of being acquired by a larger firm, the best way is through a stock purchase plan that is made available to key employees. The plans should be prepared by an attorney and provide for periodic purchases over an established length of time. Generally, the purchase price is fixed at net book value or an adjustment to net book value at the end of the year, since that figure is easy to calculate. Net book value is the difference between assets and liabilities, and adjustments may sometimes be necessary to make the figure more realistic.

Obviously, the money for employees to purchase stock must come out of salaries and bonuses. Therefore the firm must be growing and successful to make the plan worthwhile. Pricing the shares at net book value tends to understate their value because no credit is given to backlog or the reputation of the firm. However, this is an important incentive for employees because it gives them an opportunity to see their shares grow. Since the shares do not usually pay dividends, the ability to share financially in growth is what ties these employees to the firm.

Cash Flow Reports

A key report necessary for cash management is a cash flow report that shows historical information and then projects cash requirements over at least a three-month period. It is well to start with a simple cash flow report as shown in Exhibit 9–2 and examine trends such as the number of days lag between invoicing and collecting, major seasonal or one-time cash requirements, and growth patterns that will affect cash needs. After some experience, cash forecasting will become easier, and more detailed reports can be prepared, as shown in Exhibit 9–3. Generally, it is easier to forecast cash expenses because they do not vary much by month unless there are significant changes in operation. Exhibit 9–4 is a form that can be used to forecast expenses. Cash receipts are more difficult to predict because of the uncertainty of when clients will pay. Exhibit 9–5 shows a form used to forecast cash receipts by project. Exhibit 9–6 is an example of a cash flow analysis for a typical project.

One method used to forecast revenue is to take the various elements that make up a revenue forecast and estimate them separately as follows:

1. *Backlog* (work under contract that is not yet completed). This revenue will be earned over the forecast period and the amount and rate at which it will be earned should be fairly easy to predict.

9-2. This report summarizes cash status in an easy-to-read format. Receipts from clients and disbursements from operations must be estimated in detail on separate worksheets similar to Exhibits 9-4 and 9-5.

SAMPLE CASH FLOW REPORT

Month, Year __4/84__

	Current Month		Forecast		
	Actual	Forecast	Month 1	Month 2	Month 3
Beginning cash balance	$2,000	$10,000	$10,000	$10,000	$5,000
Operating cash receipts:					
From: Projects	+ 80,000	100,000	90,000	120,000	125,000
Other income	+ 10,000	10,000	10,000	10,000	10,000
Project advances	+ 0	0	0	0	0
Subtotal	92,000	120,000	110,000	140,000	140,000
Operating cash disbursements:					
Net cash flow from operations	−109,000	105,000	100,000	110,000	120,000
Other cash receipts:					
Bank loan	+20,000	0	0	0	0
Other cash disbursements					
Payment of bank loans	− 0	0	0	25,000	10,000
Ending cash balance:	3,000	15,000	10,000	5,000	10,000
Bank loan outstanding	$100,000	$80,000	$80,000	$55,000	$45,000

ABC ARCHITECTS, INC.
FINANCIAL PROJECTION AND CASH FORECAST
JUNE TO DECEMBER

Financial Projection	June	July	August	September	October	November	December
Estimated revenue	$10,000	$10,000	$20,000	$30,000	$40,000	$20,000	$20,000
Collections							
Previous month (30%)	3,000	3,000	3,000	6,000	9,000	12,000	6,000
2nd previous month (30%)	3,000	3,000	3,000	3,000	6,000	9,000	12,000
3rd previous month (30%)	3,000	3,000	3,000	3,000	3,000	6,000	9,000
Total collections	9,000	9,000	9,000	12,000	18,000	27,000	27,000
Expenses (est. at 80% of revenue)	7,200	7,200	7,200	9,600	14,400	21,600	21,600
Payment of expenses (one month lag)	7,200	7,200	7,200	7,200	9,600	14,400	21,600

Cash Forecast

	June	July	August	September	October	November	December
Cash receipts							
Collections	$9,000	$9,000	$9,000	$12,000	$18,000	$27,000	$27,000
Cash disbursements							
Salaries	3,200	3,200	3,200	3,200	5,000	7,000	9,000
Direct expenses	1,000	1,000	1,000	1,000	2,000	2,400	3,600
Office rent	2,000	2,000	2,000	2,000	2,000	3,000	4,000
Other expenses	1,000	1,000	1,000	1,000	600	2,000	5,000
Taxes	—	—	—	—	—	—	10,000
Computer purchase	—	—	—	—	20,000	—	—
Total cash disb.	7,200	7,200	7,200	7,200	29,600	14,400	31,600
Net cash gain (loss)	1,800	1,800	1,800	4,800	<11,600>	12,600	<4,600>
Cash balance (beg. of month)	5,000	6,800	8,600	10,400	15,200	3,600	16,600
Cumulative cash	6,800	8,600	10,400	15,200	3,600	16,600	12,000
Desired level of cash	5,000	5,000	5,000	5,000	5,000	5,000	5,000
Surplus/(deficit) cash	$1,800	$3,600	$5,400	$10,200	<$1,400>	$11,600	$7,000

9-3. *Factors used to develop the financial projection are based on experience and then translated into the cash forecast.*

FORECAST OF CASH FLOW FROM OPERATIONS

FISCAL YEAR _1984_

Month	Gross Payroll	Payroll-Related Costs	Facil. and Rent	Other Operating Expenses	Bonuses and Profit-Sharing	Income Taxes, City & State	Federal Income Taxes	Capital Items	Debt Repay.	Total Cash Disb.
Jan.	$62,000	$8,000	$15,000	$12,000	0	$1,000	$7,000	0	0	$105,000
Feb.	60,000	6,000	15,000	14,000	0	0	0	$5,000	0	100,000
Mar.	64,000	7,000	16,000	13,000	0	0	5,000	0	$5,000	110,000
Apr.	70,000	10,000	16,000	12,000	0	1,000	0	9,000	2,000	120,000
May	70,000	10,000	16,000	12,000	0	1,000	0	9,000	2,000	120,000
Total	$800,000	$80,000	$190,000	$160,000	$40,000	$4,000	$20,000	$30,000	$20,000	1,344,000

9-4. *Cash disbursements are estimated on this worksheet and the totals transferred to the "net cash flow from operations" column in Exhibit 9-2.*

FORECAST OF CASH RECEIPTS FROM PROJECTS

FISCAL YEAR *1984*

Project	Contract Type	Construction Cost Est.	Contract Amount	Amount Paid to Date	Balance Owed	Estimated Payments Schedule					
						Jan.	Feb.	Mar.	Apr.	May	June
123 Proj. X	Lump Sum	$2,000,000	$100,000	$26,000	$74,000		$18,000	$20,000	$16,000	$20,000	
142 Proj. Q	Lump Sum	4,000,000	240,000	0	240,000			10,000	10,000	20,000	20,000
248 Proj. U	% Const.	1,000,000	70,000	60,000	10,000		10,000				
542 Proj. S	Hourly	Study	15,000	2,000	13,000	6,000	6,000	1,000			
014 Proj. T	Hourly	Study	35,000	20,000	15,000	10,000	5,000				
Total Cash Receipts						$100,000	$90,000	$120,000	125,000	125,000	125,000

9-5. *Cash receipts are estimated on this worksheet and the totals transferred to the "operating cash receipts from projects" column in Exhibit 9-2.*

EXAMPLE OF A CASH FLOW ANALYSIS FOR A TYPICAL PROJECT

	Total	July	August	September	October
Project Y					
Collections	$40,000	0	$10,000	$10,000	$20,000
Disbursements					
Labor & overhead	27,000	14,000	10,000	3,000	
Reimbursable expenses	2,000	1,000	1,000		
Consultants' costs	7,000			3,000	4,000
TOTAL DISBURSEMENTS	36,000	15,000	11,000	6,000	4,000
Diff. between collect./disb.	4,000	⟨15,000⟩	⟨1,000⟩	4,000	16,000

2. *Current Proposals Outstanding.* The estimated fees for currently outstanding proposals are multiplied by a percentage that represents the likelihood of obtaining the project. This figure is then used in the projection. For example, if the firm has a proposal outstanding for $100,000 and there are two other firms in competition, then this proposal is weighted by one-third, or $33,000. An estimated start date is determined and the $33,000 is projected by month at a certain level of earnings.

3. *New Business Development.* An estimate is made of the number of new proposals expected to be written in the forecast period times the percent probability of success times the average contract size. This calculation gives the balance of the revenue estimate. For example, if the firm expects to write 40 additional proposals in the forecast year beyond what are currently outstanding and their probability of success is one out of three (33 percent) and the average size of each proposal is $50,000, then this represents an additional $660,000 in revenue that is added to items 1 and 2 above. The $660,000 is projected to be earned at an estimated monthly level during the forecast period.

It is important that the total revenue estimated be reviewed by the marketing director who is charged with obtaining the new work and the operations director who is responsible for seeing that it gets done. They must both agree that it can be reasonably attained. Furthermore, the marketing and operations directors must analyze the revenue projection to see that it is balanced with the disciplines and capabilities of the people on staff. Finally, the financial manager must review it and convert it to a cash receipts estimate by applying the factors to determine when payments can be expected.

Another area of difficulty in preparing a cash forecast is in determining when consultants can be expected to submit their invoices. The best way to estimate is to use the terms of the contract, coupled with any past experience working with the consultant.

New Techniques of Cash Management

There are several methods available to speed the flow of cash receipts into a central depository account and then to manage the outflow of funds so that excess cash is not sitting idle and not earning interest. Most of these techniques are applicable to larger firms or those that may receive cash at several different locations. However, each firm should discuss its cash management needs with its banker to determine if there is a more efficient way to handle the receipt of funds.

1. *Lock boxes.* This is a special post office box that appears on the firm's invoices and directs clients to send their checks to this address. Only the bank has access to the box and it collects the checks several times during the day and deposits them directly into the firm's account. This procedure saves at least a day in getting checks deposited and is particularly useful if the firm does work in several cities. The bank will study the various locations where cash is received and can recommend the most efficient locations for lock boxes.

2. *Depository transfer checks.* These checks are really drafts that one bank writes on another to authorize the transfer of funds to the writing bank. They are a useful device for moving funds quickly to a central depository account from regional bank accounts, because they move through the Federal Reserve system rather than through the mails.

3. *Wire transfers.* This is a method of transferring funds even more quickly than by means of depository transfer checks. Funds are transferred the same day and often in a matter of hours. The cost of wire transfers is higher than that for depository transfer checks.

4. *Zero balance accounts.* This is a method of disbursing funds from several bank accounts without allowing any idle funds to remain in these accounts. Zero balance accounts have no balance, but when a check is drawn against them and presented for payment, the bank automatically draws from a central depository account just enough money to cover the check. Likewise, any receipts into these accounts go directly to the central depository account. To keep track of these transactions, the bank's customer receives a daily cash balance report, generally by Telex, describing all the transactions that have occurred that day.

All these cash management techniques cost the bank money, the same as every transaction that occurs within any bank customer's account, such as receiving deposits and paying checks. The bank earns revenue by investing any excess funds held in customers' accounts and through loans, trust services, safe deposits, and all the other services a bank provides. When determining the charges for cash management services, the bank will look at the firm's entire banking relationship, including services provided to the principals of the firm as well. Sometimes the cash management service can be accommodated at "no charge" if the bank receives sufficient revenue from other sources.

Importance of Cash Flow

Cash flow is so vital to the existence of a firm that it must be constantly monitored. While the person in charge of finance is closest to the cash situation on a daily basis, the proper management of cash requires more than merely reacting to situations as they occur. It requires careful planning in order to have the necessary cash available when it is needed while at the same time minimizing bank borrowings or disturbing short-term investments.

Discussion Problems

1. Background. For many years Gale Marine Engineers concentrated on work for the private sector, designing facilities for several shipbuilders on the East Coast. Several years ago they opened an office on the Gulf Coast in response to increased projects in that part of the country. Last year they acquired a large project from the government working for the Navy Department at an installation on the West Coast.

The firm has a line of credit with a bank on the East Coast and for years has had a $50,000 limit on the line, which has been adequate in the past. Borrowings have averaged around $20,000 for many years. There have been a few bad debts, but the firm has been free of borrowing for about 30 days a year. The bank has renewed the line annually without question.

When the firm obtained work from the federal government, it found itself in a position where it had to begin work on a project before a contract was awarded and based on a notice to proceed. However, because of its inexperience in government work, there were often problems with the preaward audits that frequently were not resolved until months after the work was started. Very often it was as much as six months before problems were resolved and a contract was signed. At that time the firm would send its first invoice for services to date.

Project managers were paid bonuses on the volume of work they produced so there was considerable pressure to obtain as much work as possible. One project manager recently obtained a large assignment from a developer of marinas on the West Coast. After the project was underway for three months the developer unexpectedly went bankrupt, and the firm will likely have to write off $25,000 in losses.

One project manager obtained most of his work as a consultant to architects or other engineering firms. He had many acquaintances in these firms. However, because his clients did not pay him until they were paid, he generally had an average of 90 days outstanding on accounts receivable.

Gale Marine Engineers prospered as volume and manpower steadily increased over the years. Profits consistently averaged about 5 percent before taxes. Early in 1984 borrowings exceeded the credit line limit and did not show any signs of declining. At this point, the financial manager became concerned and both he and the managing principal visited the bank and were told that, based on the firm's previous performance, the bank would increase their credit line to $75,000, but the interest rate was also raised from 2 percent to 2½ percent over the prime rate. The increase proved satisfactory for six months, but after another government contract was acquired, the $75,000 credit limit was reached and the financial manager went back to the bank for another increase. At that point the banker had to reluctantly tell him that, because of tight money conditions, he could not increase the line any further.

Assignment. List the various mistakes the firm was making from a cash flow standpoint. What options are available to the financial manager at this point? How can he or she bring the situation under control?

What kinds of cash flow reports are necessary and how often should they be prepared?

2. Background. Your 35-person interior design firm has been with the same bank since you founded the firm 18 years ago. You never forgot their help at the beginning when they loaned you $2,000 for working capital, with your automobile as security, to get the firm started. Occasionally you have had to borrow for short periods of time to meet a payroll, and the bank was always accommodating. Other than maintaining your checking account there was little expected from the bank and you saw the bank president rarely or only at social functions. You recently obtained an assignment as a consultant to a London architectural firm on a hotel project. The project is in Central America. You need help with such matters as letters of credit, foreign currency transactions, and foreign business procedures.

You approach your banker because the architectural firm has indicated that you must obtain a separate letter of credit for your portion of the project. The architect also asks you to open a bank account in London because you will be paid partially in pounds and will have expenses for the office you open there.

At a meeting with your local banker he tells you that he has little experience in foreign operations and directs you to another bank in a nearby large city.

Assignment. How should you establish a relationship with the new bank that will allow them to accommodate your needs now and in the future? List the kinds of information that the new bank will want to have. How would you organize the package of information to give to the bank?

10
Accounting Systems: Emphasis on Computers

1. How detailed should my chart of accounts be to give me the information I need?

2. How is project revenue recorded in a project accounting system?

3. Where can I find computerized systems tailored to the needs of professional service firms?

4. What is an integrated accounting system and why is it important?

5. What should I look for in purchasing a computerized accounting system?

6. What are the alternatives to purchasing a system?

7. What are some of the advantages of a service bureau?

Most firms establish accounting systems when they first begin operation and the system is usually set up by an accountant familiar with small business operations. The problem is that design firms have certain unique characteristics that do not fit the general mold of small businesses. In fact, they are more of a hybrid between a small business and a professional practice, such as a doctor or attorney, when it comes to accounting.

General Accounting Systems

A general accounting system consists of the cash receipts and disbursements system, payroll, general ledger, and those accounting functions similar to all businesses. This portion of the system does not require special knowledge of design firms to set up and operate. Some firms, particularly smaller ones, function successfully with only a general accounting system.

The system is built around a chart of accounts that lists all account classifications which the firm needs to monitor. These accounts include revenue, expenses, assets, liabilities, and net worth. All accounting transactions are coded to these items. Generally, a smaller firm can use a simpler chart of accounts with fewer breakdowns. As a firm grows, a more detailed chart of accounts becomes necessary. When the accounting system is mechanized, the chart of accounts has to be numbered in such a way that the computer can accept subclassifications which can then be summarized into a single account. Furthermore, the method of numbering has to be established to allow for sufficient growth in a computerized system so that the entire chart of accounts does not have to be rewritten as a firm increases in size, number of departments, and locations.

The American Institute of Architects (AIA) and the American Consulting Engineers Council (ACEC) have uniform charts of account that can be adapted to almost any practice and are recommended for adoption rather than having a firm develop its own unique chart of accounts. An example of an abbreviated chart of accounts, which generally follows the pattern of the AIA and ACEC charts, is shown in Exhibit 10–1.

The books and records of the general accounting system can be kept either by hand or by computer. Many accountants will provide all transactions posted by machine and a monthly profit and loss statement and balance sheet, together with all the necessary quarterly and end of year tax reports and reconciliation of the bank account. This is called "write-up service" and is useful to many small businesses that cannot afford full-time accounting help. Frequently, financial statements are prepared on a cash basis because that is easier from the records, but accrual statements can be produced by incorporating the net changes month by month in work in progress, accounts receivable, and accounts payable.

Most firms, after they have been operating for awhile, recognize that they need more than monthly financial statements to properly manage the firm.

Computerized General Accounting Systems

There are many software systems on the market today to accommodate the general accounting needs of any business, large or small. They are often sold as individual packages such as:

1. *General ledger:* Maintains financial records and prepares financial statements.

2. *Payroll:* Keeps payroll records, writes checks, and prepares tax reports.

3. *Accounts payable:* Records payables and writes vendors checks.

4. *Accounts receivable:* Keeps track of what is owed and paid by clients and prepares periodic reports.

These systems are not unique to any business and are readily adaptable to almost any firm. They have also been programmed to run on the very smallest micro computers and are heavily promoted to the small businessperson. The problem with them, as far as design firms are concerned, is that they do not address the very important needs of a project accounting system. Some standard packages have been developed by the large hardware vendors to run job costs, but in many instances they are designed for small construction firms and are not readily adapted by an architect, interior designer, or consulting engineer. Examples of computer-generated financial statements are shown in Exhibits 10–2 and 10–3.

10-1. *This example gives the major account headings and organization of the chart of accounts. Additional account listings under each heading can be added as needed.*

SUMMARY EXAMPLE OF CHART OF ACCOUNTS

BALANCE SHEET

1.0 Series—Assets

1.1   Current Assets
1.2   Fixed Assets

2.0 Series—Liabilities

2.1   Current Liabilities
2.2   Long-Term Liabilities

3.0 Series—Equity

3.1   Capital Stock: Common
3.2   Capital Stock: Preferred
3.3   Retained Earnings

INCOME STATEMENT

4.0 Series—Income

4.1   Professional Service
4.2   Other Income

5.0 Series—Direct Project Expenses

5.1   Direct Project Payroll
5.2   Direct Project Expenses

6.0 Series—Indirect Costs

6.1   Indirect Payroll Cost
6.2   Indirect General and Administrative Costs

INCOME STATEMENT
FOR THE PERIOD 1/30 THROUGH 4/30

	THIS MONTH	% OF TOTAL INCOME	YEAR-TO-DATE	% OF TOTAL INCOME
INCOME				
Professional fees	$80,000	89%	$280,000	89%
Reimbursable expenses	10,000	11	35,000	11
TOTAL INCOME	90,000	100	315,000	100
DIRECT PAYROLL EXPENSE				
Staff payroll	28,000	31	100,000	32
Principals' salaries	4,000	4	15,000	5
TOTAL DIRECT SALARIES	32,000	35	115,000	37
Direct project expenses	8,000	9	30,000	10
TOTAL DIRECT EXPENSES	40,000	44	145,000	47
INDIRECT EXPENSES				
Indirect payroll costs	10,000	11	40,000	13
Indirect payroll	4,000	4	15,000	5
Rent/utilities/maint.	15,000	17	55,000	17
Professional activities	2,000	2	7,000	2
Auto/truck expense	2,000	2	9,000	3
Business insurance	6,000	7	22,000	7
Library & ref data	1,000	1	4,000	1
TOTAL INDIRECT EXPENSE	40,000	44	152,000	48
TOTAL EXPENSES	80,000	89	297,000	95
NET PROFIT/LOSS	$10,000	11%	$ 18,000	5%

10-3. *Usually a balance sheet requires footnote explanations of such items as a description of the notes payable. These footnotes are a part of the financial statements.*

BALANCE SHEET
AS OF 4/30

ASSETS

Cash	$ 40,000	
Accounts receivable	1,200,000	
Notes rec./capital assets	56,000	
Prepaid expenses	18,000	
TOTAL CURRENT ASSETS		$1,314,000
FIXED ASSETS		
Office equipment	40,000	
Technical equipment	15,000	
Transportation equipment	30,000	
Buildings	50,000	
TOTAL FIXED ASSETS		135,000
TOTAL ASSETS		$1,449,000

LIABILITIES & CAPITAL

Accounts payable	60,000		
TOTAL CURRENT LIABILITIES		60,000	
Notes payable (Long Term)	$ 890,000		
TOTAL LONG-TERM LIABILITIES		890,000	
TOTAL LIABILITIES			950,000
OWNER'S EQUITY			
Capital stock		100,000	
Retained earnings		$ 399,000	
TOTAL CAPITAL			499,000
TOTAL LIABILITIES & CAPITAL			$1,449,000

Project Accounting Systems

A project accounting system enables a firm to identify revenue and expenses by project, which is extremely important in controlling operations. In fact, if projects are monitored properly and overhead kept under control the firm is more than likely to prosper.

Project accounting starts with timesheets, which should be filled out by every person in the firm. A timesheet adapted to the format of a computer input document is shown in Exhibit 10–4. The frequency of reporting is a matter of how often management needs to know the status of projects. Generally, timesheets are turned in to the accounting office at the end of each payroll period. The timesheets are summarized into a report that records total time charges against each project (direct labor) and against indirect labor categories, such as administration or marketing. Exhibit 10–5 is a simplified example of this report. Overhead costs are entered into the system as a percentage of direct labor.

In the project control system reimbursable expenses are also assigned to projects by proper coding when they are presented to the accounting department for payment. Consultant expenses also fall in this category. Reimbursable expenses include such items as telephone calls, printing, data processing, and travel. These expenses must be segregated in the reimbursable category, which is charged directly to projects, and the remaining portion, which cannot be identified and which is included in overhead expenses. As a matter of policy, the firm should try to assign as many costs directly to projects as possible. Clients are more likely not to question direct charges whereas, if left in overhead, the total overhead rate may be unusually high and therefore open to question.

The project accounting system should record revenue in accordance with the terms of the contract. That is, hourly projects should earn revenue as effort is expended. Revenue on lump sum projects should be recorded in accordance with the project manager's estimates of work remaining to complete the project. Other types of contracts should be accounted for under one of these options. That is, multiplier contracts, standard billing rates, and cost plus fixed contracts should have revenue recorded on the basis of time expended. Percentage of construction contracts should be determined on the basis of estimates to complete (for example, the project may be 75 percent completed) times the estimated contract price (for example, $100,000, in which case $75,000 of the contract price has been earned).

Since the project accounting system is on an accrual basis, revenue is accounted for when it is earned rather than when it can be billed. That is, projects that can only be billed after certain milestones are completed still earn revenue each month based on the project manager's estimate.

The difference between revenue earned and expenses incurred on the project will be the profit or loss. Exhibits 10–6 and 10–7 are examples of project control reports printed by computer.

Computerized Project Accounting Systems

In recent years a number of software vendors have developed packages specifically for design professionals. In these systems timesheet and expense information is entered and the program generates reports on the basis of hours and dollars showing the status of projects against budgets. Many vendor packages are very effective, and knowing of them is important so that you do not have to develop your own system from scratch. An excellent reference source is *Design Compudata* published by one of the authors of this book, Frank Stasiowski, 126 Harvard Street, Brookline, MA 02146.

10-4. *Example of a time sheet that can be adapted to computer processing.*

TIMESHEET

CLASSIFICATION CODE: ______ TIME RECORD FOR PAY PERIOD BEGINNING ______ AND ENDING ______ NAME: ______

JOB NUMBER	JOB NAME	PHASE CODE	SERVICE CODE	S	M	T	W	T	F	S	S	M	T	W	T	F	S	TOTAL HOURS

INSTRUCTIONS FOR COMPLETING TIMESHEET

Identify your time by entering the correct *job number* and *job name* in the spaces provided. *Phase codes* are the single letters defined below. *Service codes* are the single numbers representing specific tasks within each phase. Include both a phase code and a service code from the list associated with the particular phase. If you work on separate phases and/or services of the same job during a single pay period, list the separate phase or service on a separate line.

Overtime hours should be listed separately by reentering the job number and job name, phase code and service code beginning at the bottom line of the time sheet.

P = PRELIMINARY/SCHEMATIC
   1 = Research/programming
   2 = Schematic drawings
   3 = Presentation

D = DESIGN DEVELOPMENT
   1 = Research/programming
   2 = Working drawings
   3 = Specifications
   4 = Word processing/typing

W = CONTRACT DOCUMENTS
   1 = Working drawings
   2 = Specifications
   3 = Word processing typing

N = CONTRACT NEGOTIATION
   1 = Specifications
   2 = Word processing/typing
   3 = Consultation

A = CONTRACT ADMINISTRATION
   1 = Contract admin./office
   2 = Contract admin./job site
   3 = Color selection

X = EXTRA SERVICE/REIMBURSABLE
   1 = Working drawings
   2 = Specifications
   3 = Word processing/typing
   4 = Contract admin./office
   5 = Contract admin./job site
   6 = Consultation

I = INTERIOR DESIGN
   1 = Research/programming
   2 = Schematic drawings
   3 = Presentation

U = URBAN PLANNING/LAND USE
   1 = Research/programming
   2 = Schematic drawings
   3 = Presentation

K = CONTRACT ADMIN., POSTCOMPLETION
   1 = Contract admin./office
   2 = Contract admin./job site

E = ENGINEERING IN-HOUSE
   1 = Research/programming
   2 = Working drawings
   3 = Consultation

G = GENERAL OFFICE
H = HOLIDAY
M = MARKETING/PROMOTION
S = SICK LEAVE
V = VACATION
C = CHARGEABLE HOURS
O = SICK LEAVE w/o PAY
T = TIME OFF w/o PAY

The preceding INDIRECT EXPENSE CODES should be entered in the phase code block. Enter 0000 as the job number. No service code is required.

JOB NUMBER	JOB NAME	PHASE CODE	SERVICE CODE	S	M	T	W	T	F
1077	PARISIAN	W	1	3	5	2.5		6	4
1077	PARISIAN	W	2		.5	3	2		
78037	CMMC DECK ADON	A	1		.25			2	
0000	GENERAL OFFICE	G					4	1.5	

PROJECT TIME SUMMARY
(Prepared in Hours)

Week Ending 3/31

Graphics Department Employees	Projects					Overhead					Total Time
	1	2	3	4	5, etc.	Admin.	Mkg.	Holiday	Vac.	Sick	
S. Blake	6	14	12						8		40
R. Donohue			16	16		4	4				40
T. Gates			36			4					40
Total	140	800	205	68	42	101	58	0	40	20	1500

10-5. *This report summarizes the information on timesheets and is prepared at the close of each timesheet period.*

PROJECT SUMMARY REPORT

Period: 12/1–12/31
Manager: Smith

| | Project Costs | | | | | | Revenue Earned | | | | |
| | Direct Labor | | Overhead | Direct | Sub- | Total | | | | Profit/ | Project |
	Hours	Dollars	at 1.8%	Expense	Contractors	Cost	Fee	Reimb.	Total	Loss	Budget
Project A—Current	24	$ 2,808	$ 5,054	$1,300	$ 0	$ 9,162	$ 15,050	$ 1,500	$ 16,560	$ 7,398	
—To Date	2,620	43,230	77,814	6,502	18,000	145,546	125,500	20,000	145,500	(46)	$150,000
Project B—Current	13	260	468	20	0	748	1,500	250	1,750	1,002	
—To Date	13	260	468	20	0	748	1,500	250	1,750	1,002	20,000
Project C—Current	40	700	$ 1,260	100	1,500	3,560	5,000	2,000	8,000	4,440	
—To Date	200	3,600	6,480	500	2,000	12,580	14,000	2,500	16,500	3,920	16,500
Project D—Current	56	840	1,512	500	0	2,852	1,000	500	1,500	(1,352)	
—To Date	150	2,550	4,590	500	1,000	6,090	3,500	1,500	5,000	(1,090)	5,000

10–6. *This report presents project information in a two-line summary. Project cost information is taken from timesheets, payroll records, and expense reports. Fee earned is calculated according to contract terms and the difference between total costs and total revenues represents profit or loss on the project. Project budget is the total amount established for the project.*

MANAGEMENT SUMMARY REPORT

Period: _12/1–12/31_

(List each project under appropriate project manager.)	Activity Status (Project to Date)					Billing Status		
	Budget	Revenue Earned	Remaining	% Compl.	% Spent	Invoiced	Received	Accounts Receivable
Jim Smith, Proj. Mgr.								
Project A	$150,000	$145,500	$ 4,500	80%	97%	$120,000	$100,000	$20,000
Project B	20,000	1,750	18,250	10	9	0	0	0
Project C	16,500	16,500	0	90	100	10,000	10,000	0
Project D	5,000	5,000	0	100	100	5,000	0	5,000

10–7. *This report shows the status of a project by comparing the percentage complete based on a technical evaluation of the project with the amount spent. Note that Project A is only 80% complete, but almost all the budget has been spent.*

A representative listing of some vendors with software packages specifically developed for design professionals is as follows. These systems were designed to operate on several different kinds of hardware configurations.

ACCI Business Systems, Inc.
4625 North Freeway, Suite 109
Houston, TX 77022

Alpine Data Systems
2821 Northrup Way
Bellevue, WA 98004

Applied Computer Services, Inc.
4915 Waters Edge Drive, Suite 170
Raleigh, NC 27606

Architectural Computer
3835 Connie Way
Santa Barbara, CA 93110

BST Data Systems, Inc.
P.O. Box 23425
Tampa, FL 33623

Breuer & Company
54 Middlesex Turnpike
Bedford, MA 01730

Brilling Data Systems
681 Market Street, Suite 541
San Francisco, CA 94105

Concept Group, Inc.
4849 North Mesa, Suite 101
El Paso, TX 79912

DFI/Systems
11801 S. Apopka-Vineland Rd.
Orlando, FL 32811

Data Basics
11000 Cedar Road, Suite 110
Cleveland, OH 44106

Datasystems Designers, Inc.
1004 Baltimore, Suite 800
Kansas City, MO 64105

Data Lab Corp.
200 West Monroe, #1106
Chicago, IL 60606

Engineering Design Corporation
160 Old Derby Street
Hingham, MA 02043

Engineering Science Computer Service
57 Executive Park South, Suite 590
Atlanta, GA 30329

Harper & Shuman, Inc.
68 Moulton Street
Cambridge, MA 02138

J. L. Heiniger Associates
636 West Jefferson Street
Morton, IL 61550

Microtech
3180 Pullman
Costa Mesa, CA 92626

Numeri/Comp., Inc.
703 Grove Street
Rockford, IL 61108

Sys Comp Corporation
2042 Broadway
Santa Monica, CA 90404

Vickrey & Assoc.
7334 Blanco Rd., Suite 109
San Antonio, TX 78216

Yandell & Hiller
2805 Fort Worth National Building
Fort Worth, TX 76102

Yeakel Electronic Systems
P.O. Box 17011
Irvine, CA 92713

Of course, buying a packaged system means that the firm must accept the input and output formats that come with it. While the programs can be individually tailored in some cases, this is often expensive and can sometimes cause problems with the system. Furthermore as the software vendor continually upgrades and improves the system it is often difficult to incorporate these changes into a customized system.

Integrated Accounting Systems

There are systems on the market today that combine general accounting and project accounting into a single integrated system designed to operate on a micro or mini computer. The cost of these systems is well within the reach of all but the smallest firms. Many of these systems have been developed specifically for design professionals so they highlight the features important to these firms. Many systems incorporate other capabilities, such as word processing and financial forecasting, as well.

An integrated system is helpful in that a single entry transmits the data to all the systems where needed. For example, a timesheet entry goes to both the payroll and project control systems. This is very important and helpful in that it eliminates the need for duplicate entries and therefore minimizes errors as well as the work effort involved in maintaining the system. Integrated systems currently require a greater memory capacity than that found in the small micro computers, although the computer industry is changing rapidly and improvements are constantly being made.

Purchasing a Computer System

Purchasing a computerized accounting system is a major undertaking, which the firm will have to live with for a long time. Therefore it is important to do it in a systematic way. Exhibit 10–8 is a checklist of items to be considered. First, the firm should look at its requirements for information and be certain that the computer is the right answer. In some cases, a very adequate manual system is in place and operating; it may only need some improvements to adequately serve the firm for several more years in its growth cycle. Once the decision has been made to move forward with a computerized system, the best procedure is to document your present system and then make the necessary changes for it to conform with the system you want to mechanize. Often an outside consultant not affiliated with any vendor can be helpful in this changeover. This review of the present system will often point out the need for changes in outmoded procedures and often reveal unneeded records. Project managers and other users of the system should be consulted so that the system will produce the reports they need and in a format that they can understand.

10-8. *Note the emphasis on preplanning before any consideration is given to specific hardware or software.*

CHECKLIST FOR BUYING A COMPUTERIZED ACCOUNTING SYSTEM

YES	NO	
☐	☐	Has the firm determined that it needs a computerized accounting system?
☐	☐	Have the people who will be working with the system agreed to its installation?
☐	☐	Have you researched the market to determine what systems are available to fit your needs?
☐	☐	Have you determined whether a standard package system is appropriate or will you develop your own software?
☐	☐	Has the system been developed specifically for design professionals?
☐	☐	Do you have adequate space for the hardware and peripheral equipment?
☐	☐	Have you examined the possibilities of using a service bureau or timesharing service?
☐	☐	Have you examined your present system and procedures and taken steps to correct any deficiencies in operation?
☐	☐	Have you visited the computer installations of other similar firms?
☐	☐	Have you considered backup facilities in case of temporary system failure?
☐	☐	Have you considered the security aspects of the computer installation?
☐	☐	Do you have someone on staff to take charge of the computer installation or will someone be hired for this purpose?
☐	☐	Have you analyzed the costs and payment terms offered by the vendor?
☐	☐	Has your attorney reviewed the legal documents involved?

After the analysis is complete the firm is then in a position to draw up a list of specifications outlining the requirements needed in the new system. Further information on the background of the firm and a description of its present system are added, and this document then becomes the basis of a request for a proposal that is prepared and sent to several vendors whose software and hardware appear to meet the needs.

The responses are reviewed and likely candidates are asked to demonstrate their systems and to answer further questions. Prior to making a final selection the firm should call and perhaps visit several installations where the vendor's system is in operation. The firm should also consult with an attorney who has experience with computer systems to review the contract documents.

A systematic approach will minimize the chances for making an error in the selection process.

Timesharing and Service Bureaus

There are alternatives to the outright purchase or lease of a computerized accounting system, and before making a final decision, the firm should investigate them. Timesharing and service bureaus allow the firm to use computerized accounting systems without making a large initial capital investment or regular lease payments.

Timesharing. Buying time on large computer installations is called "timesharing." The firm may use a small terminal in its office to gain access to the larger system, which then processes its data and issues reports. The firm pays only for the time it uses the larger system and in some cases for data storage. Timesharing is advantageous when there are knowledgeable people on the firm's staff who can use the resources of the large computer installation effectively.

Service Bureaus. These computer companies process data for outside clients. They are well adapted to handle accounting data, since they are equipped to process batches of information on a periodic basis, such as monthly. The firm can either bring the data to the service bureau or transmit the data automatically, depending on whether the firm has terminals that can communicate with the service bureau's equipment. Service bureaus are useful when a firm is getting started in computerized accounting systems and it wants to learn more about computers before making an investment. Service bureaus are also a way to begin training personnel in the use of computers. One of the most prominent timesharing firms and service bureaus working with design professionals is the Harper & Shuman firm listed on page 133.

Discussion Problem

Background. Your 25-person interior design firm has grown rapidly in the last few years. However, you are still receiving quarterly financial statements on the cash basis prepared by an outside accountant. You have a micro computer that you use for technical work and also for word processing. Recently, a member of your staff who is proficient with computers prepared a simple program to accumulate time by project. This has piqued your interest and you would like to develop further information on projects by using the computer.

Assignment. How do you go about investigating and selecting the right system? List the factors to consider in evaluating the software systems on the market. What outside sources would you investigate to get an independent and unbiased opinion on various vendor packages?

11
Reporting to Achieve Results

1. How can good financial reporting improve performance?

2. How can I evaluate my present reporting system?

3. What four characteristics identify an effective reporting system?

4. Why should "information only" reports be minimized?

5. What is "exception reporting" and why is it important?

6. How can reports be used in the decision-making process?

7. Why are variance reports useful to a busy executive?

A good financial reporting system can make a significant impact on overall financial results. Firms with good reporting systems generally are the most profitable and also do the best work for clients.

Impact on Overall Financial Performance

Strange as this may seem, it works because a good reporting system focuses on results and measures these results against goals that were established in advance. How well these results measure up is a key element in evaluating staff. Project managers and department heads will soon discover that it is easier to perform well than to make excuses about why they fell short of expectations. A good financial reporting system will have everyone pulling in the same direction, since they are all working toward the same set of goals.

It should be recognized, however, that a good reporting system will not turn a poor performer into a good performer. A poor performer may have problems unrelated to overall performance, and these need to be discovered through discussion and counseling. However, good reporting will turn a good performer into an even better performer. This is because the reports encourage people to do well, since they are a way to gain recognition in management's eyes. People's abilities are brought to the forefront and periodic reporting of results sparks healthy competition among high-achievers.

Evaluation of a Reporting System

To discover whether a firm has a good financial reporting system, a number of questions need to be asked. First, are the reports being read and acted upon? Reports distributed without any feedback are an indication that the system is not too effective. Project managers and department heads should be asking questions about the numbers and the derivation of certain allocation methods for the financial manager to know for certain that the reports are being read and understood. Second, do the reports give warnings in time for management to take corrective action where necessary? The main purpose of reporting is not simply to tell the firm where it has been but, more importantly, where it is going. If this kind of information cannot be gleaned from the reports, then they are simply not doing their job. Third, can the reports be prepared routinely with the financial staff available? Most financial staffs are stretched thin at the time financial statements are being prepared, but they should be able to handle the regular workload, perhaps with a certain amount of extra effort, but without excessive overtime.

Finally, if the financial system is computerized, is correct information being generated without an unusually large number of manual corrections having to be made? Mistakes will creep into almost any system, but the computerized reports should be basically correct most of the time. Exhibit 11–1 is a checklist for evaluating your reporting system.

11-1. Use this checklist to evaluate your current reporting system to determine what improvements may be necessary.

CHECKLIST FOR EVALUATING A REPORTING SYSTEM

YES	NO	
☐	☐	Have you asked the users of the reporting system for their comments and suggestions?
☐	☐	Can you determine instances where the reporting system has helped you become a better manager?
☐	☐	Do you and other managers look forward to receiving the reports?
☐	☐	Do you read the reports when received or are they stacked on your credenza to be examined later when you "have time"?
☐	☐	Can new people in the firm quickly understand and use the reports?
☐	☐	Do people have the information they need to manage without being overloaded with information?

Elements of a Good Reporting System

For a system to meet the needs of management, it must have credibility. How a system gains credibility is as follows:

1. *It must be accurate.* This does not mean that the numbers must just add up, but rather that any mistakes in the system must be corrected in the next reporting period. There is nothing more discouraging to project managers and department heads than to have mistakes go uncorrected after they are reported to the financial manager. If they persist the people using the system will just ignore the reports.

2. *The reports must be timely for them to be useful.* How timely the reports are depends on how the firm is organized and how much it is willing to spend in the financial area. Some of the largest companies gather data from all over the world and have their financial reports within a few days after the close of the month. Of course, these companies spend large sums of money on their reporting systems. The typical architectural or engineering firm should not have to wait longer than two weeks after the close of the accounting period to receive financial statements. As it is, this is halfway into the next reporting period, and any longer wait means that virtually nothing can be done to make corrections on what the statements reveal. Any firm having to wait longer than two weeks should consult with its independent auditors to see what can be done to speed up the accounting process.

3. *The reports should be fair.* By fair it is meant that cost allocations to the various profit centers should be made on an equitable basis. Overhead must be distributed in such a manner that those receiving a portion of it understand the basis of allocation, and while they may not like it, they should recognize that there is no fairer way possible to distribute the burden. Generally, direct labor is the basis for distributing overhead costs, but this may not always be the best way if, for example, one profit center manager uses outside contract labor while another uses in-house staff.

4. *The reports should be clear, which means that they must be quickly and easily understood.* The reports should not require further analysis or additional calculations on the reader's part. One of the best ways of presenting clear reports is through charts and graphs. This type of visual presentation is easier to read than columns of figures, and graphics keep people interested in the presentation.

The sample reports shown in Exhibits 11–2 through 11–16 have all been used in presentations to management. While the data are fictitious, the charts can be used to develop a firm's own reporting presentations. Graphics look more attractive if they are presented in color, but color charts take longer to produce and, in presenting the latest financial information, there is often not enough time to prepare color charts.

Exhibit 11–2 is a bar graph showing revenues over a 10-year period. At first, a simple presentation such as this may appear not to have enough information to justify the chart. However, the more information displayed in a chart, the more difficult it is to read and comprehend. Therefore, in this case, rather than showing a detailed breakdown of revenue by type on the one chart, it is more effective to use another, such as the pie chart shown in Exhibit 11–3. Exhibit 11–4 is another bar chart showing a 10-year history of operating profit. Exhibit 11–5 illustrates a ratio, in this case percentages of profit to net fees earned over a 10-year period. The ratio is compared with a profit goal of 25 percent. Whenever ratios are portrayed in graphic form, it is important to compare them with some base or goal, otherwise the ratio has little meaning except for historical purposes. Exhibit 11–6 is a graphic portrayal of productivity factors, or the percent of direct labor to total labor by office or profit center. In this case, the actual productivity factors are compared with the factors needed to meet budget.

Exhibit 11–7 is a line graph comparing cumulative fees earned during a fiscal year with the budget. Note how quickly the comparison between actual and budget figures can be made without studying a large number of figures and making mental calculations.

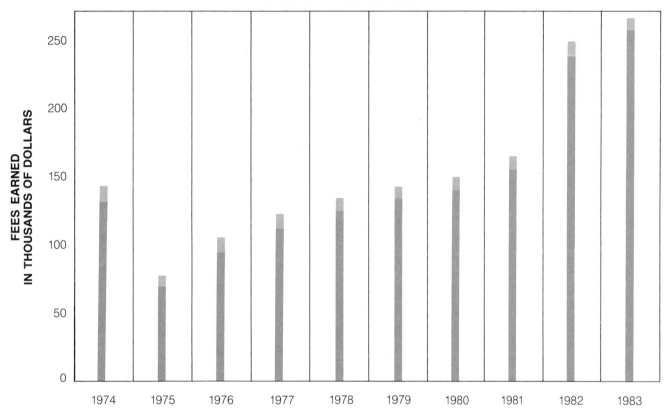

XYZ CONSULTANTS, INC.
GROSS & NET FEES EARNED
FISCAL 1974 THROUGH 1983

**SUBCONTRACTORS AND
REIMBURSABLE EXPENSES**

NET FEES EARNED

11-2. *This chart shows a steady growth rate in revenues after recovery from the 1974–1975 recession. Note the sharply higher revenues in the last two years.*

11-3. *This chart shows the distribution of revenue by client type for the last two years. Note the sharply higher dependency on the federal government for revenue.*

BREAKDOWN OF REVENUES BY CLIENT TYPE

XYZ CONSULTANTS, INC.
BREAKDOWN OF REVENUES BY CLIENT TYPE,
FISCAL 1982 & 1983

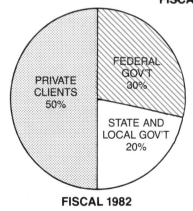

FISCAL 1982

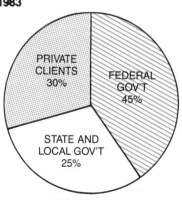

FISCAL 1983

XYZ CONSULTANTS, INC.
OPERATING PROFIT (PRETAX AND PREBONUS/PROFIT SHARING),
FISCAL 1974 THROUGH 1983 (IN THOUSANDS)

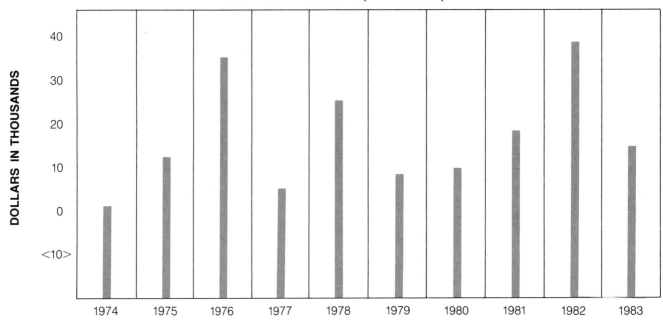

11-4. *A 10-year history of operating profit is likely to fluctuate in this manner in a professional service firm, particularly a smaller one.*

XYZ CONSULTANTS, INC.
PERCENTAGE OF PROFIT TO NET FEES EARNED,
FISCAL 1974 THROUGH 1983

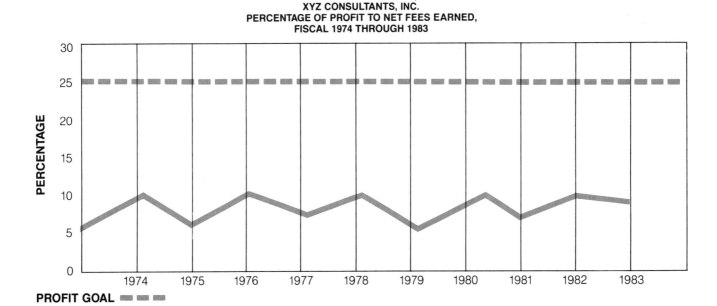

PROFIT GOAL ▬ ▬ ▬

11-5. *The firm has set a high profit goal that it has not come close to achieving. Perhaps the goal is unrealistic.*

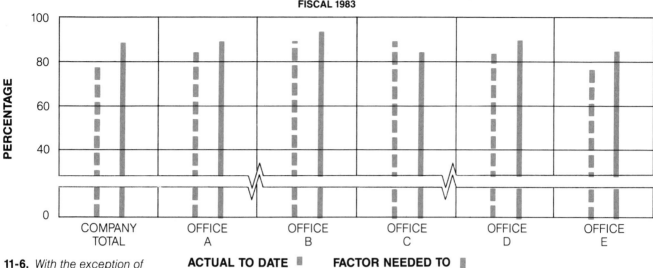

XYZ CONSULTANTS, INC.
PRODUCTIVITY FACTOR (% DIRECT LABOR TO TOTAL LABOR),
FISCAL 1983

ACTUAL TO DATE **FACTOR NEEDED TO MEET BUDGETS**

11-6. *With the exception of Office C none of the other offices has achieved a sufficiently high productivity factor to meet budget. The budgets may have to be revised.*

COMPARISON OF CUMULATIVE FEES EARNED VERSUS BUDGET

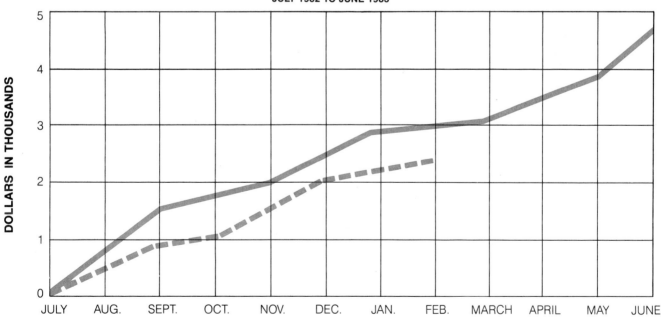

XYZ CONSULTANTS, INC.
COMPARISON OF CUMULATIVE NET FEES EARNED VERSUS BUDGET,
JULY 1982 TO JUNE 1983

F/Y 1983 BUDGET
F/Y 1983 ACTUAL

11-7. *Actual net fees have remained under budget since the first of the year. With higher revenues budgeted for the latter part of the year it appears to be unlikely that the budget will be met.*

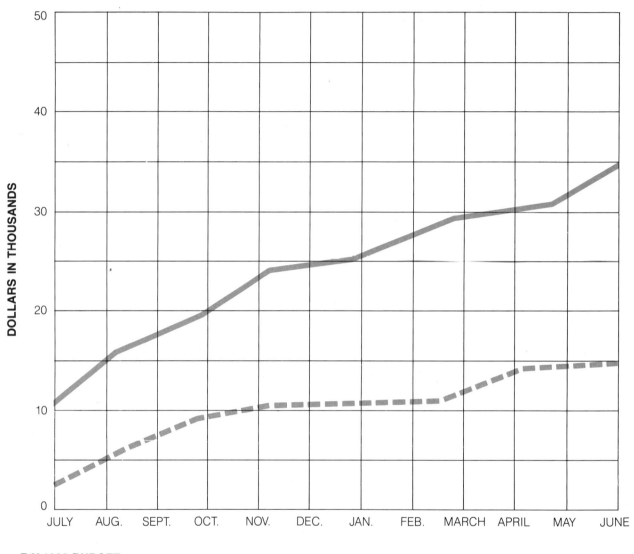

**XYZ CONSULTANTS, INC.
COMPARISON OF CUMULATIVE PRETAX PROFIT VERSUS BUDGET,
JULY 1982 TO JUNE 1983**

F/Y 1983 BUDGET
F/Y 1983 ACTUAL

11-8. *Actual profit for the year
was well below the budget.
This requires an explanation.*

Exhibit 11–8 is a similar chart showing the same comparisons for pre-tax profit. The people who can most appreciate these charts are chief executive officers and managing principals who have little time to spend analyzing data. These people must be able to glean the status of a situation quickly in order to make decisions.

Other Methods of Presenting Understandable Reports

Limiting Account Breakdowns. There are other ways beside the use of graphics to present clear and useful reports. One method is to limit the number of account breakdowns as reports are submitted on top management. For example, Exhibit 11–9 is a detailed presentation of a profit and loss statement that is useful for a profit-center manager in a larger firm. It shows in detail the various charges to his or her profit center. Exhibit 11–10 is a profit and loss statement for a smaller firm. The item labeled "miscellaneous" is kept to a minimum to eliminate questions about this account. By contrast, Exhibit 11–11 is a financial report to senior management in a larger firm that eliminates detailed breakdowns and concentrates instead on comparisons with forecasted results. The practice of limiting account breakdowns presented to higher levels of management is generally effective. However, it should be recognized that there are some profit-center managers who are simply not interested in knowing the details and some senior management personnel who insist on detailed reports. Therefore, the first rule is to know the audience for the reports and to give them what they need and want.

Exception Reporting. Another effective way of presenting financial reports is through exception reporting. Exception reporting operates on the premise that managers are usually flooded with too much information and therefore have difficulty recognizing the important material that they should know. By highlighting information that is out of the ordinary and not reporting certain information that is within established parameters, the manager can concentrate on what is important. Exhibit 11–12 is a report listing projects in trouble, that is, projects that have exceeded budgets by 10 percent or more. A manager need only scan this list to know which projects need attention. One problem with a listing like this is that once a project makes the list, it is not likely to be removed until completed, so the list becomes increasingly lengthy. Exception reporting can be readily adapted to computerized reports, since information out of the ordinary can be asterisked or highlighted in some way. In a manual system of reporting, red circles can be drawn around the information to be highlighted.

People should only receive reports on which they can take action. This means that reports "for information only" should be minimized in the interest of reducing the information glut. For example, project managers need to have detailed information on the projects they control, but they do not generally need information on other managers' projects. Routine status reports should be examined and eliminated after they have served their purpose. A good illustration is a crisis report generated to meet a specific need. For example, the principals of the firm may need to monitor cash on a daily basis when there is a severe cash shortage. But once the situation has passed, only the financial manager may need to monitor cash daily. Therefore, a daily cash report to the principals is no longer necessary.

Comparative Reporting. Another effective way of reporting financial information is through comparative data. Comparative data are presented in the form of variance reports where data are compared with a budget or historical period. Comparisons are easy to grasp, but it is important to have a method for highlighting the significant variances. One method, as shown in Exhibit 11–13, is to bracket the unfavorable information. That is, where revenues are lower than budget, which is unfavorable, the difference is bracketed. Where expenses are higher than budget, which is also unfavorable, the difference is bracketed. Where profit is lower than budget, which is unfavorable, the difference is bracketed. The reader of the report then need only scan the variance column for the larger bracketed amounts, and he or she has the significance of the report in a very short period of time. He or she can then concentrate on finding the reasons for the variances, which is the important matter.

11-9. *A large firm needs many account breakdowns in order to control costs. In this case merging accounts would create large balances that would require further breakdowns in order to be analyzed properly.*

PROFIT AND LOSS STATEMENT FOR A LARGE FIRM

XYZ Consultants, Inc. (Large Firm)
Office A Income Statement
February 1983

REVENUE	Current Month	Year to Date
Project revenue	$304,830	$2,434,640
Other income	29,820	250,560
Total revenue	$334,650	$2,685,200
OPERATING EXPENSES		
Salaries: Direct	$121,725	$ 981,800
Indirect	28,392	343,241
Payroll taxes	4,653	37,224
Vacations	6,489	51,912
Sick leave	7,048	56,384
Holidays	9,355	74,840
Group insurance	1,100	8,800
Severance pay	801	6,408
Consultants	3,658	29,264
Data processing	1,791	14,328
Legal & accounting	2,743	21,944
Temporary secretarial	2,330	18,640
Travel	7,580	60,640
Promotion	6,001	48,008
Rental of space	22,104	196,832
Supplies	6,703	53,624
Furniture & equipment lease	2,292	18,336
Depreciation	3,800	30,400
Insurance & bonding	1,605	12,840
Printing & reproduction	8,200	65,600
Repairs & maintenance	9,097	72,776
Dues & subscriptions	4,032	32,256
Employee procurement	1,698	13,584
Telephone	4,302	14,416
Postage & freight	9,642	77,136
Interest	5,618	44,944
Conferences	2,491	19,928
Miscellaneous	2,892	23,136
Other direct expenses	9,968	79,744
Total operating expenses	$298,110	$2,488,985
Net profit before taxes	$ 36,540	$ 196,215

PROFIT AND LOSS STATEMENT FOR A SMALLER FIRM

ABC CONSULTANTS, INC. (Small Firm)
INCOME STATEMENT,
FEBRUARY 1983

REVENUE	Current Month	Year to Date
Project revenue	$29,423	$102,980
Other income	1,542	5,397
Total revenue	$30,965	$108,377
OPERATING EXPENSES		
Salaries: Direct	$10,121	$ 35,423
Indirect	4,732	16,562
Payroll taxes	1,527	5,344
Vacations, holidays, sick leave	951	3,329
Group insurance	89	312
Data processing	284	994
Legal & accounting	580	2,030
Promotion	3,131	10,958
Rental of space	4,297	15,040
Supplies	147	515
Furniture & equipment lease	289	1,011
Depreciation	816	2,856
Liability insurance	115	403
Printing & reproduction	680	2,380
Dues & subscriptions	1,412	4,942
Telephone	115	403
Miscellaneous	100	350
Other direct expenses	1,012	3,542
Total operating expenses	30,398	106,394
Net profit before tax	$ 567	$ 1,983

XYZ Consultants, Inc.
Office A Income Statement (In Thousands)
February 1983

	Current Month		Year to Date	
REVENUE	**Actual**	**Forecast**	**Actual**	**Forecast**
Project revenue	$305	$300	$2,435	$2,650
Other income	30	40	250	250
Total revenue	$335	$340	$2,685	$2,900
OPERATING EXPENSES				
Project expenses	$132	$140	$1,062	$1,120
General overhead	166	160	1,427	1,570
Total expenses	$298	$300	$2,489	$2,690
Net profit before tax	$ 37	$ 40	$ 196	$ 210

11-11. *Note how easy it is to grasp the meaning of a report that contains a few key numbers.*

11-12. *This exception report listing projects in difficulty would be very useful for managing principals with little time to read reports. Figures in parentheses in the last column represent the dollar value of losses on projects.*

PROJECTS IN TROUBLE

XYZ Consultants, Inc.
Projects Exceeding Budgets by 10%
February 1983

Office A	Project Revenue ($)	Profit/Loss ($)
Project C	$ 7,489	($121)
Project E	129,834	26
Project F	60,234	19
Project H	9,834	(14)
Office B		
Project K	$ 19,334	($ 42)
Project M	12,468	4

11-13. *Note how easy it is to grasp the meaning of this report by looking for the large bracketed numbers in the last column.*

VARIANCE REPORT

XYZ Consultants, Inc.
Office A Income Statement/Variance Report (In Thousands)
February 1983

REVENUE	Actual	Budget	Variance
Project revenue	$305	$315	[$10]
Other income	29	28	1
Total revenue	$334	$343	[$ 9]
OPERATING EXPENSES			
Salaries: Direct	$121	$116	[$ 5]
Indirect	29	26	[3]
Payroll taxes	5	5	—
Vacations	6	6	—
Sick leave	7	7	—
Holidays	9	10	1
Group insurance	1	1	—
Severance pay	1	1	—
Consultants	3	3	—
Data processing	2	3	1
Legal & accounting	2	2	—
Temporary secretarial	2	4	2
Travel	8	10	2
Promotion	7	6	[1]
Rental of space	22	22	—
Supplies	7	3	[4]
Furniture & equipment lease	2	2	—
Depreciation	3	3	—
Insurance & bonding	1	1	—
Printing & reproduction	9	11	2
Repairs & maintenance	9	9	—
Dues & subscriptions	5	4	[1]
Employee procurement	2	3	1
Telephone	5	6	1
Postage & freight	9	11	2
Interest	6	1	[5]
Conference	2	2	—
Miscellaneous	3	3	—
Other direct expenses	10	10	—
Total operating expenses	$298	$291	[$ 7]
Net profit before tax	$ 36	$ 52	[$16]

Highlighting Important Information. Still another method of presenting effective financial reports is shown in Exhibit 11–14 where the current information, which is the most important information, is highlighted by shading the comparative data. This concentrates the reader's attention and is quite effective when presenting a large number of figures. Rounding to the nearest meaningful dollar amounts, whether hundreds or thousands, also makes reports easier to read.

Use of Ratios. Ratio analysis is another technique often used to present financial information. Ratios present key indicators of performance, such as average collection period and sales per employee, and they are particularly useful when compared with averages of other similar firms. Exhibits 11–15 and 11–16 are examples of such comparisons.

Using Financial Reports

The most important factor in presenting financial reports is to know your audience and to present them with the information they need and want in order to manage effectively. Generally, readers of reports want summaries and conclusions. The financial manager should try to anticipate any questions that might be asked about the reports. He or she should be prepared to explain the reasons for any unfavorable results.

Reports should be directed to the people who can take action and achieve results. These people need a minimum of key information that tells them what they should know quickly and succinctly. They should not be overwhelmed with a lot of reports and data. Reports that emphasize the profit and loss approach are generally the most effective when comparing results of a single project, a profit center, or the firm as a whole. Ratios are also very effective in conveying a lot of information with a very few numbers, but to be really effective, they must be compared with a base or with other firms in order for meaningful comparisons to be drawn.

Reports should present the latest financial information available, which means that meetings should be scheduled when reports are issued. At the meeting the financial information should not be read aloud line by line; only the significant items should be mentioned and comparisons drawn. Then, as questions are raised, the financial manager can discuss whatever additional detail is required.

After the meeting it is well to follow up on the reports by requesting suggestions for improvement. It is possible that the financial manager may still be providing more information than is necessary or required, and you will discover this by asking for suggestions. The financial manager should also examine what other firms are doing by discussing reporting techniques with counterparts in other firms.

11-14. *Rounding figures to thousands where appropriate is very effective in improving the readability of reports.*

INCOME STATEMENT WITH CURRENT INFORMATION HIGHLIGHTED

XYZ Consultants, Inc.
Office A Income Statement (In Thousands)
February 1983

	Current Month			Year to Date		
	Last Year	Actual	Forecast	Last Year	Actual	Forecast
REVENUE						
Project revenue	$291	$305	$300	$2,105	$2,435	$2,650
Other income	22	30	40	190	250	250
Total revenue	$313	$335	$340	$2,295	$2,685	$2,900
OPERATING EXPENSES						
Project expenses	$121	$132	$140	$ 998	$1,062	$1,120
General overhead	158	166	160	1,302	1,427	1,570
Total expenses	$279	$298	$300	$2,300	$2,489	$2,690
Net profit before tax	$ 34	$ 37	$ 40	($ 5)	$ 196	$ 210

COMPARISON OF SELECTED RATIOS

XYZ Consultants, Inc.
Comparison of Selected Ratios,
Fiscal 1983

Dun and Bradstreet Survey*

	Upper Quartile	Median	Lower Quartile	XYZ Consultants, Inc.
Return on sales (%)	8.7	4.11	2.03	3.5
Return on net worth (%)	47.4	26.4	16.6	13.6
Sales per employee ($)	52,680	29,920	23,220	22,614
Collection period (days)	91	61	33	158
Sales (in thousands of $)	4,370	2,110	1,460	9,836
Net working capital to sales (%)	20.3	11.0	5.0	16.9

*"Financial Analysis of Engineering, Architectural and Surveying Service," *Dun and Bradstreet*, 1979.

11-15. *This report is useful for comparing your firm's experience with averages in the industry.*

BALANCE SHEET ACCOUNTS AS PERCENTAGE OF NET SALES

XYZ Consultants, Inc.
Balance Sheet Accounts as Percentage
of Net Sales,

Fiscal 1983

	Dun and Bradstreet Survey* (Median, %)	XYZ Consultants, Inc. (%)		Dun and Bradstreet Survey* (Median, %)	XYZ Consultants, Inc. (%)
Cash	2.5	1.8	Accounts payable	2.0	3.3
Accounts receivable	17.0	43.2	Bank loans	5.0	5.1
Inventory	4.5		Notes payable	2.0	
Notes receivable	1.5		Other current liabilities	7.0	19.9
Other current assets	4.0	0.2	TOTAL CURRENT LIABILITIES	8.0	28.3
TOTAL CURRENT ASSETS	18.0	45.2			
			Long-term liabilities	6.0	0.5
Fixtures & equipment	6.0	4.3	Stock/net worth	19.0	26.1
Real estate	4.0	3.2	TOTAL LIABILITIES & CAPITAL	30.5	54.9
Other noncurrent assets	2.0	2.3			
TOTAL ASSETS	25.0	54.9			

*"Financial Analysis of Engineering, Architectural, and Surveying Service," Dun and Bradstreet, 1979.

11-16. *The reader of this report should highlight the amounts with significant variances and ask the financial manager for possible explanations.*

Reporting as a Basis for Decision Making

How financial reports are prepared and presented is important and, to a certain degree, influences whether they are read and used. Reports to the principals of the firm should be typed on $8\frac{1}{2} \times 11$-inch paper and bound into a folder with dividers or colored tabs for ease in reading and carrying in a briefcase. Do not present reports on lined accounting paper that is difficult to read. The reports should have a summary narrative on top for the benefit of those people unable to attend the meeting where they are discussed.

In presenting the reports, the financial manager should point out highlights and interpret the results. The financial manager must be prepared to answer questions. If he or she does not have an answer it should be obtained later and reported back to the questioner. The entire focus of the presentation should be on the future and what the figures mean in terms of future results. There is nothing anyone can do to change what has already happened, but the past gives us the best indication of what is likely to happen in the future.

When presenting financial information that will be the basis for significant policy decisions, such as opening or closing an office or deciding to enter a new market, it is most important that the financial manager clearly present options and alternatives and discuss their pros and cons. However, the financial manager should not make a recommendation unless asked. Generally, three options should be presented, if possible, and the effects of each described.

If a recommendation is requested, the financial manager should present it and make it clear that this is an opinion. Of course, it is necessary to support the conclusions, and the financial manager should be prepared to answer questions that may arise. If there is any controversy or disagreement with the numbers it is most important that it be settled beforehand. Nothing can demoralize a meeting or lead to ineffective decision making more than having two people disagree over numbers while the rest of the participants do not know whose numbers to believe. Since the financial manager is generally the one to give the presentation, there should be an arrangement beforehand to get clarification and agreement, particularly if the financial manager has cause to believe that someone at the meeting will take exception to the figures. There may still be disagreement, but if everyone understands the reason for it and why the numbers are different, then they can at least make an intelligent decision.

Reporting in Smaller Firms

The principals in a small firm do not have time to review voluminous reports, any more than their large-firm counterparts. Therefore it is just as important that they have a system that meets their needs. In some cases an outside consultant may have to be hired to review the system and design the necessary reports in the proper format. When this has been set up, the bookkeeper can be shown how to follow the system and produce future reports.

Graphics systems are now available on some of the smaller computers, and they can be very effective in producing charts and graphs from accounting data similar to those shown in Exhibits 11–2 to 11–8. Not only are the computer graphics more accurate than hand-drawn charts, but the system can be set up to produce these reports on a routine basis. As technology improves and the cost of this equipment comes within reach of smaller firms, reporting systems can be effective and meaningful to firms of all sizes.

Certain key reports listed in Exhibits 11–9 to 11–16 can and should be adapted for use in smaller firms. For example, Exhibit 11–10 shows how a smaller firm should combine accounts in the income statement so as to present a more readable report with significant numbers for comparison. The principle of exception reporting should be used by firms of all sizes, and therefore the report showing profits exceeding budgets in Exhibit 11–12 is applicable to smaller firms as well. Variance reporting is another technique that is useful to the smaller firm, and the principals will appreciate a report such as that shown in Exhibit 11–13 which they can quickly scan to find significant deviations from the budget. The use of ratios for comparison purposes is also helpful to firms of all sizes. In this case, if the survey data are broken down by size of firm it will be particularly helpful to the smaller firm.

Discussion Problem

Background. The President of XYZ Architects is in his late 60s and has been thinking about retirement for several years. However, he has been overwhelmed with the day-to-day task of running the firm for so many years that he has not devoted any time to finding a prospective buyer or thinking about any other aspects of ownership transition.

One day he receives a call from the senior vice-president of a larger firm on the East Coast, whom he had met casually a while back. The senior vice-president was frank in stating that his firm was looking to acquire an architectural firm of about the size of XYZ Architects, and he was holding very preliminary discussions with several candidates at the moment. The president said he would be willing to explore the possibilities unofficially, with the stipulation that these talks be held in strictest confidence. Since the senior vice-president was going to be in town, dinner was arranged and the senior vice-president stressed that they would be spending only a little time on financial details at these preliminary discussions and suggested that the president put together some data in a highly visual form that they could review together.

Assignment. Attached are examples of the reports prepared by XYZ Architects. Review each one to determine whether it is pertinent for discussion at the meeting. If so, sketch a rough outline of how it might be presented in graphic format. What other kinds of graphic presentations would be effective?

WORK IN PROGRESS/AGED RECEIVABLES

XYZ Architects, Inc.
Work in Progress/Aged Receivables
As of 12/31/—

Client	Total ($)	Work in Progress ($)	Current ($)	Accounts Receivable 30 Days ($)	60 Days ($)	90 Days and Over ($)
Bailey Builders	$ 15,500	$10,000	$ 5,500			
Joe McDermott	42,520	6,520	16,000	15,000		5,000
First Federal	10,000	1,500	8,500			
Tom Jackson	19,000	6,500			12,500	
Demontrond	5,123	2,560	2,563			
Cy-Fair Schools	12,350	4,500	4,850	3,000		
Harris County	4,600	3,600	1,000			
Montgomery County	4,511	1,200	750	2,561		
City of Humble	4,486	1,890	2,596			
Totals	$118,090	$38,270	$41,759	$20,561	$12,500	$5,000

Listing of unbilled work in progress and accounts receivable by client is broken down according to the number of days that accounts receivable are outstanding.

INCOME STATEMENTS

XYZ Architects, Inc.
Income Statements 1980–1983 (est.)

	1980	1981	1982	1983 (est.)
Income				
Fees Earned	$233,880	$280,734	$325,481	$470,000
Reimbursable Expenses	2,975	9,514	11,123	20,000
Other Income	812	612	1,012	5,000
Total Income	237,667	290,860	337,616	495,000
Direct Expenses				
Direct Salaries: Principals	17,089	19,225	20,441	25,000
Direct Salaries: Employees	61,916	74,235	88,040	100,000
Total Direct Salaries	79,005	93,460	108,481	125,000
Outside Services	15,901	10,009	11,049	10,000
Other Direct Expenses	5,311	12,618	12,808	5,000
Total Direct Expenses	100,217	116,087	132,338	140,000
Indirect Expenses				
Admin. Salaries: Principals	16,327	22,225	30,462	28,000
Admin. Salaries: Employees	18,714	20,234	32,564	33,000
Temporary Employees	6,021	5,618	2,618	2,000
Vacation/Holiday/Sick Time	10,427	11,812	13,002	14,000
Payroll Related Expenses	7,227	8,002	9,382	10,000
Office Expense	22,536	26,018	28,888	30,000
Legal/accounting	2,601	3,101	4,014	3,000
Automobile Expense	4,228	5,600	6,437	6,000
Depreciation	916	1,114	1,445	2,000
Business Development	2,806	3,418	4,055	5,000
Other Indirect Expense	8,302	14,718	28,061	27,000
Total Indirect Exp.	100,105	121,860	160,928	160,000
Total Expenses	200,322	237,947	293,266	300,000
Profit/Loss before Taxes	$ 37,345	$ 52,913	$ 44,350	$ 55,000

Here are projected balance sheets for the current year and estimated for the following year.

INCOME STATEMENTS AND BALANCE SHEETS

XYZ Architects, Inc.
Pro Forma Income Statements & Balance Sheets, 1984–1985

	1984 ($)	1985 ($)
INCOME STATEMENTS		
Project revenue	$500,000	$550,000
Other income		
Total revenue	$500,000	$550,000
Operating expenses		
Project expenses	200,000	225,000
General overhead	248,000	270,000
Total expenses	$448,000	$495,000
Net profit before taxes	$ 52,000	$ 55,000
BALANCE SHEETS		
Assets		
Cash	48,000	33,000
Accounts receivable	120,300	135,300
Work in progress	78,200	98,200
Other current assets	25,600	25,600
Fixed assets	85,000	85,000
Total assets	$357,100	$377,100
Liabilities & equity		
Liabilities		
Accounts payable	75,000	57,000
Notes payable	25,000	20,000
Other liabilities	42,000	30,000
Total liabilities	$142,000	$107,000
Equity	$215,100	$270,100
Total liability & equity	$357,100	$377,100

Actual and estimated revenue earned on major projects is listed according to type of client.

PROJECTED REVENUE BY CLIENT TYPE

XYZ Architects, Inc.
Projected Revenue by Client Type,
1982, 1983 (Est.), 1984 (Est.)

	1983 ($)	1984 ($)	1985 ($)
Private Sector Clients			
Bailey Builders	$ 25,500.00	$ 15,000.00	$ 35,000.00
Joe McDermott	85,200.00	40,000.00	65,000.00
First Federal	47,500.00	50,000.00	70,000.00
Tom Jackson	80,300.00	80,000.00	90,000.00
Demontrond	60,250.00	20,000.00	40,000.00
Subtotal	$298,750.00	$205,000.00	$300,000.00
Projected sales			
City bank		45,000.00	35,000.00
Office plaza		20,000.00	25,000.00
Subtotal		65,000.00	60,000.00
Total		$270,000.00	$360,000.00
State/Local Government			
Cy-Fair Schools	45,500.00	15,000.00	30,000.00
Harris County	26,300.00	20,000.00	30,000.00
Montgomery County	24,600.00	30,000.00	15,000.00
City of Humble	99,850.00	20,000.00	20,000.00
Subtotal	$196,250.00	$ 85,000.00	$ 95,000.00
Projected revenue			
Hobby Airport		100,000.00	70,000.00
Houston Port Authority		45,000.00	25,000.00
Subtotal		145,000.00	95,000.00
Total		$230,000.00	$190,000.00
Grand total	$495,000.00	$500,000.00	$550,000.00

This schedule of fixed assets by type of equipment is necessary to determine depreciation expense.

XYZ ARCHITECTS, INC., DEPRECIATION SCHEDULE AS OF 12/31/—

| | Date Purchased | (In Thousands) | | |
		Original Cost ($)	Depreciation ($)	Net Book Value ($)
Furniture and Fixtures				
4 Executive desks	06/18/76	$ 8	$ 6	$ 2
4 Executive chairs	06/18/76	2	2	0
4 Side chairs	06/18/76	2	2	0
4 Credenzas	06/18/76	4	3	1
4 Secretarial desks	06/18/76	4	3	1
4 Secretarial chairs	06/18/76	1	1	0
4 Side chairs	06/18/76	1	1	0
15 Standard wood desks	07/20/76	12	10	2
Etc.				
Total furniture & fixtures		$432	$205	$227
Leasehold Improvements				
Telephone installation	03/21/75	$ 12	$ 12	$ 0
Security system	04/03/76	7	7	0
Etc.				
Total leasehold improvements		$668	$ 26	$342
Transportation Equipment				
3 Oldsmobile sedans	02/28/78	$ 30	$ 30	$ 0
Etc.				
Total transportation equipment		$412	$ 80	$332

12

Special Problems of Interior Design: Purchasing

1. What is involved in establishing a purchasing service in an interior design firm?

2. What is the key to a profitable purchasing service?

3. How do I handle purchases from funds in an escrow account?

4. What should I establish as the usual markup on furniture purchases?

5. What deposits are usually required on furnishings to be ordered?

6. What are some drawbacks to establishing a purchasing function?

7. How can the financial manager be of assistance?

I nterior design firms operate on a basis similar to architectural firms to the extent that they are both project oriented. There are, however, some characteristics of interior design firms that set them apart. The fee structure may be quoted on a square foot basis, hourly rate, or percentage of the furnishings cost. The square footage and percentage of cost calculations eventually must relate back to the hours of labor needed to accomplish the task, and this provides the firm with a measure of its productivity. In some cases rates per square foot have been established by building developers that are customary for interiors work of a standard commercial grade, and it is expected that these rates will be quoted in proposals for this type of work. When trying to attract these clients, the firm must gear its efforts to produce at these rates and still be able to make a profit in order to stay competitive. Otherwise, it must select potential clients who are looking for a better product or more complex design and convince these people that they are getting a superior service for a higher price.

Summary Bid Form

Interior design firms usually prepare detailed floor plans and specifications for their clients to enable dealers in furniture and equipment to prepare their bids. Comparison of bids is facilitated when a summary bid document is prepared, such as that shown in Exhibit 12–1. This summary permits the interiors firm and the client to prepare a spread sheet analysis of the various bids. It also quickly isolates those dealers who are unable to bid on all items.

Preparing the summary in this fashion enables the interiors firm and the client to compare discounts offered by the manufacturer to the various dealers. The form also isolates the dealer's add-on costs and profit, and those dealers who do not wish to disclose this information are eliminated from bidding. The form also clarifies the application of sales tax only to the furniture portion of the cost.

Purchasing Services

The interior design firm that offers clients a purchasing service presents a whole new set of problems to the financial manager. These firms go beyond specifying the furniture and furnishings to be provided. They order the material and arrange for the installation as well. This function is often handled by an expediter in the interiors firm or else a separate department may be necessary, depending on the size and volume of orders. The expediter is responsible for working with the designers to select manufacturers, place purchase orders, expedite deliveries, and arrange for supervision of the installation crews. It is a large and important reponsibility and one that many interior design firms are not set up to handle. For that reason many firms, particularly the smaller ones, only perform this service for a few clients or else for smaller projects. On larger projects, the client may be referred to a company that specializes in large-scale purchasing of furnishings and supplies.

In some cases the purchasing service may be a necessary part of the project, such as the design of hospital or hotel facilities in one of the Middle Eastern countries. In this case there is no one on the client's staff and no readily available service in the country to perform the task. The architect or interior designer must be knowledgeable enough to take on this responsibility as part of the design contract or else subcontract with a firm that has this capability.

Purchasing Forms and Procedures

Following are some sample forms and procedures used in the purchasing function:

Project Product List. This form as shown in Exhibit 12–2 is used to list specific quantities, manufacturers, specifications, and costs for all items purchased through the interiors firm. When the list is completed to the designer's satisfaction and accepted by the client, it is forwarded to the expediter who fills out purchase orders for the items listed.

The project product list is kept by the expediter until all purchase orders have been prepared and signed. The list is then sent back to the designer who uses it to check purchase orders. After approval, the list is returned to the expediter who retains it as

SUMMARY BID FORM

Proposal for Furniture, Furnishings, and Equipment
Dollar Bank
First Floor of Smith Building

FROM: _____

Amount

Section 1 Gilbert   _____

Section 2 Gunlocke   _____

Section 3 Howe   _____

Section 4 IIL   _____

Section 5 JG   _____

Section 6 Modern Mode   _____

Section 7 Stendig   _____

Section 8 Stow Davis   _____

    Total Dealer Net   _____

Plus _____% profit   _____

    Subtotal "A"   _____

Plus _____% overhead, freight, delivery, and installation   _____

    Subtotal "B"   _____

Plus sales tax (where applicable) on subtotal "A"   _____

Plus net packing charges   _____

    GRAND TOTAL   _____

_____% Discount for immediate payment within 15 days of invoice   _____

    Total   _____

Submitted by: _____

                    Authorized Signature   Date

12-2. *This report is a comprehensive listing of all items purchased.*

PROJECT PRODUCT LIST

SOLD TO: ABC Interiors
CONTACT: J. Glenn

INSTALLED AT: Haven Motel
CONTACT: R. Rosen

SHIPPED TO: Haven Motel
CONTACT: R. Rosen

JOB #: 7002
CUSTOMER ORDER: 1346

QTY	MFG. NUMBER	DESCRIPTION		SHIP DATE	UNIT LIST	INVOICE	RECEIPT TICKET	FREIGHT	ITEM INVEN.
15	416	Custom Table Lamps	Blue Shades	4/2	$25.00	$375.00		$12.00	Yes
26	2118	T.V. Sets	Std. Commercial Grade	5/1	$400.00	$10,400.00	181	$250.00	Yes
50	11617	Framed Prints	Seascapes	6/1	$25.00	$1,250.00	132	100.00	spec. order
40	211	Floor Lamps	Green Shades	4/2	$35.00	$1,400.00		50.00	Yes
		Total				$26,000		$840.00	

PURCHASE ORDER

TO: _Able Lighting Mfging. Company_

121 East Street

New York, N.Y.

SHIP TO: _Haven Motel_

211 South Avenue

Norfolk, Virginia

DATE	DELIVERY DATE	SHIP VIA	F.O.B.	TERMS	PURCHASE ORDER NO.	
2/28	4/12	Smith Transport	Dest.	30 Days Net	1645	

QUANTITY	DESCRIPTION	PRICE	AMOUNT
15	#446 Cust. Table Lamps (Blue Shades)	$25.00	$ 375.00
40	#211 Floor Lamps (Green Shades)	35.00	1,400.00
20	#121 Ceiling Fixtures (Modern)	50.00	1,000.00
	Total		$17,500.00

☒ NOT FOR RESALE ☐ FOR RESALE TAX NUMBER _____

JGR

Authorized Signature

TMG

Designer

12-3. _Purchase orders are standard documents used by most businesses to purchase supplies and equipment._

an original design document. A separate form is used for each manufacturer so that no original information is erased when change orders occur. All additions or subtractions are listed on separate lines.

Purchase Order. Upon receipt of the project product list the expediter prepares a purchase order shown in Exhibit 12–3 with six copies as follows:

1. White: original copy to manufacturer.

2. Blue: copy to chief executive.

3. White: copy to job file, expediter.

4. Yellow: copy to master file.

5. Pink: copy to accounting.

6. Orange: copy to unbilled file.

The expediter types purchase orders with the information shown and signs in the appropriate place. The yellow copy is filed immediately in the master file. All other copies together with the project product list are sent to the designer for checking and distribution.

The chronological numbering of purchase orders must be maintained by the expediter to ensure that unauthorized purchases are not made. Purchase orders containing errors in typing are marked void and sent to the accounting department for filing. The yellow copy of all purchase orders including the voided ones should be kept in the master file. If blank purchase orders are used to replace voided ones the voided copy should be noted as such.

Purchase Order List. As the expediter generates purchase orders, each one is listed chronologically on the purchase order list shown in Exhibit 12–4 with the date issued, identification of the person taking the purchase order, manufacturer, project number, and amount. As invoices that correspond to project purchase orders are received by the expediter from manufacturers the expediter posts the amount invoiced on the purchase order list and calculates the open purchase order balance. In the case of repeated invoicing on one purchase order the amount invoiced and open purchase order balance are erased and updated each time an additional invoice is received. Each week the expediter makes one copy and forwards it to the accounting department for preparation of the cash flow report. The accounting department totals all open purchase order balances and transfers the appropriate number to the cash flow report. The copy of the purchase order list is stapled to the cash flow report for backup support.

Financial Aspects of Purchasing Services

The key to a successful purchasing service is to avoid committing the firm's own money to it. The profit margins available by marking up furniture purchases by, say, 10 percent are simply not sufficient to offset the carrying charges on the money outstanding with manufacturers. That is the reason why many firms do not provide the service.

One method is to request a deposit from the client of from one-third to one-half of the total amount of the furnishings to be ordered. This money is placed in an escrow account and not deposited with the firm's funds. As individual orders are placed with the manufacturers, a portion of the money is withdrawn to pay the deposits required by certain manufacturers to begin production. Particularly in the case of large custom orders the manufacturers may want from one-third to one-half as a deposit. In other cases manufacturers will want full payment before delivery.

Other manufacturers with whom the interiors firm has dealt in the past will ship the merchandise on open account. This generally means payment in 30 days, with perhaps a discount for payment in 10 days. If there are sufficient funds in the escrow account, the interiors firm may be able to pay in 10 days, in which case it gets to keep the discount, depending on the terms of the agreement with the client. In any event, the interiors firm should immediately invoice the client for any furnishings

12-4. *This report is useful to show unfilled purchase orders.*

PURCHASE ORDER LIST

PURCHASE ORDER	DATE ISSUED	TAKEN BY	MANUFACTURER	PROJECT NUMBER	AMOUNT	AMOUNT INVOICED/ DATE	OPEN PURCHASE ORDER BALANCE
1645	2/28	RMG	Able	7002	$17,500.00	$ 375.00 4/12	$ 17,125.00
1646	2/2	JJR	Baker	7002	$20,000.00	$ 20,000 4/16	0
1647	3/5	BRG	Charlie	7002	$15,000.00		15,000.00
TOTALS					$415,000.00	$200,000.00	$215,000.00

that have been shipped. The interiors firm expects to be paid in full on these shipments and not out of the escrow account. These terms need to be carefully explained to clients so they understand the purpose of the escrow account. It is only to take care of advance deposits that may be required, and eventually it is credited against the last shipment of furnishings.

On smaller projects the interiors firm can sometimes ask for and obtain a deposit of 100 percent of the furnishings costs. These instances are rare, but when they occur the interiors firm is in a much better position to take advantage of all discounts for prompt payment offered by manufacturers. The purchasing service then becomes profitable enough to make it attractive.

Disadvantages of Purchasing

There are several drawbacks to providing a purchasing service to clients. In the case of damaged merchandise the expediter is required to spend time negotiating with the manufacturer, the freight carrier, and the insurance company. If the merchandise delivered is not as ordered—say, it is the wrong model or color—time must be spent straightening out this problem. If a client should suddenly go bankrupt or otherwise be unable to pay for the merchandise, the interiors firm, as agent for the client, is likely to be involved in working out a settlement with the manufacturer. This is particularly true if the merchandise was custom ordered. An attorney should therefore be involved in preparing the standard contract used for purchasing services.

Coordination with Financial Manager

It is very important in an interiors firm that the expediter work closely with the financial manager. The purchasing service requires large sums of money, and it must be carefully controlled so that the client's deposits are used most effectively. Escrow accounts also give the financial manager an opportunity to invest these funds so that they earn maximum interest up until the time they are needed.

The financial manager can also monitor the entire purchasing service to see whether it is a profitable endeavor. Some principals of the firm may wish to provide this service as an accommodation to their clients, but if it is not profitable, their attitude toward it may change.

An excellent reference source for further information on the business and financial aspects of interiors firms is the revised edition of *A Guide to Business Principles and Practices for Interior Designers* by Harry Siegel with Alan Siegel (Whitney Library of Design, 1982). Note especially Chapters 9, 15, and 25. The book also has sample forms that may be used in an interiors practice.

Discussion Problem

Background. Your 10-person interior design firm has been asked by your largest client to undertake the purchasing function for a chain of small hotels they are opening in the South. Previously, you had done the interior design work for their hotels and your specifications were then given to the client's purchasing department to obtain the furnishings. The client has been unhappy with the turnover in its purchasing department and the problems this has caused its management. As a result the client has reduced the staff and limited the purchasing department's duties to normal routine purchases of consumable supplies and equipment for the hotels.

You know that if you do not accept this responsibility the client will probably contract with another interiors firm in the city to perform this service. It will then be only a matter of time before the new firm replaces you completely.

The most important question is who will do the purchasing: Can someone within the firm be trained to handle it or must you hire someone from outside? You arrange a meeting with the other principal in your firm to discuss this matter.

Assignment. What considerations should you give to the formation of a purchasing department in your firm? List the advantages and disadvantages, and on balance, what course of action you will take. List the qualifications for the person assuming the purchasing function. Where can you find information on the salary range for this position?

13
Special Problems of Government Work

1. What makes working for governmental agencies different from other types of work for the design professional?

2. What are some of the advantages of governmental work?

3. How can a firm improve its chances of being selected for a project?

4. What are some useful reference sources to assist the design professional in governmental work?

5. What are some helpful hints to follow during the course of a government audit?

6. What appeals are available on decisions of government auditors?

7. Where can the design professional turn for help if he or she is accused of violating the regulations?

For those firms that seek work from the federal government, as well as from state and local governments, the experience can be quite satisfactory or highly frustrating. The key is knowing the rules and playing by them. Contracting with the government requires the design professional to operate under a set of accounting rules established by the government. These rules determine which type of costs are recoverable under the contract. The problem is that the regulations were written for the large defense contractors and are often not easily adapted to smaller firms. Furthermore, large companies have staffs of people who keep up to date on the latest regulations in government contracting. Unfortunately few design firms can afford to have specialists in this field on their staffs so they must rely on their financial personnel or else hire outside consultants who are knowledgeable. In addition the government has the right to inspect a contractor's cost records to determine that they are kept in accordance with the regulations. The government officer can use the findings of this inspection to help him negotiate the contractor's price.

Because certain elements of overhead are disallowed, such as interest expense, entertainment, and donations, profit margins are generally kept within the lower ranges. Working for the government is usually less profitable than commercial work. Adherence to governmental regulations requires the firm to maintain its accounting records in certain prescribed formats, and there is considerable extra paperwork, negotiating procedures, and other overhead expense involved.

The plus side of doing work for the government is that frequently the projects are quite large and stretch over long periods of time. This can add a degree of stability to a firm that must rely on a heavy turnover of work which often lasts only a few weeks. Long-term work will keep a team of people busy and cover overhead expense while the principals and marketing personnel search for new work. Frequently, the government investigates state-of-the-art techniques that permit a firm to learn new design concepts while working on these projects. By the same token, a firm can become overly dependent on the government for one segment of its business, which can be disastrous if this work is suddenly withdrawn.

The pluses and minuses therefore have to be weighed carefully before a firm decides to enter the field of government contracting.

Proposing on Government Work

Proposing on government work can be expensive so care must be taken to only submit proposals for that work which the firm feels it has a good chance of winning. By law the government must advertise all requests for proposals (RFPs) over $25,000 in the *Commerce Business Daily*. This publication is issued every business day, and subscriptions are available from the Government Printing Office, Washington, D.C. 20402. Design firms normally must have a statement of qualifications (Standard Form 254) on file with the office seeking the procurement and must update it with a Standard Form 255, which lists recent projects that are directly appropriate to the procurement.

Because of heavy competition for government work, it is rare for a firm to win a significant contract merely by responding to a request for proposal and making a formal presentation unless the firm has unusual qualifications. Generally, it is necessary to have some familiarity with the project when responding to the request for proposal. Many firms use friends and contacts in Washington to alert them to new construction projects of various agencies. The firm then has a headstart in preparing its response and can do a better job than its competition. In some cases when working in a particular location near governmental facilities the firm can suggest a project to the government officials and help them draft the request for proposal. In any event the firm should develop a greater familiarity with the project than just reading the RFP. You need to visit the government officials who will be making the award and thoroughly understand the project so that your response will stand out from the others and the firm's capabilities will directly match the government's needs.

Six Percent Fee Limitation

Federal Procurement Regulations stipulate that no firm will be compensated for design effort in excess of 6 percent of the construction cost of the project. Yet many firms who consistently work with the federal government earn fees well in excess of that amount. The following are steps to maximize your fee potential in government work:

1. Obtain a copy of the Federal Register (Vol. 41, No. 15) for January 22, 1976, page 3293, and read what is and is not included within the 6 percent fee limit. Some items not included are

   a. Investigative services for feasibility studies, measured drawings for existing facilities, subsurface borings, surveying, program definition for schematic or preliminary plans and estimates.

   b. Specialized consulting services not normally found in an architect/engineering/planning firm.

   c. Supervision of construction, review of shop drawings or samples, travel and per diem allowances, presentations, models, renderings, and lab reports.

   d. Reproduction of documents for bidding.

2. Define the project scope in detail to highlight what is considered to be within the 6 percent limit and what is outside the limit and therefore subject to extra compensation.

3. Find out who did the government fee and construction estimate and how old it is. Many government estimators are young and inexperienced and often will not include appropriate task/hour figures for construction costs. Also, their estimate could be three or four years old and based on old construction methods and costs.

4. If you disagree with the government's construction cost estimate, suggest a feasibility study for extra compensation to verify the figures and to see that the actual construction cost estimate is realistic.

5. Be certain that the government contract includes a provision whereby changes in scope during the work automatically change the construction cost estimate. Without this, you may design a $12 million facility and be paid on the basis of an original estimate of $6 million.

6. Be prepared to perform only those services that are paid for in your contract. Don't redo programming just because you disagree with it unless you will be compensated.

Finally, prepare for every part of the negotiation by systematically reviewing each aspect and term of the contract with those who will actually negotiate the contract.

Accounting Regulations

Different government agencies have different accounting regulations, and it is important for the financial manager to become familiar with those that affect the firm. For example, the Defense Acquisition Regulations govern work for the Department of Defense, and the Federal Procurement Regulations (currently undergoing change to become the Federal Acquisition Regulations) affect most of the civilian agencies. A good reference source for design firms is the *Code of Federal Regulations, Public Contracts and Property Management*, published by the American Consulting Engineers Council (ACEC), 1015 Fifteenth Street, N.W., Washington, D.C. 20005. Another source is the audit guides published by the various governmental agencies. The latter publications are now available under the Freedom of Information Act, and they should be requested from the agency performing the audit. For example, the Defense Contract Audit Agency (DCAA) has auditing responsibility for the Department of Defense. DCAA offices are located in several large cities and near large defense contractors.

While work can be contracted for in a number of ways including lump sum, level of effort, and time and materials, the method most often favored, particularly for larger work, is cost plus fixed fee with an upset limit. This procedure places the design professional in a double bind of only getting paid for actual costs plus the fixed fee for anything less than the limit. The design professional is paid nothing more than the upset price if the project goes over that amount. Obviously, the design professional must be very aware of costs in this situation as well as the regulations affecting the agency that is requesting the work.

What Is a Government Audit?

One of the most unusual and unfamiliar characteristics of government work has to do with the special accounting regulations and the accompanying audits. An audit consists of a review of the firm's finances by an agency of the government or an independent contractor hired for that purpose. The auditor's task is not only to determine the reasonableness of the firm's figures in developing its cost proposal but also to determine whether the firm is following governmental procedures in its accounting. If the audit is made prior to the award of a contract, the government contracting officer has the benefit of knowing the firm's costs while negotiating the contract.

A firm seeking government work must agree to undergo an audit as a condition for obtaining the work. This procedure may sound unusual to a design firm that is new to government contracting, particularly since none of the firm's private clients are likely to make it a condition in their contracts. However, the practice of investigating and auditing another firm's books is not unusual in the business world, particularly when a smaller firm seeks to obtain a long-term supply contract with a large retailer, for example, and the retailer wants reassurance of the financial viability of the supplier.

Government Audit Considerations. A government audit can be made before, during, or after a project has been completed. Generally, an audit will be conducted in advance, particularly if the firm is new to government contracting and has never been audited before. It is important to segregate costs that are allowable in calculating the overhead rate from costs that are not and to have this documentation ready to show the auditor. Definitions of allowable/unallowable costs can be found in the ACEC bulletin cited above.

Government auditors are trained to look for instances of discrimination, where the government is charged more for the same service than commercial clients. Therefore it is important to make certain that the firm handles government and commercial clients in the same manner and on a consistent basis.

In addition, the auditor will be looking for instances where reimbursable expenses are mixed with overhead costs, usually inadvertently, where the government would be charged twice for the same expense. Exhibit 13–1 is an illustration of reimbursable expenses mixed with overhead costs. Another area to be prepared for questions and possibly unallowed costs is where there are transactions between the principals and the firm. An example of this is where the principals own a building or equipment and lease it to the firm. The burden of proof is on the firm to prove that the transactions are conducted the same as if a third party were involved. Charges of excessive compensation to the principals of the firm is another popular area of contention by auditors.

Suggestions for a Successful Audit. Maintaining good communications is the key to a successful government audit. You should schedule an opening conference with the auditor, learn something about his or her background, the purpose of the audit, and what data are to be examined. Then assign the auditor to a private office or workplace, give instructions that he or she is to deal with a single contact for all information in the firm, and make the materials available that are requested, but nothing more. The audit should be confined to an examination of the accounting records in support of the cost proposal submitted. The auditor should not have freedom to examine all financial records. If there is a question, you should ask the

13-1. *Every item of expense that could be considered reimbursable should be recorded by two methods in the accounting records, either as a direct expense or as part of overhead. The accountant must then have sufficient information on each expense to make the proper designation.*

EXAMPLE OF REIMBURSABLE EXPENSES MIXED WITH OVERHEAD COSTS

Assume Overhead Rate Was Calculated as Follows:

Payroll burden	$ 30,000
General and administrative expense	140,000
TOTAL OVERHEAD EXPENSE	$170,000
Direct labor	100,000
Overhead rate	1.7

Within General and Administrative Expense Were the Following:

Telephone $ 8,000   (of which $3,000 in telephone and $4,000 in travel were directly related to projects and recovered as reimbursable expenses.)

Travel $10,000

Your accounting system did not distinguish between the two types of expense (direct and indirect) and recorded telephone and travel in one account that was considered part of overhead.

Correct Method

Included under General and Administrative as part of overhead:

Telephone	$5,000
Travel	$6,000

Included in a separate expense account that is not part of the overhead calculation:

Other direct expenses $7,000

reason for the need to examine a particular record. For example, the auditor is supposed to audit costs. Therefore there is no need for an examination of the complete financial statements that include revenue and profit.

It is wise to check with the auditor periodically throughout the course of the audit and as any problems arise. It is much easier to try to resolve differences at the field auditor level before they are written into the audit report and reviewed by the audit supervisors. If differences of opinion continue to exist, you should ask to have a meeting with the audit supervisor and, if necessary, with the head of the local audit office.

At the conclusion of the audit, schedule an exit conference to go over the auditor's findings and recommendations. Recognize that the auditor's opinions are subject to interpretation of the regulations. Furthermore, the auditor's report is only advisory to the contracting officer, who makes the final decision. In practice, however, contracting officers rarely substitute their judgment for the technical opinion of the auditor.

Nature of Contracting

Government contracting is a highly specialized method of operation. Most architectural and engineering firms learn from their own trial and error and through the experience of others. Those firms that do considerable work in this area often train their financial managers to become knowledgeable in the techniques of government contracting. There are numerous books available and some loose-leaf accounting/law services that keep the reader abreast of the latest regulations, such as Government Contracts Reports published by Commerce Clearing House, 4025 West Peterson Avenue, Chicago, IL 60646. In addition, the financial manager can learn through seminars and professional society meetings, as well as through the experience of friends in other firms.

If a firm gets into a problem, even unwittingly, you should be aware the government has a standard set of appeal procedures. This is a new experience for most firms, particularly when they hear charges of "defective pricing" and sense that they have run afoul of the law for the first time. Unfortunately, the firm can become embroiled in a time-consuming and expensive controversy with the government. Many firms are anxious to reach a quick settlement because the two parties are unevenly matched; the government can afford to spend unlimited time and resources on the problem, whereas a firm cannot. When these situations arise, it is important to seek expert assistance from an attorney and accountant who specialize in government contracting. They can help the firm make the proper judgments.

Discussion Problem

Background. Your 12-person architectural firm has never been involved with any governmental projects. Since your firm was founded three years ago it has prospered until you are now the largest woman-owned architectural firm in the state. Two larger engineering firms have asked you to form a joint venture with them in conjunction with some large projects involving the installation of a major rail transportation terminal in the city. Your qualifications and experience on a high visibility project in the city (a performing arts center that won a design award) coupled with your success as a woman-owned business enterprise have brought you some attention in the media. The engineering firms feel you would be an important asset in obtaining the contract.

Assignment. Assuming that you want your firm to grow in this direction, how would you prepare yourself for government work? What sources of help are available to assist the firm in structuring its accounting system to meet governmental regulations? List the considerations that have to be weighed in deciding whether to submit a proposal on a governmental project.

14
Elements of Tax Planning

1. What are the advantages/disadvantages of the sole proprietorship form of organization?

2. What is an S corporation and what is its principal benefit to a design professional?

3. How does a slow growing or declining firm face exposure to a possibly large tax bill?

4. Why should tax planning be done early in the taxpayer's year?

5. What is the tax on accumulated earnings and why is it important for the design professional to be aware of its implications?

6. What kinds of tax shelters should be of interest to the design professional?

7. What are the tax advantages/disadvantages of equipment leasing as a tax shelter?

Most design professionals need help in structuring their personal and business affairs to carry out their financial plans and at the same time minimize the impact of taxes. This is an area that requires the advice of specialists, including an attorney, accountant, insurance advisor, and financial planner. To the extent practical, the design professional should convey his or her wishes and ideas to these professionals and then let them develop the methods for achieving the goals. The design professional needs to ask questions and make certain that agreement is reached on the plans developed or else ask for new suggestions. In some cases, it may even be necessary to get new advisors, if the ones selected are not sensitive to the thought processes and temperament of the design professional.

The design professional does not need to keep up on the latest tax laws and court interpretations; specialists can be relied upon for that. However, the design professional needs to have a general knowledge of tax planning in order to get the most from these specialists.

Decisions on Organization

Design firms can be organized as individual proprietorships, partnerships, or corporations. There are advantages and disadvantages to each form of organization. No one right method exists for any firm regardless of size.

Sole Proprietorship. Generally, firms start as a sole proprietorship and may stay that way until they reach a size that makes it economically justifiable to form a partnership or corporation. A sole proprietorship is not a separate entity for either legal or tax purposes. That is, it is indistinguishable from the owner. The advantages of a sole proprietorship are that there are no extra taxes to pay or reports to file, except for the additions to the owner's tax return at the end of the year. This is the simplest and most economical way to operate. The disadvantages of a sole proprietorship are that it does not give the owner any tax protection or continuity beyond the owner's lifetime. For example, if there are profits in the proprietorship they flow directly to the owner as ordinary income. Since the owner is not an employee the deduction is lost for any group insurance carried on the proprietor (but not on any employees).

Partnership. The partnership form of organization differs from the sole proprietorship in that a partnership is a separate entity and files an information tax return. Losses and gains from the partnership activity flow directly to the individual partners in the form that they are earned. That is, ordinary income becomes ordinary income to the partners and capital gains to the partnership are treated as capital gains on the individual partners' income tax returns. The advantage of a partnership is that it creates an equity interest that can later be sold by a partner as a capital gain. The transferability of partnership interests enables the partnership to survive the death or disability of a partner. The disadvantages of partnerships are that these interests cannot be sold so easily as stock in a corporation and a partnership is not so easy to manage as a corporation.

Corporation. The corporate form of organization is preferred by many firms since it is flexible and permits the firm to grow without restraint. Some states permit professionals to incorporate under special provisions in the corporate law that addresses professional corporations. They also permit design firms to incorporate under the laws governing regular corporations. Since state laws vary, it is necessary to have an attorney guide you in these decisions. The advantages of a corporation are that it is easier to transfer ownership than in any other form of organization and it also permits the stockholders to do some tax planning, as you will see later in this chapter. The disadvantages of a corporation are that more expense and paperwork is involved in filing state and federal tax returns, census data, and so on.

Within the corporate structure there are Subchapter S corporations, (now called "S corporations"), which avoid the double taxation of dividends—once as income to the corporation and a second time as income to the stockholders. S corporations are similar to partnerships in that they permit losses and gains to flow directly to the stockholders, who report their losses or gains on their individual tax returns. At the same time, the stockholders have the corporate protection from liability, although this is sometimes questionable in the case of professional liability. That is why it is necessary to have the professional liability insurance policy written to protect the individuals as well as the corporation. S corporations are useful to a firm at the beginning if losses occur because the stockholders can take credit for them immediately. The usefulness of the S corporation diminishes later on as most design firms do not pay dividends. Instead profits are distributed as bonuses and profit sharing.

Tax Aspects of Corporations

Most design firms that are organized as corporations pay their income taxes on the cash basis of accounting, so as not to pay taxes on money not yet received. The cash basis of accounting recognizes income when received and expenses when paid. This is distinguished from the accrual basis of accounting that recognizes income when earned and expenses when incurred, regardless of when cash is received or disbursed. The Internal Revenue Service (IRS) permits service firms to pay taxes on the cash basis as long as the firm's records are prepared on that basis or else are converted to the cash basis at the end of the year in workpapers that can be traced in a audit.

Because of the difference between cash and accrual, it is not unusual in some years for a firm that is not growing rapidly to be faced with a significant tax bill. That is because accounts receivable are being paid off, but new projects are not taking their place and building up unbilled work in progress and new accounts receivable. On the other hand, rapidly growing firms are constantly adding to their work in progress and accounts receivable and can find themselves in a loss position for tax purposes and therefore not subject to tax. Exhibit 14–1 illustrates this situation.

When a firm is first incorporated it has the opportunity to select its fiscal year, and the fiscal year does not necessarily have to conform with the calendar year. In fact, it is better if the fiscal year is different, because the two separate dates permit some time for tax planning between the stockholders and the corporation. Once the fiscal year has been set, however, it cannot be changed without IRS approval.

14-1. *A declining firm generates cash as accounts receivable are paid off and new work does not take its place. On the other hand, a growing firm needs cash to expand and support its increasing level of accounts receivable and work in progress.*

EXAMPLE OF TAXES INCURRED BY DECLINING FIRM VERSUS GROWING FIRM
(Assume Both Firms Pay Taxes on Cash Basis)

	Declining Firm			Growing Firm		
	Year 1	Year 2	Year 3	Year 1	Year 2	Year 3
Accrual revenues	$500,000	$400,000	$300,000	$500,000	$600,000	$700,000
Accounts receivable/work in progress less accounts payable	170,000	140,000	100,000	170,000	220,000	255,000
Cash excess of revenues over expenses in the current year on which the firm would normally expect to pay taxes	25,000	20,000	15,000	25,000	30,000	35,000
Reduction/increases in acc'ts rec./ work in progress less accounts payable (reflecting changes from previous year)		30,000	40,000		⟨50,000⟩	⟨35,000⟩
TOTAL EXCESS OF CASH RECEIPTS OVER DISBURSEMENTS (TAXABLE)	$25,000	$50,000	$55,000	$25,000	⟨20,000⟩	0

End of Year Tax Planning

The corporation itself is often considered a tax shelter because the stockholders have control over their salaries and bonuses and therefore can shelter their income to some extent. The IRS requires that stockholders who are officers pay themselves "reasonable compensation," which is open to considerable interpretation.

The tax laws permit an accumulation of up to $150,000 in earnings in a professional corporation under the current laws without penalty and without having to prove a business need. Funds beyond that level can be left in the corporation and remain untaxed for as long as the firm can prove that they are needed for a justifiable business expense, such as office equipment, working capital, or purchase of another business. If the firm has an annual business plan and can document its needs beyond $150,000, it can escape the corporate penalty tax on accumulated earnings.

Tax planning, or taking prudent action to minimize taxes, is a legitimate activity so long as there is a valid business purpose for the actions taken and the intent is not to defraud the government. In fact, tax planning makes good business sense the same as any action that reduces expenses. However, tax planning is a highly specialized activity requiring the expertise of accountants and attorneys who make it their specialty. These people keep up with the tax laws that change practically every year, and they keep abreast of the latest interpretations of the regulations by both the IRS and the courts. The most important thing for the design professional to remember is to do planning early in the year while there is still time and to hire experts for this purpose.

Accountants maintain libraries of tax services that are kept current with the latest regulations. One of the best for planning purposes is *Tax Planning* published by Institute for Business Planning, Prentice-Hall, Inc., Englewood Cliffs, NJ 07632. These services are expensive and directed primarily toward the tax practitioner. The design professional might be better off subscribing to a newsletter for the general public, such as the Kiplinger Tax Letter, 1729 H Street, N.W., Washington, D.C. 20006. In addition, many public accounting firms prepare client bulletins and brief synopses of the latest tax laws, which are distributed to their clients and made available to others on request.

Tax Shelters

Much has been written about tax shelters and a potential investor who expresses any interest at all is likely to be deluged with information from promoters. Tax shelters can be both good and bad, but they require the services of an attorney and accountant to determine whether they are appropriate for the individual investor. If you determine that your potential tax liability will be significant and a tax shelter seems like a possible alternative, it is well to investigate them early in the year. Exhibit 14–2 is a listing of the more common types of tax shelters and the advantages/disadvantages of each. An excellent unbiased reference source for tax shelters is called *Tax Shelters: The Basics*, published by Arthur Andersen & Co., 69 West Washington Street, Chicago, IL 60602.

Generally, by September most of the best shelters are fully subscribed and anything that is promoted in November or December has the possibility of being a fly-by-night operation with questionable benefit. Furthermore, tax shelter investments extend over a number of years, so it is important to know that the general partner or promoter will be around for a long time.

A trusted advisor should be used to investigate the merits of the shelter. It must have economic merit above its tax-saving possibilities in order for it to be acceptable. In addition, it should be structured in such a way as to avoid the likelihood of challenge by the IRS, which can disallow the deduction and make the taxpayer liable for substantial penalties and interest.

Profit-Sharing Plans. Design professionals have methods for sheltering income that relate directly to their firms. The creation of a profit-sharing plan is an excellent tax-sheltering device that has the added flexibility of not requiring fixed payments. Payments can be made in relation to the overall profitability of the firm, and in poor earning years, no payment need be made. It is important to have an experienced attorney prepare the plan documents that require IRS approval in order to gain the

14-2. *This table is a highly abbreviated summary of a very complex subject. There are many considerations and factors that depend on the individual's circumstances. Professional help is necessary in evaluating the advantages and disadvantages of tax shelters.*

ADVANTAGES/DISADVANTAGES OF SOME COMMON TAX SHELTERS

Type	Advantages	Disadvantages
Real Estate	1. Sound, traditional investment	1. Needs expert to judge value
	2. Appreciation, hedge against inflation	2. Investment not liquid
	3. Ability to spread risk with other investors	3. Usually requires a large investment
Oil and Gas	1. Deduction for intangible drilling costs	1. High degree of risk.
	2. Deduction for percentage depletion	2. Recapture of certain tax benefits upon disposition of property
	3. Potential for capital gain	3. Investor may be subject to certain minimum taxes, windfall profits tax
Farming	1. Certain costs that are normally capitalized, such as for soil and water conservation, are allowed to be expensed	1. Farm income has not kept pace with inflation
	2. Capital gain treatment for live stock	2. Vagaries of the weather
	3. Certain corporations can use cash basis of accounting	3. High risk
Timber	1. Capital gains treatment on timber transactions	1. Extraordinary risks from natural and man-made causes
	2. Current deduction for certain costs after planting	2. Cyclical demand for timber
	3. Certain losses given special treatment	3. Local tax structures and environmental issues
Motion Pictures	1. Special accelerated depreciation allowed	1. Box office failures
	2. Motion pictures qualify for investment tax credit	2. High cost of production and distribution
	3. Major advertising deductions taken in first year	3. Substantial investment required

deduction for tax purposes. The plans often call for the establishment of a trust with trustees appointed by the firm who have fiduciary responsibilities to the members of the plan. It is important that the plan not discriminate unfairly in favor of the principals in order for it to be acceptable to the IRS. An attorney familiar with the current tax laws can be very helpful in structuring the plan so that it will be accepted by the IRS.

Pension Plans. Pension plans are another method for sheltering income and they are divided into two types. Defined benefit plans establish the amount of benefit each employee will receive (generally related to his or her most recent earnings prior to retirement), and then actuarial calculations are made to determine the amount of contribution the firm must provide each year.

Defined contribution plans, on the other hand, establish the amount of the firm's contribution, and then the benefits for retiring employees are determined actuarially. Both plans require a fixed contribution each year. Defined benefit plans require the firm to take on the burden of providing for past service liability, or the liability immediately incurred when the plan went into existence to cover employees at their current salaries. For example, someone close to retirement at the time the plan goes into existence will take a significant sum of money out of the plan in a few years to buy an annuity at time of retirement. Funds are taken from the general pool when the time comes for retirement. The past service liability for all employees must eventually be funded, and it is accumulated through additional contributions to the plan over the years. In the case of a young person, the plan has many years to acquire the necessary funds. Obligations for past services are not required to be reported on a firm's balance sheet as a liability but are only disclosed in footnotes to the financial statements. However, there is discussion in accounting circles that may eventually change the regulations and require the reporting of the past service liability on the balance sheet. This would weaken the firm's ability to obtain additional credit. Many pension plans are now insured by an agency of the federal government to prevent them from going bankrupt if the firm suffers financial difficulties. Such insurance premiums are another cost that must be absorbed by the plan.

Other Tax Shelter Devices. *Individual retirement accounts* (IRAs) are an obvious source of tax planning for most individuals. Other sources include *short-term trusts* and *interest-free loans* to the design professional's children for college expenses. Obviously, an attorney must be consulted when considering the establishment of trusts and loans, but the design professional should be aware of the existence of these devices for tax planning.

A good source of information on tax-sheltering devices and plans are the financial service companies and banking houses. For example, Merrill Lynch has a wealth of literature on all types of plans and other firms publish an equally large assortment. As other companies, such as Sears and American Express, move into the financial service business, there will be no end to the information available at little or no charge. While most of the literature is directed at sales, you can still find a great deal that is educational and directed toward the new investor.

Equipment Leasing

In some cases the principals of a design firm form a partnership to buy equipment and then lease it to the firm. This can be an effective tax-sheltering device by giving the partnership the advantages of accelerated depreciation of the equipment and, in some cases, an investment tax credit. At the same time it provides a source of funding for the purchase of expensive equipment, such as CAD systems.

The problem with equipment-leasing tax shelters between the same parties is that the IRS examines them very closely because it knows they are set up primarily for tax reasons. Therefore the arrangement has to pass certain stringent tests. It must be a valid lease between the parties, which means that the terms should be about the same as that granted by a third-party leasing company. Otherwise the IRS will consider the transaction to be a conditional or installment sale and not allow the lease terms. For example, a three-year lease with an option to purchase the equipment for $1 at the end of the three years has the obvious appearance of a sale, regardless of what the parties call it. The lessor must have some risk in the transaction and there must be a valid business purpose.

To get the investment tax credit, an equipment-leasing partnership must pass two additional tests according to current tax laws. First, it must incur business expenses in excess of 15 percent of the rental income, not including taxes, interest, or depreciation. That is, these expenses must be for servicing and managing the lease to prove that the lessor is really in the business of leasing equipment. Second, the lease term must be for less than 50 percent of the useful life of the equipment. That means that equipment with a life of seven years cannot be leased for longer than 3½ years. The equipment-leasing partnership must make other arrangements, since renewing the lease to the firm for another 3½ years would defeat the purpose. Because of these tests, many equipment-leasing partnerships must pass the investment tax credit along to the firm.

The accelerated depreciation of the equipment allows the partnership to create a tax loss that flows directly to the partners. An illustration of an equipment-leasing partnership is shown in Exhibit 14–3. When the depreciation is used up, a "crossover" point occurs when the partnership begins to generate profits. Then there

ILLUSTRATION OF EQUIPMENT-LEASING PARTNERSHIP
($100,000 CAD System Leased to Firm over 3 Years)

	Year 1	Year 2	Year 3
Principals' Partnership			
Lease revenue	$20,000	$20,000	$20,000
Lease expenses	7,000	7,000	7,000
Interest, other costs	1,500	1,500	1,500
Accelerated depreciation	14,250	20,900	19,950
TAXABLE INCOME	⟨$2,750⟩	⟨$9,400⟩	⟨$8,450⟩
Design Firm			
Cash income	400,000	450,000	500,000
Cash disbursements (excluding lease)	350,000	375,000	425,000
Lease payments	20,000	20,000	20,000
Total Cash Disbursements	370,000	395,000	445,000
Excess of cash receipts over disbursements	30,000	55,000	55,000
Federal income tax on above (1983 rates)	4,650	9,750	9,750
Invest. tax credit (assume no carryback)	⟨4,650⟩	⟨5,350⟩	
TAX LIABILITY	0	$4,400	$9,750

has to be new planning, such as contributing the equipment to the corporation or starting over by buying new equipment and leasing it to the firm. The equipment-leasing tax shelter enables the partnership to retain the profit that an equipment-leasing firm would earn, and at the same time, it creates a tax shelter that the principals of the firm can understand and control. This should be distinguished from other types of shelters that may be involved in activities foreign to the professional, such as cattle feeding lots or oil and gas drilling ventures.

However, because of the complexities of the tax laws it is vital to have experienced counsel assist in planning these activities. Tax shelters of all types are under constant surveillance by the IRS, and the penalties imposed on those that are not allowed are very heavy. In the case of design firms faced with the need to acquire capital equipment, the first test of whether a tax shelter has a legitimate business purpose may be met, but as we have seen, that is only the beginning. Furthermore, the tax laws change and they are constantly tested in the courts, which makes any regulations cited subject to frequent revision.

Equipment Purchases through Pension/Profit-Sharing Plans

Pension and profit-sharing plans can also be used as vehicles to finance equipment purchases. The plan documents must be amended by an attorney to permit the plan to do this and still maintain its fiduciary relationship. It is important that the equipment lease terms be set up as if it were a third-party transaction. That is, the terms of the lease must be the same as if the firm financed the equipment using a third-party leasing company. Otherwise, there is a risk that the IRS will not allow the transaction.

The advantage to the plan is that these transactions often allow a better rate of interest to be earned than is possible from conventional sources of investments. Sometimes these arrangements follow a two-step procedure. The principals in the plan borrow up to the maximum permitted, and they, in turn, purchase the equipment and lease it to the firm. This is necessary, in some instances, because a corporation is prohibited from borrowing directly from a pension plan, since current tax laws have tight restrictions on such borrowing.

As with all these matters, the advice of an attorney is necessary before proceeding.

Background. Your 30-person interior design firm has been successful since you began five years ago. Bonuses have been generous over the years and you consider your employees to be well paid. Your insurance advisor now recommends the installation of a pension plan and presents you with the following data on the taxes paid for the past year:

	1983
Cash receipts	$950,000
Cash disbursements	820,000
Taxable income	130,000
Taxes paid	$ 40,050

He explains that the firm is in the 46 percent marginal tax bracket, which means that almost half the profit above $100,000 is taxed away. A qualified pension plan is deductible for tax purposes, and the benefits to employees are subject to deferred taxation. The firm could contribute up to a maximum of 15 percent of payroll, or $45,000 based on last year's payroll, which would fund the plan and provide a benefit for retiring employees who met the obligations of service with the firm.

Assignment. What are the advantages/disadvantages of installing a pension plan? Develop an analysis of the tax implications of installing a qualified pension plan. What are the motivational aspects and advantages in personnel relations to installing a pension plan?

15
Acquiring Capital Equipment

1. What are the advantages/disadvantages of the outright purchase of capital equipment?

2. What is the difference between leasing and renting?

3. What are the risks of a third-party lease?

4. Why can a leasing company sometimes make an offer even more attractive than a bank loan (even though the leasing company must borrow its funds at a bank and still make a profit)?

5. How can I best arrange to finance my equipment through a leasing company?

6. What are the important clauses to look for in a rental contract?

7. How do I prepare a cost analysis to compare purchasing, leasing, and renting costs?

All professional service firms use capital equipment, and indications are that more and more of this equipment will be used in the future. Word processing equipment, mini and micro computers, and computer-aided drafting and design equipment are destined to become commonplace in the offices of the future. The method of acquiring this equipment will largely be delegated to the financial manager, who must analyze the various options of purchasing, leasing, or renting.

Purchasing

The outright purchase of equipment is the easiest and quickest method and, in addition, has the following advantages:

1. Outright purchase is often the least expensive because you are not paying a leasing company's fee, but this is not always the case as will be seen later in this chapter.

2. In the case of a purchase, there is no question that the owner is entitled to the investment tax credit and can take advantage of accelerated depreciation.

3. When the equipment is fully depreciated, the owner can operate it at "no charge," which can be a competitive advantage or else give the owner a higher profit margin.

4. The owner has full control over the equipment. That is, the owner can move it, sell it, modify it, rent it, or do anything else, provided it is not pledged against a bank loan that may have restrictive covenants regarding the equipment in the agreement.

5. The initial outlay of cash means that no further outlays will be required, and therefore no further cash planning is involved in this transaction.

The disadvantages of the outright purchase are as follows:

1. It ties up funds that might better be used for working capital purposes.

2. If the firm must borrow additional funds to make the purchase, its limited borrowing capacity is used up.

3. With a purchase the firm takes on the full risk of obsolescence, which can be significant in the case of new equipment coming on the market.

4. The owner must handle the insurance and maintenance costs on the equipment, which may not always be the case with leased or rented equipment.

Leasing

Leasing differs from renting in that the former generally includes some provision for eventual ownership of the equipment by the lessee. Leasing combines the advantages of having the equipment available when needed with some of the advantages of owning. Other advantages of leasing are

1. A major advantage is that you do not have to come up with the full amount of cash all at once.

2. The lessor can often buy equipment for less than an individual purchaser because the lessor often buys in quantity.

3. Equipment breakdowns may be the responsibility of the lessor, depending upon how the contract is written. In addition, the lessor assumes responsibility for obsolescence of the equipment. Of course, the lease price takes the factor of obsolescence into account.

4. Upon disposition of the equipment, the lessor can often obtain a higher selling price for the same reason that the lessor can purchase it at a lower price because of the volume of transactions.

5. The lessor can pass along the investment tax credit to the lessee, or if it is kept, the lessee can often negotiate more favorable terms.

The disadvantages of leasing are as follows:

1. The firm is undertaking a fixed obligation that must be paid in good times as well as bad.

2. The leasing cost includes a profit to the leasing company over and above the cost of equipment and financing.

3. To deal with a leasing company, a firm needs a "track record," similar to what it needs when borrowing from a bank. The leasing company must to be assured that the firm has sufficient financial strength to pay the lease, and this requires that financial information be disclosed to the leasing company.

4. The firm is at the mercy of current interest rates at the time it makes the transaction. The leasing company bases its charges on its own cost of borrowing money, which may be higher than what a bank would charge if the firm went directly to borrow from the bank.

Renting

Renting does not involve any acquisition of ownership of the equipment and is generally considered to be a short-term expedient. The advantages of renting are

1. You have the equipment when you need it and are not burdened with payments when the need has passed.

2. It enables a firm to try out new equipment or different types of equipment without making a financial commitment.

3. It enables the firm's personnel to get training, particularly on computer equipment.

4. Rental equipment may be able to handle a temporary overload situation.

The disadvantages of renting are as follows:

1. It is generally the most expensive method of acquiring capital equipment.

2. The equipment may not be available when you need it, and it is usually not in new condition.

3. Rental agreements are tightly worded documents written by the equipment owner's attorney. They generally place most of the obligations on the renter and few on the owner.

Important details, like who is responsible for insurance and maintenance and who pays for equipment installation and removal, need to be clearly understood at the time a rental agreement is signed. It is important to know what is reasonable to expect in the way of response time to service calls and what constitutes excessive downtime. If the firm needs to acquire additional liability insurance to protect the equipment, this needs to be known.

Obviously, it is important for the firm's attorney to review a rental agreement. Just because an agreement is printed and is made to appear like a standard contract is no reason to believe it cannot be modified with clauses added or deleted.

Cost Analysis

When a firm decides to acquire capital equipment, the financial manager should prepare a detailed cost analysis listing the various options available. An example of a cost analysis is shown in Exhibit 15–1. If the principals of a smaller firm are not comfortable with making their own analysis, they should ask their accountant to assist them. They should also not hesitate to ask his or her advice regarding the

COST COMPARISON FOR LEASE, PURCHASE, OR RENTAL OF $100,000 EQUIPMENT

Lease		Purchase[2]		Rental[4]	
Total purchase price + interest	$137,500[1]	Total purchase price + interest	$137,500	Total rental price + interest	$111,750
Less: Tax savings @ 46% rate (top tax bracket) on $137,500	63,250	Less: Interest	37,500	Less: Tax savings @ 46% tax rate on $111,750	51,405
Net cost over 5 years	$ 74,250	Depreciation	95,000[3]	Net cost over 3 years	$ 60,345
		Subtotal	$132,500		
		@ 46% tax rate	$ 60,950		
		Invest. tax credit	10,000		
		Total deductions	70,950		
		Net cost over 5 years	$ 66,550		

[1]Assume straight lease with no pass-through of investment tax credit, and because lessor can purchase equipment at lower price, he can finance at same rate as bank (15 percent) and still make a profit.

[2]Financed by $100,000 bank loan at 15 percent.

[3]The 1982 tax law reduces basis for depreciation by one-half of the investment tax credit in 1983.

[4]Assume renter of equipment wishes to recover 90 percent of cost over three-year period of rental agreement at 15 percent.

15-1. *This analysis indicates that the least expensive alternative is an outright purchase financed over a five-year period.*

contemplated purchase. Many accountants are involved in acquiring computers for their own practice and they can give advice from personal experience.

While financial considerations are an important element in the final decision, very often nonfinancial reasons, such as better service to clients or competitive pressures, can be the overriding consideration in the acquisition of capital equipment.

Discussion Problem

Background. Your architectural firm is interested in acquiring CAD equipment because you recognize that it will be important to your future growth and ability to remain competitive. You are presently using a service bureau, but you want to own your own equipment. One equipment manufacturer has offered to train your staff at another architectural firm where he has installed this equipment. The other firm agrees and arrangements are made to hold classes once a week after hours. Members of your firm participate on a voluntary basis.

You examine the alternatives in financing the equipment and decide that leasing is your best alternative. The equipment manufacturer recommends a leasing firm that he uses. Several years ago you leased some furniture from another leasing company, and you decide to ask both firms to submit a proposal.

Assignment. List the advantages and disadvantages of using a leasing company for this transaction. What clauses to protect you should be included in the lease document? What other considerations beside price should be examined when deciding between the two firms?

16
Internal Financial Controls

1. What are internal financial controls and why are they important?

2. Why is an end of year audit no substitute for proper financial controls?

3. What can a smaller firm do to establish controls over the handling of funds?

4. Is fidelity bond coverage appropriate?

5. How can splitting financial duties help achieve better financial control?

6. How can I split financial duties in a small firm?

7. What can a principal do to assist in this area?

One place where most design firms have a weakness is in the area of internal financial controls. This is an accountant's term and it has to do with assuring that the financial transactions of the firm are carried out in accordance with management's directives. For example, the principals of a firm expect that the payroll checks will reflect each individual's current salary, or the number of hours worked times the current hourly rate. There should be no fictitious names on the payroll. What proof do the principals have that their wishes are being carried out? In smaller firms the managing principal may sign all checks and is probably familiar enough with everything to spot any obvious discrepancies. However, as a firm grows the managing principal does not have time to check everything personally, particularly in the financial area. More and more reliance is placed on others. Fortunately, most people hired are honest and this trust in them is not misplaced. Occasionally, a dishonest employee will be hired and this person can wreak havoc in an office, often for long periods of time, before being discovered.

The establishment of a good financial management function is so new to many firms that the firm may not have had time to consider the possibilities of theft or embezzlement. Furthermore, many principals believe that any discrepancies will be discovered in the course of an end of year audit. Unfortunately, that is not the purpose of an audit. An audit is performed to express an opinion on the financial statements. Auditors are trained to look for discrepancies, of course, and if any are found they will be pursued. However, an audit is designed to test only a sample number of transactions so it cannot be relied upon to discover fraud.

Nevertheless, the end of year audit is a good starting point to begin to establish internal controls. The auditor is trained to look for weaknesses in this area during the course of the audit and will report the findings following the completion of the audit. In many cases the auditor will prepare a formal letter to management disclosing the findings, but in any case, the principals of the firm should meet with the auditor and discuss possible improvements.

In smaller frims that do not have an end of year audit, it may be worthwhile to ask the outside CPA firm that prepares the tax returns to do a special internal controls review. The one-time charge for this service would be a very worthwhile investment if the firm implements the changes that are suggested.

Insurance is available to cover some of the exposure, and it should be purchased as part of a complete liability coverage program. This insurance is called "fidelity bond coverage" and it protects the firm from theft by anyone who handles funds. Premiums are generally inexpensive and the firm should discuss the amount of coverage it needs with its insurance broker.

Suggestions for Better Internal Control

Splitting up accounting duties is one of the most effective ways to improve internal controls and to remove temptation from otherwise honest people. When key duties are split, it then requires collusion on the part of two or more people to accomplish the same theft and that becomes more difficult. For example, whoever prepares checks should not have the responsibility for reconciling the monthly bank statements. Otherwise there is no control over what checks can be written. Likewise, checks received in the mail should be logged in by someone other than the bookkeeper who prepares the bank deposit, so there is a duplicate record of incoming receipts. Exhibits 16–1 and 16–2 are simple forms that can be kept by someone other than the chief accountant or bookkeeper to keep track of cash.

The problem in most smaller design firms is that there is no one available for these duties to be split. In that case, someone from outside the accounting department, like the receptionist, could open the mail and record the checks before giving them to the bookkeeper.

The managing principal can become part of the internal control procedure by periodically inspecting the financial records and tracing one or two transactions. An

16-1. *In a smaller firm the receptionist can maintain this log of incoming checks as the mail is opened and sorted.*

WEEKLY LISTING OF CASH RECEIPTS

DATE ___2/28___

CHECK		FROM	AMOUNT
NO.	DATE		
1896	2/24	ABC Development Corp	$ 15,000
289	2/24	Junction City, Texas	2,489
1602	2/25	Johnstown Independent School District	21,621
143	2/26	General Hospital Corp.	4,000
2962	2/27	Schenectady County Hospital	13,500
TOTAL			$ 91,028

CASH STATUS REPORT

Month: ___2/28___
Account name: ___First Bank of Smithtown/Operating Account___ Account number: ___1234___

Date	Beginning Balance	Deposits	Check		Other Adjustments*	Balance
			Numbers	Amount		
2/7	$ 18,000	$ 26,000	189-215	$14,500	0	$ 29,500
2/14	29,000	9,000	216-235	36,000	+ $18 ✳	1,982
2/21	1,982	40,000	236-261	29,000	0	12,982
2/28	12,982	14,000	262-280	19,000	0	7,982

TOTAL _____

*Other Adjustments (Explain)___ Bank service charge deducted in error in January.___

Prepared By: ___J.D.T.___   Date: ___2/28___
Approved By: ___P.M.H.___   Date: ___3/1___

16-2. *This form should be prepared by someone other than the person who writes the checks. It should then be reconciled with the books of account.*

obvious starting point is to examine the payroll records of everyone in the accounting department. Another fairly obvious check is to make certain that accounting personnel take their vacations. Beyond this, the managing principal can demonstrate an interest in good financial recordkeeping and show that he or she does not take these matters lightly. The managing principal can use the checklist shown in Exhibit 16–3 to examine the firm's procedures and make some necessary improvements right away.

Discussion Problem

Background. Your 15–person interior design firm has had the same bookkeeper since shortly after you founded the firm 22 years ago. Mrs. Smith has been diligent in her duties since her first day on the job and her attendance record has been outstanding. She has kept books on a manual basis all these years and you have never had a problem in the accounting area that she could not handle. Your firm has never been audited and your outside accountant prepares the tax returns from information supplied by Mrs. Smith. You often wonder how you could ever function without her.

You get your opportunity when she is suddenly taken ill and must be confined to the hospital for six weeks. Your outside accountant offers to provide you with one of his bookkeepers to help during this period. After working in your office a few days the new bookkeeper tells you that the accounting records are in poor shape. Bank statements have not been reconciled for three months, there are errors in posting, and the general ledger has been out of balance for almost a year. Mrs. Smith has been covering up discrepancies since 1975, although there is no evidence of fraud.

Asssignment. How do you go about correcting this situation? List the key ingredients in an internal control system in even the smallest of firms. What steps can you take to minimize the likelihood of this situation ever happening again?

16-3. *This checklist can be used to begin a review of the firm's internal financial controls.*

CHECKLIST FOR INTERNAL CONTROL

1. General

a. Are accounting records kept up to date and balanced monthly?

b. Is a chart of accounts used?

c. Does the managing principal use a budget system for monitoring income and expenses?

d. Are cash projections made?

e. Are monthly or quarterly financial reports available to the managing principal?

f. Does the managing principal take a direct and active interest in the financial affairs and reports that are available?

g. Are the personal funds of the principals and their personal income and expenses completely segregated from the firm?

h. Is the managing principal satisfied that all employees are honest?

i. Is the bookkeeper required to take annual vacations?

2. Cash receipts

a. Does someone other than the bookeeper open the mail?

b. Does someone other than the bookkeeper list mail receipts before turning them over to the bookkeeper?

c. Is the listing subsequently traced to the cash receipts journal?

d. Are receipts deposited intact daily?

e. Are employees who handle funds bonded?

f. Do two different people reconcile the bank records and make out the deposit slip?

3. Cash disbursement

a. Are all disbursements made by check?

b. Are prenumbered checks used?

c. Is a controlled, mechanical check protector used?

d. Is the managing principal's signature required on checks?

e. Does the managing principal sign checks only after they are properly completed?

f. Does the managing principal approve and cancel the documentation in support of all disbursements?

g. Are all voided checks retained and accounted for?

h. Does the managing principal review the bank reconciliation?

i. Is a petty cash fund used and is it reconciled periodically?

j. Does the managing principal never sign blank checks?

k. Do different people reconcile the bank records and write the checks?

4. Accounts receivable and sales

a. Are invoices prenumbered and controlled?

b. Are clients' accounts balanced regularly?

c. Are monthly statements sent to all clients?

d. Does the managing principal review statements before mailing them?

e. Are account writeoffs approved only by the managing principal?

5. Notes receivable and investments

a. Does the managing principal have sole access to notes and investment certificates?

6. Property assets

a. Are there detailed records available of property assets and allowances for depreciation?

b. Is the managing principal acquainted with property assets owned by the company?

c. Are retirements of assets approved by the managing principal?

7. Accounts payable and purchases

a. Are purchase orders used?

b. Does someone other than the bookkeeper always do the purchasing?

c. Are suppliers' monthly statements regularly compared with recorded liabilities?

d. Are suppliers' monthly statements checked by the managing principal periodically if disbursements are made only from invoice?

8. Payroll

a. Are the employees hired by the managing principal?

b. Would the managing principal be aware of the absence of any employee?

c. Does the managing principal approve, sign, and distribute payroll checks?

17
Outlook for the Future

Predictions indicate that the market for design services is likely to become more competitive as it has for other professional services. The bans on advertising are being lifted and professionals are beginning to understand that they are going to have to compete in the marketplace against other professionals. This places a premium on effective marketing and business development. One of the keys to effective marketing is to know where to invest your marketing dollars for the greatest return. The marketing staff needs answers to such questions as what types of projects are most profitable, what proposals are most successful, and how much does it cost to prepare different kinds of proposals? Many of these answers must come from the financial manager. Business planning is going to become a necessity because firms are going to have to chart a course and follow it instead of spending valuable resources trying to go after all markets.

Design firms will be changing from labor-intensive practices, where everything is done by hand, to those with a greater reliance on equipment, such as word processors and computer-aided drafting equipment. This means that the firm will have to make financing decisions involving more money than it has ever spent before. The decisions will be ones it will have to live with for years to come. Change is coming at a faster rate than ever before and those that do not keep up will become expendable and obsolete. Young people coming out of school expect to be working with computers, and if your firm is not at the state of the art, they will seek firms that are. Smaller firms will have to make the necessary capital investments the same as larger firms. This means they must obtain the best financial advice they can get from accountants and other advisors. The penalty for poor management decisions is going to be harsher than ever before because we are dealing with capital resources and not people who can be laid off in a downturn. We can expect to see bankruptcies occurring in some firms.

Interest rates are likely to remain high for the foreseeable future even as they continue to fluctuate in the short run. This means that many projects will not be funded and certain design work will be completed and "put on the shelf." Cash flow will continue to be a problem for the design firm as well as for its clients.

Competition is likely to come from different sources in the future. For example, some businesses and manufacturers of furniture are getting into design. Smaller and medium-size firms that have not developed a unique expertise and strength are likely to become victims of more aggressive competitors.

These signs of the future indicate that the role of financial management in design firms is likely to increase and the accompanying need for better management will be greater than ever before. It is a challenge that will be met by the well-managed firms that continue to grow and prosper.

Long-Term Outlook

During the next 10 to 15 years we will see fully computerized working drawings with capital-intensive design firms operating at a much larger and more cost effective scale than today. Better design will become a commonplace because more time will be allowed at the design stage of a project, due to the ease of developing working drawings once a design has been finalized. More design professionals will learn how to sketch; yet fewer will be required to do hardline working drawings. Computer communications will allow for the development of CAD systems that will automatically produce specifications. Drawings on paper will be rare because contractors in the field will be hooked electronically to databases on CAD systems that will allow them to call up any part of a drawing for review on hand-held computer screens.

There will be significantly more competition from nonprofessionals in design. Personal computer companies will develop software packages that will allow consumers to design their own homes, to perform their own mechanical engineering specifications, and even to prepare their own structural engineering specifications.

There will be personnel problems, because people will not know what to do with careers outmoded by new technology. The impact of these changes will be felt as more smaller design firms are created. The 1980s is the age of the entrepreneur and will see a trend toward more startups as individuals become dissatisfied with larger firms. This will be particularly true in the case of women- and minority-owned firms as more of these are created. Federal government policies will act as a stimulus to the creation of these firms. On the other hand, larger firms will grow even larger as the need for greater amounts of capital are required for expansion. Medium-size firms without access to capital for expansion may have difficulty in the future. We will probably see a wave of mergers and acquisitions take place as firms try to position themselves for market penetration and expansion.

Medium-Term Outlook

We are seeing many technological changes already that will be commonplace. Color plotters with high resolution and speed will replace black-and-white plotters. Video disk storage will replace magnetic media as a more dense and durable form of retaining information. There will be modeling and simulations of three-dimensional design in the computer-aided drafting area.

Programming will become more simplified and more English language–oriented as computer firms realize the need to make it easier for professionals to use the equipment. We will see three-dimensional graphic systems come into existence. Do-it-yourself software will allow even inexperienced designers to achieve structural, mechanical, and architectural integration of their project work. Computers will allow many staff members to work at home and to communicate with the office via telephone. Desk terminals will be used for timecard input, engineering calculations, architectural design, as well as word processing. Many reprographic companies will offer computer services, allowing even the smallest architect or engineer to use some of the most powerful computer equipment to produce working drawings. We will see computerized catalogs and other graphic information available for rent.

Short-Term Outlook

We are now seeing voice-activated typewriters, and they will soon become commonplace. System networks will become common in which one computer talks to another or a service bureau talks to an in-house computer.

We will see significant fee competition from firms that are computerized and have taken advantage of productivity improvements. These firms can quote fees below others and will continue to as long as fee pressure exists. In fact, firms will find it difficult to operate without computers. Too much paper and too little selectivity will cause major problems in firms entering the computer age without proper planning. Computers will often be required by clients seeking design services.

We will see developers building office buildings specifically for design professionals. These buildings will not only contain normal drafting and office space but have a computerized drafting system available for the tenants as part of the lease package.

It is obvious that computerization is the wave of the future and change is the byword of the eighties.

Selected Bibliography

Books

Burstein, David, and Frank Stasiowski, *Project Management for the Design Professional*. New York: Whitney Library of Design, 1982.

Class, Robert Allan, and Robert E. Koehler. *Current Techniques Institute of Architectural Practice*. Washington D.C.: American Institute of Architects, 1976. (Particular attention should be paid to Chapter 6.)

Drucker, Peter. *Management: Tasks, Responsibilities, Practices*. New York: Harper & Row, 1974.

Eyerman, Thomas J. *Financial Management Concepts and Techniques for the Architect*. Chicago: Skidmore Owings & Merrill, 1973.

Foote, Rosslyn F. *Running an Office for Fun and Profit*. Philadelphia: Dowden, Hutchinson & Ross, 1978.

Foxhall, William B. *Techniques of Successful Practice for Architects and Engineers*. New York: McGraw-Hill, 1975.

Getz, Lowell V. *Financial Management and Project Control for Consulting Engineers*. Washington, D.C.: American Consulting Engineers Council, 1983.

Mattox, Robert. *Financial Management for the Architect*. Washington, D.C.: American Institute of Architects, 1980.

Reports and Manuals

American Consulting Engineers Council. *A Manual of Practice for Consulting Engineering*. Washington, D.C., 1977.

———. *A Practical Guide to Professional Engineering and Architectural Procurement*. Washington, D.C. 1979.

American Institute of Architects. *Standardized Accounting for Architects*. Washington, D.C., 1978.

———. *Compensation Guidelines for Architectural and Engineering Services*, (and Supplement), 2nd ed., Washington, D.C., 1978.

———. *Architects' Handbook of Professional Practice*. Washington, D.C. (date varies for each chapter).

———. *Financial Management for Architectural Firms: A Manual of Accounting Procedures*. Washington, D.C., 1970.

Bevis, Douglas. *Profit: Planning for It, Making It, and Keeping It*. Chicago, 1976.

Case and Company. *An Analysis of the Impact of Federal Government Overhead and Profit Allowances on Architectural Firms*. San Francisco, 1976.

Clarke, Jon O. *The Overhead Rate*. Professional Engineers in Private Practice Division, National Society of Professional Engineers. Washington, D.C., 1982.

Dun & Bradstreet, Inc. *Financial Analysis of Engineering, Architectural and Surveying Services (SIC 8911)*. New York, 1978.

Professional Services Management Journal. "Executive Salary Survey," 1983.

———. "Operating Statistics Survey for Professional Services Firms," 1980.

———. "Overhead Survey of Professional Services Firms," 1979.

Reece, James S. *A Survey of Management Control Practices in Large Architectural and Architectural Engineering Firms*. Cambridge, Mass.: Harvard Business School, 1975.

Robert Morris Associates. *Annual Statement Studies*. Philadelphia, 1978.

Vining, G. William. *Financial Management Handbook for Engineering Firms*. Professional Engineers in Private Practice Division, National Society of Professional Engineers. Washington, D.C.

Articles

Barker, Bradley. "Profit Planning in Design Firms." *Professional Services Management Journal*, June 1977, p. 1.

McDonald, Howard R., and T.L. Stromberger. "Cost Control for the Professional Service Firm." *Harvard Business Review*, January-February 1969, p. 109.

Perkins, Bradford. Series of articles on architectural firm management. *Architectural Record*, March, April, May, June, August, October 1972.

Index

Edited by Stephen A. Kliment and Susan Davis
Graphic production by Katherine Rosenbloom
Set in 11 point Times Roman